BEST SPORTS STORIES
1956

E·P·DUTTON&CO.INC

EST. 1852

OVER 100 YEARS OF CREATIVE PUBLISHING

Edited by IRVING T. MARSH and EDWARD EHRE

BEST
Sports Stories
1956 Edition

●

A Panorama of the 1955 Sports Year

INCLUDING THE 1955 CHAMPIONS OF ALL SPORTS

*WITH THIRTY OF THE YEAR'S BEST
SPORTS PICTURES*

E. P. DUTTON & CO., INC.
NEW YORK   ●   1956

PRINTED IN THE UNITED STATES OF AMERICA
BY THE WILLIAM BYRD PRESS
RICHMOND, VIRGINIA

Library of Congress Catalog Card Number: 45-35124

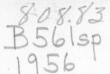

TABLE OF CONTENTS

BASKETBALL

RACING

TENNIS

DOGS

HUNTING AND FISHING

GENERAL

FOR THE RECORD

ILLUSTRATIONS

PREFACE

This, the twelfth in the series of Best Sports Stories annuals, is a little different in at least one respect: There are more prize-winners than in any of the previous eleven volumes.

Maybe it's because the quality of the stories is increasing from year to year. Maybe they're all so fine (and the editors like to think so) that it's difficult for the judges—John Chamberlain, Bob Considine and Quentin Reynolds, who have been doing this sort of thing for many years now—to choose among them.

At any rate, for the first time in its dozen years, the Best Sports Stories annual has shared prizes in the News Coverage Division *and* the News Feature Division. Only the magazine story won outright, and that by only the margin of a single point.

Faced with these ties, the editors decided to share the wealth. They split the $250 prize in both the deadlocked divisions. And in so doing they added a couple of new names to the list of prize winners. Jesse Abramson, whose story of the Indianapolis 500-mile race shared the news coverage prize with Joe Trimble's account of the seventh World Series game, has won the prize twice before, but this is the first time that Trimble has entered the winner's circle. John Gillooly, whose story on blind golfers won the news coverage award a year ago, shares this year the news feature prize with his piece on Harry Agganis, but Bob Goethals, the co-winner, is a first-timer. As a matter of fact this is the first time he has appeared in Best Sports Stories.

And Dick Young, whose efforts have been reprinted here many times before, is making his debut as a victor with his magazine piece on Preacher Roe and the spitball.

As in the past, the judges received each story not knowing who wrote it and where it appeared. Each story was "slugged" for identification and nothing more.

And here is the final box score of the judging:

News Coverage Division

Author and Story	Chamberlain	Considine	Reynolds	*Pts.
Abramson's *The Checkered Flag*...	3	1	—	4
Trimble's *Paradise at Last*........	1	3	—	4
Nason's *12 Minutes Short of 70 Days*	—	—	3	3
Povich's *Up from the Floor*........	—	2	—	2

Author and Story	Chamberlain	Considine	Reynolds	*Pts.
Rendel's *Midnight for Kippax Fearnaught*	—	—	2	2
Danzig's *Tennis Turnabout*........	2	—	—	2
Condon's *Thunder in Los Angeles*..	—	—	1	1

News-Feature Division

Gillooly's *Sox Apollo*.............	3	—	2	5
Goethals' *Locker Room*...........	2	—	3	5
Maule's *They Never Hurt Me*......	—	3	—	3
Gallagher's *He Wouldn't Harm a Fly*	—	2	—	2
Cooke's *Saga of Plainfield Teachers*.	1	—	—	1
Rosenbaum's *The Important Part*...	—	1	—	1
Cartwright's *The Merciful Executioner*	—	—	1	1

Magazine Division

Young's *The Outlawed Spitball*.....	3	—	3	6
Heinz's *Young Fighter*...........	—	3	2	5
Perry's *Brooklyn's Mad Golf Course*	—	2	—	2
Hirshberg's *Roommate: Bob Cousy*.	2	—	—	2
Seamon's *Big Man from Nicetown*..	—	1	—	1
Frank's *Coaching the Pros Is a Cinch, He Says*	1	—	—	1

* Based on 3 points for a first-place vote, 2 for a second and 1 for a third.

To explain why they selected as they did, this is what the judges said:

JOHN CHAMBERLAIN

News Coverage

The obvious first choice to me is the story of the death of Bill Vukovich (Abramson's *The Checkered Flag*). The reporter was handed a routine assignment which turned before his eyes into a tragedy. The horrifying details are handled with fine restraint by a writer who rose to one of those opportunities which nobody ever wants to come his way.

Second best is the Davis Cup doubles story (Allison Danzig's *Tennis Turnabout*). It wouldn't have mattered very much to the Australians if they had lost the doubles, since they were pretty sure bets to win three singles anyway after winning the first two matches. Nor could a double victory have saved the day for the Americans. But the writer makes you feel that something terrific hinged on every serve and volley. A fine job on something that could have been routine.

Third is the story of the victorious Dodgers (Joe Trimble's *Paradise at Last*). I count it a good job because the writer handled delirium without getting (a) inarticulate or (b) drunk on his own words.

Honorable mention should go to the piece on "Dogs" (John Rendel's *Midnight for Kippax Fearnaught*) and to the Marciano-Moore story (Shirley Povich's *Up from the Floor*). The account of the Southern California-Notre Dame game (David Condon's *Thunder in Los Angeles*) is pretty good, too.

News Features

For No. 1 I pick another story of death, "Agganis" (John Gillooly's *Sox Apollo*). This is really a heart-wringer, and again it's handled with fine restraint. It's also a lesson in the art of packing a lot of information into a very few words. The author wrote it out of deep knowledge of his subject, and knew just what to include and what to throw away.

No. 2 in the features is the one about Ben Hogan waiting for Fleck to finish (Bob Goethals's *Locker Room*). It makes you feel for Hogan without taking anything away from the guy he had to meet in a play-off the next day.

The third best feature is the story of Morris Newburger's mythical football team, "Plainfield Teachers." (Bob Cooke's *The Saga of Plainfield Teachers*). I could believe in Plainfield Teachers College myself, even after the hoax had been exposed. That means that the author of the story can create the illusion of reality.

The parody on Davy Crockett (Jerry Mitchell's *The Saga of 'Davy' Berra*) is worth an honorable mention, as is "1st Series" (Roger Birtwell's *Two Men Gambled*), which features Jackie Robinson and Billy Martin each dashing for home.

Magazines

For first choice I like the conversation with Preacher Roe about his dirty work over the years with the spitter (Dick Young's *The Outlawed Spitball*). I suppose it's just plain immoral to choose this brazen admission of illegality, but the Preacher makes such an engaging crook that it is hard to resist him. The planning and the capture of the story are examples of high journalistic enterprise, which ought to count too in awarding a prize.

And now I come to a confession and a terrible surprise (to myself). The confession is this: basketball bores me. The surprise is that I think the story of a swing around the basketball circuit with Bob Cousy (Al Hirshberg's *Roommate: Bob Cousy*) is marvellously full of homely human interest. Clearly it is worth second place in a magazine story contest. And the third best is "Eckman" (Stanley Frank's *Coaching the Pros Is a Cinch, He Says*), also about a basketball character.

Bob Considine

News Coverage

1.—The Story of the 7th game of the World Series (Joe Trimble's *Paradise at Last*). Here, with loving care and proper respect for its place in the history of the nation, is recorded one of the great events of our time: Brooklyn's first World Series title. One has a feeling, reading this moving piece, that it may become required reading in every public school in B'klyn for the next century. I hope so.

2.—The Marciano-Moore fight (Shirley Povich's *Up from the Floor*). Here is writing as clean as the fight itself. Here a man, the writer, reaches into the soul of a great sports experience and extracts all that is worth while.

3.—The 500-mile Indianapolis race (Abramson's *The Checkered Flag*). This particular sports event seldom lends itself to good writing. The traditional punch is that somebody sat still long enough, and his pistons worked long enough, for him to win the race. But when can a writer say of the champion: "The black-and-white checkered flag, indicated a safe completed run, never fell today for Bill Vukovich?" Fine story of a slaughter.

News Features

1.—Punchy fighter (Tex Maule's *They Never Hurt Me*). Here is a true ear for the tragedy of the scramble-brained fighter. All boxing commissars should be required to read it before being sworn in. So should commission doctors.

2.—Paul Brown (Jack Gallagher's *He Wouldn't Harm a Fly*). This one gives us more insight to one of the most successful football coaches of all time than any piece I've ever read.

3.—Olympics (Art Rosenbaum's *The Important Part*). Here is a grand and intelligent view of the forest of the Olympics rather than the view we usually get—that of the trees.

Magazines

1.—The story of Billy McNeece (W. C. Heinz's *Young Fighter*). This is how a fighter talks. So few people in our business quote fighters correctly or even try to understand them. The writer is a man curious enough to have set out to explain *why* the likes of Billy McNeece goes in for this deplorable business.

2.—The story of Dyker Beach golf course (Jane Perry's *Brooklyn's Mad Golf Course*). This is delightful writing about a subject that cannot help being hilarious. Copies of this should be sent to the hallowed precincts of the U.S.G.A. to prove that the game involved is subject to certain robust influences not ordinarily connected with *B*urning *T*ree.

3.—The story of Roy Campanella (Dick Seamon's *Big Man from Nice town*).This involved the kind of research, and the brand of writing, that all of us strain for and wish for and seldom achieve.

QUENTIN REYNOLDS

News Coverage

This is always hard to decide, and usually the event makes the story. Perhaps the most exciting fight of the year was the one between Carmen Basilio and Tony de Marco. It also, I think, made the most exciting story (Jerry Nason's *12 Minutes Short of 70 Days*).

It isn't often that the judging of a dog makes for exciting reading and good reporting, but the story of Bulldog Kippax Fearnaught (John Rendel's *Midnight for Kippax Fearnaught*) was filled with drama. It is ranked second. When Notre Dame is badly beaten at football that's news, and whoever wrote the story of Southern California's 42-to-20 win over the Irish wrung every bit of excitement out of it. I'd place that story (David Condon's *Thunder in Los Angeles*) No. 3.

News Features

Some how it's easier to write about a winner than a loser. The story of Ben Hogan and how Jack Fleck tied and then defeated him for the open golf championship (Bob Goethal's *Locker Room*) is an exception. It's a "behind-the-scenes" story told in terms of

Hogan and the other golfers who were in the locker room waiting for Fleck to come home. It is suspenseful and filled with the authentic language of the men who hit a little white ball for a living. I thought the story rated the nod over the excellent story of the late Harry Agganis (John Gillooly's *Sox Apollo*) and the story on the final game of the World Series which began, "Johnny Podres was a merciful executioner. . . ." (Al Cartwright's *The Merciful Executioner*). The humorous poem about Yogi Berra deserves better than honorable mention.

Magazines

It isn't often that a magazine can beat the newspapers with a news story, but one magazine did it with Preacher Roe's confession that he'd been using a spitball for years—against all the rules. It's been common gossip around the dugouts that half-a-dozen pitchers have been getting away with the illegal delivery, but Roe was the first one to admit it. I think this ranks as the best magazine story of the year (Dick Young's *The Outlawed Spitball*). Second comes the magnificent story of the kid fighter Billy McNeece (W. C. Heinz's *Young Fighter*). The writer really got inside the fighter's skin and told us what made him click.

☆ ☆ ☆

So much for the stories.

As for the photos, it seemed to the editors that Hal Burgert's picture of the auto crash that sent cars spinning all over the track was as dramatic a shot as Best Sports Stories has ever received. And Bob Doty captured wistfulness and charm when he took the picture of Walter Alston's grandson awaiting good news. So, what better than to award *Wheel of (Mis)fortune* by Burgert and *Good News!* by Doty each a share in the $100 photo prize.

And talking of photos, the editors confess to an error in last year's volume that must now be corrected. They inadvertently credited Frank Lyerla, of the *Detroit Times*, with having taken one of the winning pictures, "Come Clean Boys." Actually the picture was submitted by Jack Weiner, also of the *Detroit Times*. The awarding of the cash prize was rectified, but here too is our apology for the error and credit where credit belongs.

So, here too is Best Sports Stories—1956, twelfth in the series. We hope you'll find it fun.

IRVING T. MARSH
EDWARD EHRE

THE PRIZE-WINNING STORIES OF 1955

Best News Stories

THE CHECKERED FLAG

By Jesse Abramson

From The New York Herald Tribune, May 31, 1955

THE BLACK-AND-WHITE checkered flag, indicating a safe completed run, never fell today for Bill Vukovich. He was burned to death in a five-car smash-up while leading the field in his all-out attempt to become the first man to win three in a row in the annual 500-mile automobile race. An estimated 150,000 spectators saw the race.

The thirty-six-year-old driver from Fresno, Calif., was roaring along the two-and-a-half-mile Speedway at record-bound speed at the 141 mile mark, in front for fifty of fifty-six laps, when he was injured fatally in one of the worst crashes in the forty-five-year history of this always dangerous, often death-dealing ride.

Bob Sweikert won the race. He was not involved in the accident.

Vukovich plowed into a pile-up as he gunned his 300-horse-power engine roaring off the southwest turn into the long back-stretch.

With machines hurtling end over end and over the walls, the drivers of the four other cars involved were not seriously hurt. Two of the track's safety patrol and a civilian were injured.

According to observers, Ed Elisian, of Oakland, Calif., who had argued his way into the race after the officials thought he had failed in the qualifying trials, was the first of the five cars to smash. Fish-tailing round the corner he had spun into the wall and turned end over end.

Rodger Ward, of Los Angeles, driving the only car which had ever won previous race, tried to swerve past and crashed into the crossover bridge which spans the track for the benefit of golfers. There's a golf course inside and outside the racing oval. Ward's car turned over.

The chain reaction was instantaneous and horrifying. Jimmy Boyd, of Fresno, Calif., swerved and cracked into the bridge, too, and Al Keller, of Green Acres, Fla., a native of New York State, smashed into the other cars. Vukovich, a lap or more ahead of all of them and about to lap them again, caught the wheel of one and went over the outside retaining wall, cracking through the foot-thick rail. One of the wheels flew off and hit Sgt. Richard Wolf, of Indianapolis, breaking his shoulder. His car burst into flames and trapped the two-time winner underneath. Fire-fighters arrived within seconds but could not pull the driver out.

Over at the finish line the officials, apprised of the smash-up, waved the yellow flag. Then followed minutes of suspense among the crowd, wondering what had happened. Soon a puff of smoke signalled something serious. Then through binoculars, through trees and partly obscuring stands one saw flames that burned fiercely for almost ten minutes.

A check of the cars quickly disclosed that some were missing. Vukovich's four-man pit crew, which had had nothing to do as yet, peered up the stretch with growing concern on their faces, hoping against hope, and finally realizing that their Bill's car had been caught in the accident.

It wasn't until a half hour later that the public-address announcer disclosed that Vukovich had been burned to death. His announcement was drowned out for thousands by the deafening roar of the machines that continued on in the race.

Treacherous gusts of wind were believed responsible for today's accidents, according to the drivers. "They caught me and shifted the car six feet on the backstretch," said Tony Bettenhausen, who finished second. "I believe that's what started Elisian on his spin."

On the 171st lap of the 200-lap race Cal Niday, thirty-nine, of Pacoima, Calif., the only one-legged driver on the big wheel of high-powered racing, slammed into the northwest wall amid an explosion of smoke, spun crazily down the track into the infield and was taken to the hospital in critical condition, suffering from burns and head injuries.

One of the most popular drivers in the sport, Vukovich, who, in recent years, left his filling-station business only for the 500, was the forty-sixth person to die since the speedway was launched in 1909. The total included drivers, mechanics and spectators.

This was the first fatality in the race itself since William (Shorty) Canton, of Indianapolis, crashed into the southwest wall in 1947.

Two years ago, when the temperature soared to a searing 130

degrees at trackside, Carl Scarborough, a driver of Clarkston, Mich., died in a hospital of heat exhaustion induced by the nerve-wracking grind over the red brick asphalt oval.

Today, for the thirty-ninth running, the crowd had just about the coldest Memorial Day in race history. The temperature was 54 degrees under heavy clouds, with a twenty-mile wind from the north chilling the unprotected devotees of high-powered cars. The sun broke through intermittently during the afternoon to splash the cameramic spectacle with vivid colors.

Nothing was more colorful than the orchid-and-cream Zink Special which twenty-nine-year-old Sweikert, a California-born adopted son of Indianapolis, drove to first place.

One of the formidable dark horses in a race which can have no authentic past-performance favorite, Sweikert had not, in his three previous tries, completed the full course, for one or another of the manifold reasons which balk these 1,800-pound special racing cars and their drivers. Today, following the accident that cast a pall over the big crowd, Sweikert, twice-married and the father of two children and two stepchildren, completed the 200 laps in 3 hours 53 minutes 59 seconds for an average of 128.209 miles.

Where a record race had been predicted by Vukovich and others, the average speed today was the slowest since 1951, due to the yellow flag that forced a slowed-up race on the field for more than 27 minutes following the big smash-up and later slows. Vukovich's win-year was 130.840. This year he switched to a blue Hopkins Special.

Sweikert, who started from the fourteenth spot, middle of the fifth row, charged into the first five at fifty miles, was second at 150, led at 225, lost it at 350, regained it at 400 and was never headed through the final 100.

He won by a lap and a quarter, 1 minute 33 seconds on the watch. His sleek borscht-colored-heavy-on-the-cream car, brand new and being raced for the first time, gave him no trouble. Sweikert went all the way without relief, which is usual, and made only two pit stops, which is minimum, for fuel and tires, consuming 1 minute 7 seconds and 46½ seconds for the repairs by his competent crew.

Bettenhausen, of Tinley Park, Ill., a thirty-eight-year-old veteran who is one of the most consistent winners in A.A.A. championship racing, but hasn't finished eight previous starts here, placed second in 3:55.32. Jimmy Davies, of Pacoima, Calif., was third; Johnny

Thomson, of Springfield, Mass., fourth and Walt Faulkner, of Long Beach, Calif., fifth.

Nine completed the 500 miles and five others were on the track when the red flag concluded the race.

Vukovich had completed fifty-six laps—140 miles—had rounded the feared southwest and southeast turns when he slammed into the pile-up that brought his death. In the fractional seconds after rounding the southeast corner he had no chance to escape the wreckage just then spewing all over the track ahead of him.

It happened on the distant backstretch, directly across the field but out of sight from the finish-line stands where Vukovich's wife, the mother of his two children, Marlene, thirteen, and William Jr., eleven, was watching the race.

The only record set today was made by Vukovich. At 125 miles his average was 136.212, eclipsing the 135.739 speed set by Jimmy Duwalt a year ago. There was a money record won by Vukovich, too. By leading fifty laps he earned $7,500, at $150 per lap. This was his fifth "500," but he had won two of them and had earned $88,863 of Speedway money on his two victories, not counting accessory revenue. His Speedway winnings, therefore, totaled $96,362, passing the $91,300 earned by Wilbur Shaw, the three-time winner who was president of the Speedway when he died in an airplane crash last fall.

Vukovich had been trying to become the fourth man to win the race three times, the first man to do it in consecutive years. He had qualified with 141.071 speed, second only to Jack McGrath's record 142.580, for the four-lap qualifying runs. When the brilliant-hued field of thirty-three cars all got away, three abreast in rows of eleven in their full-throttle start, McGrath, from the outside of the first rank, snatched the lead on the first lap, then Vukovich, driving hard as ever, forged to the head of the parade on the fourth lap.

They had a tremendous duel thereafter, their wheels almost touching once on the southwest curve with Vukovich leading fifty of the fifty-six laps, McGrath the other six.

McGrath, always a contender, never a winner, was forced out by ignition trouble after fifty-four laps. Five miles later death claimed Vukovich, and the sport went out of the race.

PARADISE AT LAST
By Joe Trimble
From The New York Daily News, October 5, 1955

THEY WON'T make Oct. 4 a red-letter day in Brooklyn. They'll print it in letters of gold from now on because it's only the greatest date in the history of the batty borough—the day those darling Dodgers finally won the World Series. At exactly 3:45 yesterday afternoon in the Stadium, the Brooks got the third out of a 2-0 victory over the Yankees in the seventh and deciding game.

And when they print calendars over there, they won't bother with Marilyn Monroe's picture. Not good enough. They'll have pucker-faced Johnny Podres, the most heroic pitcher in Dodgertown since Dazzy Vance and the only Brooklyn thrower ever to win two games in a Series. It was Podres' brilliant, crushing pitching which ruined the AL champions, sending them down to their fifth Series loss in 21.

And who do you suppose knocked in both Brook runs? No one else but Gil Hodges, the batting flop of the '52 Series.

There were many memorable events bright and tragic on this earth on past fourths of October, but the hallowed pages of history must display yesterday's momentous triumph above them all.

What kind of a date has it been? Well, on Oct. 4, 1861, the Union forces massed to form the Army of the Potomac; in 1864, the Erie Railroad opened (probably not on time); in 1940, Hitler and Mussolini met at the Brenner Pass and, in 1944, the U. S. Army broke through the German West Wall. Al Smith, the beloved Governor of New York and Presidential candidate, also died on the latter date.

As far as Brooklyn is concerned, nothing ever could match the events of yesterday, when all the years of frustration and defeat were wiped out in one blazing afternoon. It was the 49th Dodger Series game in eight appearances, and the tightest, most tense and thrilling of them all.

At the finish, when Pee Wee Reese sure-handedly threw out Elston Howard, the big park in the Bronx exploded with human

23

emotion as the entire Dodger team raced out on the field and danced and drooled in delight around Podres.

While the 62,465 customers were cheering the new champs, the proud Yankees were filing slowly into the losing dressing room; a unique experience for them. Of all, only coaches Frank Crosetti and Bill Dickey and shortstop Phil Rizzuto had ever experienced a loss before. They had it but once, when the Cardinals smeared the Yankees four in a row after losing the 1942 opener.

The Dodgers are in paradise, finally succeeding after numerous Brooklyn teams had tried for four decades. The 1916 Flatbushers were knocked off by the Red Sox and the 1920 crew by Cleveland. Then the drought set in and it wasn't until 1941 that a pennant waved alongside the tree that grew in Brooklyn. But that year they had to play the Yankees, and Mickey Owen muffed a third strike and everything went black in the borough.

Four times since then, they won the NL flag only to find those merciless Yankees on the other side of the field—and the Brooks on the losing end of the payoff. They went down in 1947 in seven games, in 1949 it was five, in '52 seven again and six in '53.

So the Brooks also went home with their heads hanging and the taunt of "Wait 'til next year!" shattering their eardrums. Now that's over. Next year came on Oct. 4 this time.

This not alone was the greatest day in Brooklyn's history. It also brought to a wondrous climax the richest World Series ever. Due to increased admission prices and the maximum number of games, the $2,337,515.34 taken in at the box office is an all-time high.

Numerous records were set, but the one the Brooklyn players will remember most was their achievement in winning four of the last five games after dropping the first two. This kind of comeback had never happened in a seven-game Series before.

To do it, they had to get a second superior pitching job from the 23-year-old Podres, their little lefthander, and also they had to whip the Yankee pitcher who had given them the most trouble, 35-year-old Tommy Byrne. Although they got the three hits off the graying southpaw before an error helped cause his removal in the sixth, they put them in exactly the right places.

Roy Campanella, who had gone hitless in 12 times up in the Stadium this Series and had a lifetime average of .070 in the big park, crashed a double to left after one out in the fourth. Duke Snider, who went all the way on his bad knee, fanned just before

Campy's hit. Carl Furillo followed with a slow grounder, Rizzuto making a fine play to get him at first as Campy reached third. Gil Hodges, with a count of one ball and two strikes, swung at an inside curve. He didn't get much wood on the ball but it went safely to left field and the Brooks were ahead.

The other safety was a lead-off single in the sixth by Reese, the veteran whose victory appetite was greatest because he had been on the losing side against the Yankees five times.

The shortstop lined a hit to left-center and was deprived of a double when Bob Cerv made a fine retrieve. Reese eventually scored the insurance run after Bob Grim had taken the mound.

But before the Brooks opened the thin gap, they nearly gave the Yankees a run. Yogi Berra opened the bottom of the fourth with a lazy fly to center, a bit to Snider's right. Junior Gilliam came over from left, invaded the Duke's realm, and then they went into an Alphonse-Gaston act. The ball tipped off Snider's glove as he made a last-second grab after realizing Gilliam was letting him take it. That fluke double gave Berra the distinction of being the ninth man ever to hit safely in every game of a full length Series. The catcher made 10 hits, topping the batters on both sides.

The Yankee fans screamed for blood after the break. It's an old axiom that you can't make a mistake against the Bombers. They break through the opening and kill you. But Podres wouldn't buckle. He got the next three batters, all strong righty sluggers. Hank Bauer hit a fly to Furillo, Bill Skowron grounded to Don Zimmer and Cerv popped to Reese in short left. The Dodger fans screamed: "Pee Wee! Pee Wee!" as he went out and Gilliam came in and the Dodger captain caught it.

The Yankee supporters applauded Gilliam when he came up to bat in the fifth, one guy screaming: "He's the best man we've got!" Junior didn't get a chance to flub anything else in the outfield because he was moved in to second base after the Brooks got their run in the sixth.

After Reese hit, Snider bunted deftly along the third-base line. Byrne fielded it and threw accurately to first base. Skowron stepped forward to meet the ball, taking his foot off the bag and forcing himself to make a tag play. He swiped at the Dodger runner's back and the ball flew out of his glove for an error.

Walter Alston, winning a World Series in his first try, sensibly ordered Campy to sacrifice and he did. Byrne handled this bunt, too. It seemed that the pitcher had a force possibility on Reese at third, Pee Wee not yet having gone into a belly-whop slide. But Byrne thought otherwise and let Reese make it, tossing to first for the out. Casey Stengel ordered an intentional pass to Furillo and then called in Grim, his relief ace who had saved the first game but was battered as starter in the fifth.

Grim's first batter was Hodges, a tough man with the bases filled. Gil took a strike and then drove a long sacrifice fly to center, Reese scoring. Grim walked Hoak, refilling the lanes, but got George Shuba, a pinch-hitter for Zimmer, on a third-out grounder.

Again the sight of a Dodger run on the scoreboard brought a Yankee threat in the bottom of the inning. This developed into a real big one and also produced the greatest fielding play of the Series—a catch by Sandy Amoros, an outfielder who was held lightly as a prospective regular in the spring because of his shabby fielding and throwing.

Podres, who passed only two, hit a wild streak and walked Billy Martin on four straight pitches. Alston came out to give the youngster a chance to get his breath. With victory so close, he didn't want the Kid to get hysterical. Johnny threw two bad pitches to McDougald, then got one over, which Gil bunted perfectly for a single, Martin taking second.

Then came the key play, the one which probably meant the title. Stengel, disdaining a bunt with Berra up, had Yogi swing away. Podres pitched outside and Berra stroked a long, high fly into the left field corner. Amoros, playing him far over toward center, had to run over 100 feet. The ball stayed up a long time, being held by the wind, and Sandy just reached it, gloving it with his right mitt in fair territory.

Martin and McDougald, not believing a catch possible, were on their horses. Billy suddenly reversed himself when almost to third and Gil was past second base before he found out the ball had been held. Amoros gracefully whirled and fired to Reese, who went into short left for the throw. Pee Wee then made another perfect throw to Hodges, just getting McDougald as he slid back. That was the 12th Brooklyn DP, a new Series record.

Bauer then hit a hopper to short and Reese couldn't get it out of his glove for a frantic portion of a second. When he did, he had to throw a blazer and it just beat the runner, according to first base umpire Frank Dascoli.

Grim was lifted for a pinch-hitter in the seventh, after Howard singled. There were two out, so Stengel sent up his hobbled husky,

Mickey Mantle. Podres fooled the Mick with a change-up, Mantle skying the ball to short left where Reese took it, with the Dodger fans again screaming his name.

Podres had a rough time in the eighth, when the Yankees got their second runner to third base. Rizzuto led off with a single to left but Martin flied to Furillo, who came in fast for the looper. McDougald then hit a sharp grounder which bad-hopped off the left arm of Don Hoak, playing third because Jackie Robinson had a sore Achilles tendon in his right foot. Rizzuto got to third as the fluke hit went into left.

The tension was terrific, with Berra and Bauer coming up. Podres really had it, getting Berra to cut under one of his slow curves. The ball went to Furillo in short right and Carl gunned it home, holding The Scooter on third. Then the youngster faced his supreme test in Bauer, who hits lefthanders very well. He took Hank to 2-2 with curves and slow-up pitches, then flung himself off the mound by putting all he could on a shoulder-high fastball which Bauer swung at and missed.

As the Yanks came up, Dodger fans stayed seated. Yankee adherents shouted for a rally.

Skowron cracked a sizzler back at Podres, the hard grounder sticking in his glove web. He was unable to get it out for a second or so, and started to run towards first base to make the putout that way. But he was able to pry it loose and make an underhand toss to Hodges. Cerv then hit a high fly which Amoros took in short left and the Dodgers were one out away from the promised land.

Podres went to 2-2 on Howard and then made him swing off stride at the change-up. Reese took one happy step towards the grounder, aimed it for Hodges and, though the toss was a bit low, Gil kept his foot on the base and the Dodgers had finally arrived in paradise.

Best News-Feature Stories

SOX APOLLO
By John Gillooly
From The Boston Record, June 28, 1955

WHEN HE WAS attending Boston University he was known as the Avenue Apollo and the sobriquet fit him snugly. For Harry Agganis had the physique, the demeanor, the superman qualities which placed him on a little Olympus all his own. He appeared indestructible; he'd pop up unpunished from under a pile of bruisers who had plummeted into him from all directions and shout fresh, crisp signals; he seemed invulnerable.

He appeared immune to pain, plague, pox, virus and that's why the death of Harry Agganis yesterday pierced the heart of the city; plunged the entire sports world into deep grief. Of late there had been ominous words, rumors about Agganis, confined to the Santa Maria Hospital in Cambridge. Glum, minatory words like "tuberculosis" and "complications" and "isolation" and "lung infection."

Harry would win over all, just as he had been winning over all through a thrill-filled young life, dedicated to physical education and sports accomplishment. He'd beat any sickness one hand tied behind his back. Intimates assured themselves of this; admirers who had watched him play football and achieve All-Everything and then work his way into the major leagues of baseball didn't see how anything could conquer him. So the untimeliest of untimely deaths yesterday was twice shocking.

Agganis was something to see—and only a few short weeks ago he was on display a few lockers away from Ted Williams' roose—after a shower in the dressing room at Fenway Park.

A Greek God for sure—all thew and sinew and shoulders. Some real Atlases in that particular nudists' colony, toweling and relaxing and cooling out after a ball game. Williams, for one, a hunk

28

of handsome man. And blond Jackie Jensen, golden boy from the Golden State. But if a sculptor walked in and wanted someone to take discus in hand and pose in the classical fashion, most likely the artists would select Agganis for his model.

Hairbreadth Harry, others nicknamed him, because of his many electric sports experiences. For Harry had a habit of narrow escapes on the athletic fields and a knack for coming through in the clutch. The facts of his life were much more like fiction.

It all began on Barry's sandy park in Lynn—this phenomenal rise to Yawkey's green acre in Boston's fashionable Back Bay—which is a football throw from the Agganis home on Waterhill St. Harry was born there and lived there—on a second-floor flat—with his widowed mother Georgia Agganis who only lately got to going a few times a week to Fenway Park and who had just recently learned to score the game herself.

Given a $35,000 bonus by the Red Sox, Agganis and his mom could have moved to much more luxurious lodgings in a more toney neighborhood but Mrs. Agganis didn't want to leave her always fastidious home and Harry was more than satisfied with his trim little room there, which his adoring mother had "wall-papered" almost completely from floor to ceiling with prints, pictures, cartoons, framed clippings.

Waterhill St. and streets for miles around must have been wretched, utterly forlorn, inconsolable yesterday shortly after noon when the tragic news flashed that the imperishable Agganis had passed on. Georgia Agganis was born in Loggonike, a suburb of Sparta in Greece but not even one with Spartan corpuscles could stand up under the weight of this tragedy.

Harry's brothers Jimmy, Demo, Philip and Paul and his sisters, Mrs. Mary Raimo and Mrs. Dema Orphanos and their many children rushed bewildered, blinded by tears to the flat upstairs on Waterhill Street to lend courage in this awful crisis, for Harry was the baby and thoroughly adored.

Each of his sisters kept a huge scrapbook on Harry's brilliant deeds even though Harry didn't exactly approve. He'd blush and giggle and find something to do in the kitchen when Georgia Agganis or one of his sisters would produce a scrapbook or a trophy or a memento and happily tell the tale it involved.

A Spring ago it happened to this correspondent, sent to Lynn to do a "life story" on Agganis, then hitting .360 for the Red Sox. Sisters and mother obliged with many clippings and anecdotes while Harry slipped away, abashed but agreeing: "If it makes them happy, that's good."

The scrapbooks bulged. Harry gave his worshipping kind plenty to clip and paste.

It began with a few small-fry achievements on Barry Park. Then Harry went to Lynn Classical and for four years was All-Scholastic in football and baseball. In the summertime he shone in Legion baseball. All his encomiums did not derive from sports, however. What is little known is the fact that he had a distinct talent as a dramatist, an actor. He was leading man in the school play, Peter Pan. He had many lines to memorize. He learned them fast, a real Barrymore. Two nights the Classical auditorium sold out. Harry was box-office as an emoter, too.

From Classical, Agganis enrolled at Boston U. He had at least 60 offers from other campuses. Some of the letters, which might embarrass athletic directors if published because they are lofty, lucrative lures, are pasted in Georgia Agganis' scrapbook. He chose B.U. because he wished to be near home and mom's fine cooking. "I cook nice Greek dishes," said Mrs. Agganis last Spring during the "life story" research, "but you know what. Harry likes my cooking best when its ravioli or spaghetti."

Grief-fractured, too, must have been Bill Joyce, Harry's coach at Classical who sent him to B.U. richly endowed with athletic and scholastic qualifications. Agganis' father died in 1946 and Joyce helped fill the void, becoming Harry's guardian angel.

Joyce has had many jolts out of sports, both as a participant and a pedagog but he still says Agganis gave him the top kick of all when Classical went to Miami for a Christmas Day, 1946, championship game with Granby High of Norfolk, Virginia, with Cluck Stobbs as quarterback. Classical won 21-14 with Harry running the team superbly as all the leading football coaches in the nation, around the South for the approaching Bowl games, looked on.

A left-handed passer, wonderful kicker, runner Agganis led B.U. out of the morass of mediocrity. The finest schoolboy athlete in 25 years around Greater Boston became one of the greatest nationally for four seasons. He made many All-America teams even though Boston U. was accorded grudging recognition. Harry forced them to focus those big prejudiced binoculars on Commonwealth Ave. He had the radiance of Yucca Flats and the mushroom cloud over the Charles could not be overlooked.

In his senior season, Agganis was forced out of a big game with U. of Maryland because of a severe chest injury. It did not permit further throwing of a football. Maybe Agganis should have been sent to the hospital then, but he refused to leave the scene. He kept warming up with the football on the sidelines the rest of the game, hoping to get back in there, but the wing would not function.

A few weeks later, Agganis returned to his generalship of the Terriers protected by a heavy cast on his chest. Asked recently if the injury might just possibly be causing his current illness, Agganis replied: "I don't think so."

Professional football clamored for Agganis who had satisfied the militia with a hitch in the Marines. The Cleveland Browns, with their Otto Graham near the exit, reportedly offered him $100,000 for four seasons.

Here was quick, certain fortune. But Agganis made Nick the Greek (Dandales), the fabulous gambler, look like a nickel-nurser. His heart was set on baseball and the Red Sox, even though the Red Sox starting price was much less and even though he wasn't sure he could ever make the varsity. Long years on the farm loomed on the horizon. While he was All-Scholastic first baseman at Lynn and a collegiate star when Spring football practice would permit him to play baseball at B.U., there was no guarantee he had major league baseball qualifications.

He could step in and sparkle immediately with the football Browns. The road to Fenway, not made for left-hand hitters, was clearly cobble-stoned. Agganis travelled it after only one season of apprenticeship at Louisville where his durability was proved when he played every inning of 154 games and encored with another show of full stamina in the lengthy play-offs.

His coach at BU, Buff Donelli, forecast Agganis' success. "Practice, study, determination should keep Agganis up there in the majors—and improving," said Buff when asked for a few words on the Avenue Apollo last summer. "He's one kid who's got active, not oral, determination. He's willing to pay the price."

Actually Agganis hand-fought his way into the majors for his fielding had flaws and his hitting wasn't wonderful. It terrified few big league hurlers. But Harry persisted, perspired and he won the first base job this season and he was hitting .313, despite Fenway's anti-southpaw dimensions, when stricken mortally by double pneumonia.

Remember the first time he went South to frivolous, frolicsome

Florida to train with the Red Sox? He was young, he was single, he had a gleaming new automobile. All rookies mix business with pleasure on this peninsular playground. But Harry with great vision and self-discipline left his car and gay clothes and his natural craving at home. "I'm going down there to make the team," he said, taking the train. "An auto down there would only get me in trouble."

Life-story in April, 1954. Death-story in June, 1955. Rough, rough indeed. A guy could bawl over this one.

LOCKER ROOM
By Bob Goethals
From The San Francisco Chronicle, June 19, 1955

BEN HOGAN had taken his shower. He was dressed in brown coat and grey slacks. His bag was packed and his locker was empty. He was ready to start home.

He was sitting on the bench in front of his locker at the Olympic Country Club and he was waiting for Jack Fleck to finish his round. At 5:45 p.m. yesterday, Hogan was presumably the winner of the National Open golf championship. Fleck's finish would make it official. Fleck was playing the 17th and he needed one birdie on the last two holes to tie for the lead and force a playoff. It was an 8000-1 chance that Fleck would come through.

Hogan's wife, Valerie, was waiting upstairs for her man. She, too, was anxious to start back to Fort Worth. The public address system blasted throughout the building: "Mrs. Ben Hogan, long distance telephone, please." Neither Valerie nor Ben heeded the words.

"I hope he (Fleck) takes a two or four on the 18th," Hogan said. He lit a cigarette. He dreaded the thought of another day of golf.

The report came in that Fleck had hit his drive on the 18th into the rough. Hogan sat with head bowed and his arms on his knees. He puffed his cigarette.

A tremendous roar from the crowd overlooking the 18th green rocked through the room. Hogan blinked. Tommy Bolt, standing nearby, couldn't contain himself and yelled out:

"The guy holed his shot from the rough!"

No, somebody quickly contradicted. That was a yell that meant Fleck had hit the green on his second shot. The report came in. Fleck was seven feet past the pin and if he dropped the putt he would tie. Nobody stirred. Then another tremendous roar erupted from the spectators. Hogan put his hands on his thighs and his back stiffened.

"Isn't that awful?" he said. Then he turned to his caddy. "Tony, you better unpack my gear."

Hogan stood up. He didn't glance at the handful of people who were standing nearby. "See you fellows tomorrow," Hogan said. He walked out of the room to join Valerie. They left the club arm in arm.

"That was the unluckiest thing I've ever heard of," said Jackie Burke. The rest of the men in the room were silent.

The time was 6:23 p.m. About 45 minutes before the locker room was a madhouse as Hogan and a mob of newspapermen chattered about Ben's apparent and unprecedented fifth National Open championship.

He had just finished his round—a par 70. He had received a standing ovation from the six or seven thousand people who were watching the show from the slope behind the 18th green. Hogan was humbled by the touching display and stood on the green with bowed head, his famous white cap in his hand. So insistent was the handclapping and yelling that he finally had to ask for silence by putting both arms in the air.

Ben was tired, dog-tired when he finally reached the locker room. He went through a club-by-club rundown on the afternoon round. Then he startled the gathering with the report that he would play no more competitive golf. He altered this when it occurred to him that he hadn't won the title yet.

"If I win this Open," he revised, "I'm going to retire from competitive golf. I don't intend to play in any more open championships. I may try a few tournaments now and then—but I won't be out to win. I intend to become a week end golfer and devote all my time to my business."

Hogan's business is the manufacture of golf clubs. He has his own line on the market and both he and Fleck use them. Hogan's intense desire to manufacture a set of clubs that suited him personally is very nearly fanatic. He revealed that he has about $130,000 worth of clubs that he will not market because they aren't perfect.

Ben's round was marked by three impressive shots. On the 14th, he hit his drive into the rough and then winged a three-wood shot 200 yards to the green; on the 15th he sank a 35-foot birdie putt, which prompted him to smile and remove his cap as the crowd clapped wildly; and on the 17th he hit a brassie shot pin high to the green.

The 17th was Ben's own crown of thorns. It's a 461-yard uphill pull and it's a par four. He had been unable to par the 17th in eight rounds—five practice and three championship. Then when he needed it the most, on yesterday's final 18, Ben parred the hole. He reached the green in two. How come?

"A doctor once told me that when a person gets excited or keyed up, his system gets a squirt of adrenalin," Hogan said. "At that time he is capable of doing things he normally couldn't do. I had the strength to reach the green in two."

Hogan's left knee was still bothering him yesterday. He said that he spent Monday and Tuesday soaking the leg in hot water.

"The more I walk the more painful it becomes," he said. "I know every hill and every rise on that course. I'm certainly glad I rested those two days."

His retirement—if he wins today—will see the end of the "Hogan Era" in golf. He has won everything in sight and then some.

"I'm all through," he said. "Tournament golf takes too much to prepare for. I've been getting ready for this tournament more than a month. I still don't think I'm ready. But this tournament playing is even rougher on Valerie. We want to settle down. The traveling here and there is murder."

Best Magazine Story

By Dick Young

From Sports Illustrated, July 4, 1955

Copyright, 1955, Time, Inc.

"Now i'm out of baseball I guess it's all right to talk about my pitching," Elwin Charles (Preacher) Roe said. He was dressed in street clothes and rested one foot on the top step of the Brooklyn dugout in Busch Stadium in St. Louis. The Dodgers were in for a three-game series with the Cards and The Preach had come up from West Plains, Mo., 155 miles away, to see his old teammates.

"Lot of people have asked me what I used to throw," Roe said, his eyes still on the Dodgers, who were taking batting practice. He turned with a self-conscious movement, as though he were taking off his shirt in public. "I like to tell 'em it was my sinker. Well, you know, the ball did drop real pretty, but it was more than a little ol' sinker. I guess it won't hurt anybody to tell the truth now. I threw spitballs the whole time I was with the Dodgers. Seven years in all."

The fact that he finally had said it seemed to give Roe a kick. He laughed.

"This isn't a confession and my conscience doesn't bother me a bit. Maybe the book says I was cheating, but I never felt that way. I wasn't the only one that did it. There still are some guys wetting 'em up right now. I know one or two of them, but it's not up to me to tell their names. When they get ready to, maybe *they* will. I'm just going to talk about me; why I did it, and why I don't think there's anything wrong with it.

"A pitcher will take any little advantage he can today, and I don't blame him. I'd pitch in front of the rubber when I had a chance. I never used a cut ball much, but I wasn't too proud to—and neither are a lot of the guys around the league.

"One time last year when I was being relieved I stood on the mound and cut a ball with my fingernail real deep. I handed it to

36

the new boy and said: 'I've got a hole in that one if you want to use it. You can get another ball if you want.'

" 'Give it to me,' he said—and he struck out the next batter on three pitches. He's still around, so I'm not gonna say who it was.

"I don't say all the little tricks pitchers use now and then should be legalized, but, hell, the spitball should be. It's not dangerous—no more than the knuckler, and nobody's outlawed that. If they want to know the real truth, you can control a spitter lots easier than a knuckler. And there ain't many things meaner than a fast ball thrown up close to the head."

Roe turned back to the field and watched Carl Erskine lazily throwing in his first warm-up pitches to Dixie Howell.

"See that little tiny plate? That's nothing. How you going to get that ball past a big guy like Kluszewski, with those big arms? The game is getting out of balance. Everything is for the batter. The ball's as live as a rabbit. They sneak the fences in on you a few more feet every year. They used to have a bigger strike zone than now and they keep speeding up the pitcher. The hitters got all the time they please.

"And look at the batters. They can put anything they want on the bats. Molasses and soda. And nobody says nothing, but we're supposed to pitch a brand-new ball all the time.

"Conscience? Hell, it never bothered me none throwing a spitter. If nobody is going to help the pitcher in this game, he's got to help himself. With Brooklyn I must of made around $100,000 and you know I couldn't have made all that kind of money not throwing my wet one."

Some time passed. Then The Preach said: "I'm not trying to fool anybody. No matter how good a pitcher is he ain't gonna win as many games as I did without that defense back of him. Say in the piece I want to thank Billy (Cox) and Pee Wee (Reese) and Jackie Robinson and Hodges for all the help they gave me. And there ain't two better guys than Snider and Furillo to go and get them in the outfield. And Campy (Roy Campanella). I couldn't have got far without all those fellows.

"I'll tell you another little secret. I wasn't always the one to load up the spitter. Once in a while, after the ball had been tossed around the infield, Pee Wee or my buddy, Cox, would come up to the mound, drop the ball easy in my glove, and say: "There it is if you want it."

"That meant they already had the ball wet for me. If I wanted to throw it, I could. If not, I'd just wipe it off. Sometimes Pee Wee would hand me the ball and say:

" 'Gimme that one good pitch now.'

"I knew then what he wanted. He wanted my 'wet curve.'

"I reckon it wasn't the best-kept secret in the world, the fact that I would wet one up occasionally. Some of the players suspicioned it, but they never could catch me at it.

"The first time I knew anybody was on to me was after my first year with the Dodgers. I was pretty crude then and hadn't gotten cute like later. Every time I was going to throw my wetter, I'd rub my glove down on my pants. I did pretty good that year. I went home feeling pretty proud. Then one day I went out hunting birds with Walker Cooper. We were moseying along toward the field when Coop said: 'Hey, Bird Dog, you been throwin' a wet one?'

"That's what he always called me, Bird Dog. I tried not to act surprised.

"I said, 'What you talking about?' I tried to think of the ones I might have thrown him. But he said:

" 'Well, in case you are, you better get a new sign. Everybody in the league knows it!'

"I didn't say yes, and I didn't say no. But when I got to camp that spring, I told Campy about it.

" 'Hell, just throw it,' he said. 'I don't need any sign. I caught spitters in the Negro league for years. You don't have to tell me it's coming.'

"It didn't take me long to find out that Campy wasn't just bragging. He was great at catching it. He'd handle most of them just as smooth as if I was throwing a fast ball. Once in a while, one of them would do a whole lot and get away from him. But Campy was always ready. He figured the umpire would ask for the ball, or the batter would call for the umpire to look at it. Campy'd toe the ball, sly-like, as he bent over to pick it up, and that would roll it dry. He'd do that if nobody was on base. If there were men on, he'd step on it, and grind it into the dirt, hard like, where he could grab it if he had to.

"But don't get Campy in Dutch. He had nothing to do with my throwing a spitter. I mean he never called for it. I decided when I'd throw it. He'd just catch it. In case the Commissioner reads this, I want that understood, hear? After all, what could Campy do? He couldn't shake me off.

"But the Commissioner, I don't think he'd mind. Fact, I hear he wants the spitter back. I'm sort of pleased that Mr. Frick has got that healthy attitude about my pet pitch. Makes me feel I was right all along."

Roe shifted his big panatella from one side of his jaw to the other.

"I started foolin' around with the spitter when I was at Columbus. Red Barrett and Harry Brecheen were there too. All three of us used to throw it around on the sidelines but I never threw it in a game. I could throw hard then. I didn't need another pitch.

"There was a left-handed boy with Indianapolis at the time, named Trimble, or Trinkle, or something like that. He threw a good spitter. I told him I wouldn't tell anyone he was using it if he'd show me how to throw it. He told me he used slippery elm to make the slick water. He'd take a piece of the elm bark, just about a quarter-inch square, and roll it up in his chewing gum to keep it hid. Then he taught me the technique.

"The idea is to get part of your grip wet, and the other dry. When the ball leaves your hand, it slips off your wet fingers and clings, just tiny-like, to the dry part of your thumb. The ball jumps on account of it. If it's a good 'un, it drops like a dead duck just when it crosses the plate.

Roe was handed a ball. He gripped it on the slick leather. Neither the thumb nor the top two fingers touched a seam.

"When you let go you squeeze a little more on the fingers," he said. "Did you ever squeeze a peach pit, or a watermelon seed, and let it shoot out? It's like that. You don't need much spit; just enough to cover the ball under the fingers, a nice thin layer. Some pitchers like to use more, but you have to experiment and find that out for yourself. Every once in a while, I'd get a little more than I needed on a pitch, and the ball would come back to me from the catcher, still wet. So, I'd get another spitter out of the same load. Why waste it?

"This ball is good and smooth. That's the best kind. If you get a scuff mark on the bottom, it might work against the spit on the top; that was one of the reasons I used to ask for a new ball so often. Another reason is that it gave me a chance to load up without being watched.

"Another thing, if you've got even one little grain of sand under your fingertip—where you grip the wet part of the ball—the spitter won't break an inch. I reckon I had 'teacher's fingers.' I could feel the smallest speck of dirt or sand. Sometimes I'd be ready to pitch, and I'd feel in my fingertips it wasn't right. Then I'd back off the rubber or throw over to first base and load it up all over again. It wouldn't make any difference if the dirt or resin was on your third and fourth fingers because you don't use them to pitch anyway.

"Sometimes, when I was ready to throw a spitter and saw that the runner on first was taking too much of a lead, I'd throw a wet one over there, and the ball would do things. But Hodges was good at catching it. He'd give me a big know-it-all grin as he tossed the ball back to me. Other times, with a man on third, I'd be in the middle of my windup, and suddenly feel a grain of sand under my fingertips. I'd have to go through with my windup, or balk, so I'd waste that pitch by throwing it wide, and then I'd make sure I did it right the next time.

"One way I figured out to keep my fingers clean, was to wipe 'em on the visor of my baseball cap. It looked like I was adjusting it on my head. I always made certain the visor was kept clean. I even went to the trouble of brushing it off with a towel on the bench between innings.

"It didn't take long for some of the hitters to figure there was something going on between my spitter and the way I fingered the cap.

"That was just fine for me. I started using the gesture as a decoy. That was as good as the pitch itself. From then on, even when I wasn't going to throw a wet one, I'd go to my cap just to cross them up.

"Jim Russell was one of the guys who suspicioned I was getting the spit from my cap. He was playing with the Braves then.

"This one day, I fingered the tip of my cap, and leaned forward to take the sign. Jim backed out of the batter's box and gave me a real hard look. He stepped back in again—and I touched my cap again. He stepped out. We did this three times. Finally, ol' Jim stood there, blind mad, and said: 'Throw the sonuvabuck and I'll hit it anyway.'

"I floated up a big, slow curve. Russell was so wound up looking for the wet one he couldn't unravel himself to swing. He just spit at the ball in disgust as it went by.

"Jim and the other guys who thought I was getting the spit when I went to my cap were close. I tried that in the early days, but I gave it up because it was too dangerous. I had to figure out a way to load up without getting caught. All one winter I wore my baseball cap. I'd be sitting in my living room with it on, and even wore it out in the woods when I was hunting."

Roe's hand strayed to his forehead. It dropped and he leaned forward.

"For hours at a time," he went on, "all I thought about was some foolproof way to get the spit to the ball without getting caught. I said to myself: 'They'll be watching me close after I come away from the resin bag. That is when they'll expect me to do the wetting. I got to set up the spitter before I go for the resin bag. I got to have a secret "source of supply" so I can squeeze the resin bag in my fingers, rub up the ball, and still keep the spit.'

"I fooled around with that idea for a long time. You know, I ain't very quick. Then one day it came to me. Look, you try it. Put your left hand up to your forehead."

Roe got up to demostrate.

"The meaty part is just in front of your mouth when your fingers touch your brow," he said from behind his hand. "Your two first fingers can just reach the meaty part. 'Spit on the meat,' I told myself, 'and when you move your hand up it looks good and natural like, like you're goin' to wipe the sweat off your forehead.'

"After that, it was just a matter of practice. I finally got so I could hit the spot on the move. Once in a while, I'd miss; not completely, but just enough so the spit would land down near my wrist. I even thought of a gimmick to fix that. Did you ever notice me snap my arm up over my head, and then bring it down sharp— like I was trying to get my arm loose? There was nothing wrong with the arm. I was snapping the spit down to where I could reach it with the flick of my fingertips. My wife used to worry when she saw me do that. She thought I was having arm trouble until I told her what I really was doing.

"When I first started I thought I needed a trick to cover me up when I reached back with my fingers to get the spit. That's when I started tugging at my belt. Try that one, too. Stick your thumb down inside the beltline of your pants, and press the knuckle of your index finger on the outside of your belt. Clench your fist when you do it. That's the natural way to hitch your trousers. And it brings your fingers right where you want 'em.

"After I'd done that a while a lot of the boys thought I was getting the wetness from my belt. So that was another decoy. Sometimes I'd tug at the belt, and some of them would think the spitter was coming. Then I'd throw a fast ball past them, or catch them taking a curve."

What persuaded Roe to start using an illegal pitch?

"Why shouldn't I have?" Roe asked. "I was about through when I decided to get me the pitch. 'If I get caught,' I told myself, 'they'll kick me out. If I don't, I'm through anyway, so how can I lose?'"

That was in the winter of 1947—a fateful year for Roe. The previous summer he had won only four games for Pittsburgh while losing 15. Branch Rickey took a chance on The Preach, bringing him to Brooklyn along with Billy Cox in exchange for the aging Dixie Walker, and Vic Lombardi and Hal Gregg.

"Some people say Mr. Rickey made the deal with a gun," Roe said, "because it turned out so lopsided. But I think even Mr. Rickey doesn't know that it wouldn't have been such a good deal if I hadn't decided that winter to use my spitter."

It *was* pretty lopsided. With Roe's help, the Dodgers won pennants in 1949, 1952 and 1953.

"Maybe you wondered why the bases usually were empty when the other team hit a home run off me," Roe said. "That's because when I was in trouble, I'd use my money pitch. Oh, I'd throw it with the bases empty too, if it was late in the game and I was protecting a one-run lead, say, but mostly I'd use it in a real tough spot, with men on base.

"I remember one game at Ebbets Field, and against the Cardinals, too. I had a 12-2 lead going into the last inning and both those runs were homers, then the Cards hit three more off me— each one longer than the other. After the third one landed upstairs in left-center, I turned around and waved toward Snider. I waved *up*. He moved a few steps to his right, thinking I wanted him to play over for the next hitter. I waved him back, then I pitched and got the last man out.

"After the game, Duke said to me:

" 'Hey, Preach. Wotinhell were you wig-wagging to me about?'

" 'I was trying to tell you that you weren't playing those guys *high* enough.' "

Roe chuckled, unperturbed by this ignominious memory.

"Another little thing I discovered," he said, "the spitter works better in warm weather. It seems to dry up quicker when it's cool.

"I never told any of these little things to the rest of the Dodgers, because I figured someday they might be traded, or maybe I would be, and then I'd get caught.

"No, I take that back; I did tell one man—my roomie, Billy Cox. We got about as close as two fellows can get, I guess, Billy and me, and there wasn't much we didn't know about each other.

"One night, while we were reading in bed, Billy put his paper down and said suddenly:

" 'Roomie, suppose they sell me. You gonna throw it to me?'

" 'What are you talking about?'

" 'You know damned well what I'm talking about,' he said. 'You gonna throw it to me?'

" 'You're darned right I am.'

" 'Well,' he said, 'go ahead, and I'll hit it out of sight.'

"I laughed and said: 'Would you tell on me? If you got traded, I mean?'

"He snickered, turned out the light, and rolled over in bed. 'I reckon not,' he said."

Roe got a slightly worried look.

"I don't want you to get the wrong idea," he said. "Some boys really laid on my spitter and if they ever read your story I want them to know that I know I didn't fool 'em.

"Some of the guys used to hit it pretty good. A lot of my best have gone out of the park. Musial hit one back at me one day, and almost tore my head off. Del Ennis always hit the spitter good; probably better than anyone. It got so bad I had to throw fast balls and sliders to him because he hit the darned things so often. I used to give him nothing but the decoys, but I wouldn't give him the real spitter."

Roe lit another cigar.

"The guys on my team used to call it 'your Beech-Nut curve,' " he continued. "That's because of the gum. On the bench, between innings, I'd dig into my pocket for a stick of it, and say: 'I'm gonna get me a new batch of curve balls.'

"I don't know why Beech-Nut was better. There seemed to be something in it that would make the ball slicker than any other gum. If this is a testimonial, then they can have it for free. I'm just telling the truth. I tried every kind of gum, and tried that slippery elm, too, but nothing worked for me like plain old Beech-Nut.

"I found out something else about Beech-Nut. It was the only kind of gum that would make the ink on a ball fade, and I think that might have been what caused it to be the best.

"I reckon when it came to complaining, Luke Sewell was about the complainingest manager, and Sid Gordon the hollerin'est hitter. But the way Sid hit me, I never could figure out why he bothered to complain. Boy, he wore me out.

"That Sewell, though, he never did stop yelling to the umpires. He'd always have his hitters make the umpire call for the ball. He'd do it three or four times a game. I usually rolled the ball to the umpire, whether I had anything on it or not. That used to make Sewell madder, and he'd call me every name he could think of—and he could think of some honeys.

"One day, while Sewell was bawling from the Cincinnati dugout, Babe Pinelli, who was umpiring at second, sneaked up behind me and asked for the ball. It so happened that I didn't have it loaded, so I just handed him the ball. He looked at it, and hollered to Sewell:

" 'Stop yelling, Luke. It's dry as a 'coon's backside.'

"Al Dark is another good hitter who complained about the spitter. He used to team up with Leo Durocher to give me hell. I told Al that it was a screwball, not a spitter. He was too smart to swallow that, though. He knew it was a spitter, but he couldn't prove it.

"There's one thing I always wondered about, where Durocher and Dark were concerned. They never hollered at me when I pitched against Sal Maglie. Any other pitcher working for the Giants, and they'd beef about spitters; never when Sal pitched against me. I still think about that."

Roe, who had suited up and tossed a few just for old times' sake, came back and sat down.

"I was lucky because I made a lot of friends, not only on my own club, but on the others," he said. "I guess I could have been a mean sonuvabuck and knocked down hitters with my spitter. It would have been a mean knockdown pitch. But I figured I was on dangerous ground, just throwing an illegal pitch, and if I ever hit anybody with it, they'd really start clamping down on me. So I let well enough alone. I'd just brush a guy back once in a while with my fast ball.

"But, hell, that's all any man should do. You ain't out there to kill a body. And as long as you don't throw at a hitter, I know it ain't dangerous, spitters or knucklers or anything you got. I know when they outlawed the pitch in the old days they let guys like Burleigh Grimes go on using it till the end of their careers, just as long as they came up with it. They couldn't have been *too* scared of the pitch.

"I didn't come up from the minors with it and I guess you would say I was a criminal with it, sort of. But it wasn't my only pitch. You don't have to believe this, but I was a wild fast-balling pitcher in my young days. Fact is, I could throw harder than most people thought when I was at my peak in Brooklyn. Folks used to make jokes about my 'hummer.' They'd say if it hit you in the nose it wouldn't blacken your eyes. I used to encourage them. It helped me fool batters with my fast ball. I didn't use it too often, but when I did, it wasn't bad. Not bad at all. Jusk ask Campy. I struck out quite a few guys with my 'hummer.'

"But my spitter was my 'money pitch.' I'd save it till I was in a jam.

"Well, who cares now? I figure I made some good money throwing my spitter for Brooklyn. That's three World Series cuts too, you know. I have a nice home, a cabin just across the Arkansas border, a small boat house and I bought a good grocery business. Not bad for a little ol' country boy. I'm for spitballs. I like 'em."

The World Series

TWO MEN GAMBLED

By Roger Birtwell

From The Boston Globe, September 30, 1955

TWO MEN GAMBLED.

Both startled 65,000 with daring dashes for home.

Both deeds were rash.

Both defied the accumulated wisdom of baseball that had been amassed through more than 100 years.

Both were made in the tenseness of the opening game of the World Series here yesterday.

One was attempted by a lean, spry fellow of 26—Billy Martin of the New York Yankees.

The other was attempted by a heavy, almost fat, man of 36—Jackie Robinson of the Brooklyn Dodgers.

Martin did it with his team two runs ahead.

Robinson did it with his team two runs behind.

Both did it with two men down.

Martin failed . . . but his team went on to triumph.

Robinson succeeded . . . but his team went down to defeat.

Record books, long years from now, will tell how two homers by Joe Collins—nee Kollings—win the first game of the 1955 World Series for the Yankees.

But I, with 65,000 others, will remember those two quick dashes for home.

In the steam of the Dodger dressing room, after the game was over, Jackie Robinson was tugging a towel back and forth across his back.

"Bush!" he declared, "so Yogi says I was bush . . . Is it better to get one run or wait for two . . . Any time they give me a run, I'll take it . . . What was bush about it—for Yogi—was that he didn't tag me out.

46

"Is it easier to score two—with one man on—than it is to score one?

"On the previous pitch, Ford didn't pay much attention to me . . . Why should he? . . . We were two runs behind—with two down —in the top of the eighth . . . Why should a man ever dream of a steal? . . . So he didn't pay much attention to me.

"If I'm out, it's bush—and I know it . . . We're still two runs behind, and the Duke doesn't get to bat . . . One swish of the bat, and the Duke might tie the score.

"So I went. I saw the white of the plate as I went across it. Yogi's mitt was at the back of the plate. And I scored."

In the dim shadows of the Yankee clubhouse, somewhat later, I walked over to the locker of Billy Martin.

His dash for home also had been a tremendous surprise.

With two down in the sixth and his team three runs ahead, he had tripled to left center.

Then, to get another run—maybe more—and increase the Yankee lead, Manager Casey Stengel had yanked shortstop Phil Rizzuto for a pinch-hitter. Stengel had sent up a lefthanded hitter —Eddie Robinson.

Because Robinson was lefthanded, it made it easier for him to pull toward the nearby right field fence. And it also made it easier for a catcher to tag a man attempting to steal from third . . . if any man were so rash as to try.

In Stengel's office, a moment before, the Yankee manager had said:

"I didn't take Rizzuto out because he couldn't play shortstop. I took him out to get some runs. But I wouldn't say a thing to discourage Martin. He knows baseball, a lot of baseball, and he makes smart plays. If I said a thing to discourage him, I might keep him from saving me a game some day."

And now I turned to Martin, as he buttoned his shirt in the dusk.

The last of the reporters were leaving him, and as they left, I could hear the words . . . "Swell try, Billy." . . . "That took guts." . . . and so on.

"The score and the outs made it unexpected," I said. "You had surprise on your side."

The little fellow stood there . . . and he thought it over.

Then he spoke.

"Do you know," he said slowly, "I don't think I'd ever do that again.

"I took a bat out of a man's hand.

"He took out Rizzuto and sent up Robby to get some runs.

"It's hard not to run when a pitcher double-pumps—and if it happened again, I might do it.

"But I don't think I would.

"I don't think I—ever again—would take a bat out of a man's hands."

A LIFE FOR THE DODGERS

By Bob Hunter

From The Los Angeles Examiner, October 2, 1955

YESTERDAY HOPE came tip-toeing back for the faithful fans of Flatbush, but this afternoon it came stomping in boldly and parked itself squarely beside the incomparable Yankees.

There is a new gleam, a new challenge, a new life tonight in Brooklyn as the Dodgers, who suddenly have become competitors instead of collaborators in this World Series, whipped the American Leaguers, 8 to 5, for the second straight game.

Suddenly, in the early evening of a Saturday night, the narrow sidewalks have become verdant parks, the dingy tenements are palaces, the tree that grows here is a fruitful forest and a pail of suds is a magnum of champagne.

Everything is wonderful in Flatbush tonight.

And just a couple of days ago, when the proposal to move the Dodgers to Jersey City again came up, the faithful of Flatbush had but one objection.

They didn't think it was far enough.

However, a magnificent performance by Duke Snider today, both in the field and at the plate, plus the expected fine relief work of Clem Labine, had changed all that.

No longer do the faithful fans of Flatbush want to give their Dodgers the Bums' rush, as the Yankees did the first two games.

Now the thing starts all over again—its a new trip on the fickle carousel, this time it's two out of three.

It means the war has to go back across the river, and the Yanks swore they'd never return there again this year.

But Brooklyn, completely dominating the day—from the singing of the National Anthem to the homicidal dash for the subway —has forced the play back to the big house on Monday.

Tomorrow, in the final game at Ebbets field, it will be a surprise starter for the surprising Dodgers, Roger Craig, with a rather downhearted Casey Stengel summoning Bob Grim to rally his disconsolate Yankees.

I want to go on record right now, so it won't be a second guess, that Ol' Smokey, or Walt Alston, is making a mistake by picking Craig.

Guys like Don Newcombe aren't going to be of much value to Ol' Smokey after next Tuesday. I hope he knows that.

He almost waited too long to come with Oiskin—that's the way they pronounce it here. Over in the Yankee Stadium it's Erskine.

But the magnificent hitting and the greater fielding of the Duke from Lynwood took care of the Dodgers and insured a glorious Saturday night in Flatbush.

There aren't any better fielders in this business than Snider.

He did what Willie Mays did in the series last year, but he did it oftener.

The Duke took a hit and a couple of runs away from Irv Noren by picking a 400-foot drive off the wall in the sixth, and on the next batter he glided swiftly in back of second base to spear Gil McDougald's dangerous low liner.

His seventh World Series homer which you saw come with two men on in the fifth, put the Maraschino cherry on the dessert for these beloved Bums.

I imagine you wondered, if you were up early enough to be in your reserved set by "Play Ball" time, just why Casey Stengel left Pitcher Don Larsen in there so long.

I did.

He was behind the batters in the first inning, although he did retire the Dodgers in rotation.

He was 3 and 1 with both Carl Furillo and Gil Hodges, and 3 and 2 with Jackie Robinson in the second.

He was 3 and 2 before walking Amoros in the third.

He was—well that's when the roof fell all the way in. The fourth, when Roy Campanella on a 3 and 1 pitch and Hodges hit the ball out of the park for three runs.

Finally, at long last, Stengel removed Larsen in the fifth, and young John Kucks came on in time to get whacked with Snider's payoff wallop.

Just before the Duke made his majestic swing, you saw Gilliam steal second base.

Perhaps you mentally blamed Yogi Berra for that, but if you were watching closely you must have noticed Larsen was not watching Gilliam closely.

He let Junior get a big jump, which is what is known to the trade as stealing on the pitcher.

When the next pitch to Peewee Reese was ball two, Stengel got the hook for Larsen.

On came Kucks, and you saw Reese tap one down the first base line, on which both Joe Collins and Kucks reacted as though it was something new to them.

The first rule for a pitcher on a ground ball hit to the right side, is to race to first base.

Collins picked up the teasing trickler, hesitated too long to make the play himself, then finally tossed to Kucks, who was too late to cover the bag.

A very un-Yankee maneuver, indeed.

Stengel could have taken out Larsen a lot earlier, too, for a couple of other reasons.

He would have saved a big lump in the throats of the Yankee fans, not to mention a bigger one on Owner Del Webb's head.

It was in the fifth, with the Dodgers leading 4-3, you'll recall, and Stengel let Larsen lead off for himself.

At that point, especially the way Larsen was conducting himself, it was much more necessary to get runs than just about anything else.

But he let Larsen bat, and the Yankee pitcher nine-ironed a shot some hundred feet above the 36,242 patrons of the art.

Webb, busily engaged talking to Commissioner Ford Frick, then tipped off the fans why his playing career lasted so quickly, because he fielded the ball with his head.

It smacked him on the right temple, and he probably was saved from serious injury by a protective helmet, a dark blue, soft fedora number that cushioned the shock.

Webb is one who agrees that Stengel was a bum for leaving Larsen in there so long.

YANKEES NEVER DIE

By Curley Grieve

From The San Francisco Examiner, October 4, 1955

CHARLIE DRESSEN, when manager of Brooklyn, once said "The Giants is dead."

There were some, in the flush of yesterday's success, who thought that the once mighty Yankees were dead—at least for this World Series.

But the Yankees never die and seldom fade away—they must be pushed off a precipice.

And so today, riding behind a Ford that never once sputtered and stuffing themselves with runs at the outset of the trip, the Bombers bounced back from three straight defeats to drub the Dodgers, 5-1, and tie up the series.

Now it's three games apiece with the seventh and final game slated tomorrow under ideal weather conditions, and the big pot of gold at the end of the rainbow as the prize.

Walter Alston has picked Johnny Podres to oppose Tommy Byrne, who is Casey Stengel's choice.

While the day was typically fall, sunny overhead and cool to the spectator army of 64,022 in the triple tiered stands, it was a dark, dreary and foreboding occasion for the fanatics across the Gowanus Canal.

Their heroes not only lost the game and the psychological advantage gained through the blood curdling show of home run power in bandbox Ebbets Field, but they very likely lost their two star performers for tomorrow's last stand.

Duke Snider, the avocado farmer from Linwood, Calif., injured his left knee when he stepped into a gopher hole in centerfield chasing a fly ball in the third inning. Something "popped" and the resultant pain forced his withdrawal.

Then Jackie Robinson, veteran Dodger third baseman, said tonight he might not be able to play in the final game because of an injured foot.

Robinson, who failed to get a hit in four times at bat and made

52

one error in today's Yankee victory, said the Achilles tendon in his left heel became sore late Sunday.

"I don't know how I got it," Robinson said, "but it pained me all during today's game. I can't tell right now whether I can play. It all depends on how the foot feels tomorrow. I want to play if I can help the club. It is up to Walt (Manager Walter Alston)."

If Robinson is unable to play, Don Hoak likely will take over third.

Snider has been the backbone in the Dodger comeback after losing the first two games.

He won Saturday's game in Brooklyn with a three run homer and collected two four basers yesterday to clinch that contest. In all, he has belted four this series and his fielding, too, has verged on the miraculous.

Snider refused to count himself out definitely but it could be that, as in Mickey Mantle's case, he would be too crippled for a top performance even if he does feel able to start.

Up to this point, the Yanks have suffered the most from casualties. Loss of Mantle, the team's big punch, and partial loss of Hank Bauer has severely sapped the Stengels, particularly at the plate.

In any event, the circumstances point once again to a Yankee World Series victory and frustration for Brooklyn, the perennial bridesmaid. A drowning man goes down only three times. The Flatbush faithful have gone down seven and this would be the eighth.

Whitey Ford and Bill Skowron thrust the daggers into the Dodger hearts today.

Ford fanned eight as he pitched a magnificently smooth four hitter, to explode once again the myth that no lefthander could shackle the Dodger batting order which started with seven right-handers and wound up with eight.

While Ford's job reminded you of an artist working with a brush, Skowron's role was more that of a blacksmith breaking a girder with a mighty blow of the mallet.

He climaxed the unhappy debut of lefthanded Karl Spooner in his first World Series starting assignment by lining the ball into the rightfield stands with two runners aboard in the first inning.

Two runs previously had crossed the plate so that Skowron's display of muscle made it a five run frame and surely inspired the grim and chunky Ford to an almost faultless performance.

He protected his cushion as if it were money in the bank and well it might be.

Whitey, though credited with the victory in the first Series game, did not finish. Bob Grim pitched the ninth inning. In fact, Ford had never finished a World Series game until today. Back in 1950 he went down to the last man then, after Gene Woodling had dropped a fly in left, Stengel called for Allie Reynolds to blow strikes by the final batter, a Philly whiz kid.

It was said, too, that Whitey, a New York product who came out of the Hearst sandlot classic, tired and tripped invariably in the eighth and ninth innings. They were like a hoodoo. But today he skimmed over those hurdles, getting three strikeouts and facing only six men.

He finished like Reynolds of yore—fanning his man, in this case, Sandy Amoros, on four pitches.

Skowron, I felt, ducked his head and closed his eyes when he belted his homer. It just didn't have the ring of authenticity. He picked off an obvious brush back fast ball from around his ears and curved it into the exposed seats that seep into right field.

Spooner, so effective in a relief role when he hurled three scoreless innings and fanned five, seemed as scared as a schoolboy giving his first concert.

He walked Phil Rizzuto, first man to face him in a lineup that Stengel revised to concentrate his righthanded power against the lefthanded Dodger rookie.

Then, after striking out Billy Martin, careless Karl walked Gil McDougald to place himself in the hole. The Yanks didn't need an engraved invitation this time, although they apparently were waiting for it in other recent situations.

Yogi Berra, with two strikes against him, hit the third pitch to the right of second. For a moment it looked like a doubleplay ball. But Junior Gilliam missed with his stab and it rolled to centerfield, Rizzuto scoring and McDougald traveling to third.

Spooner got two quick strikes on Bauer and then lost him. Hank singled through the hole at shortstop, McDougald scoring and Berra stopping at second.

Skowron, as big as a moose and so nicknamed, was down two strikes in a hurry.

Spooner, who came on the baseball horizon late last fall like a comet pitching two shutouts and fanning twenty-seven, obviously threw his fast ball high and inside, about under the chin. It surely must have been his intent at least to scare the Yankee first sacker and keep him from taking a toehold on succeeding pitches.

Skowron stepped back and swung. The ball sailed into the stands and three runs trotted across the plate.

That was the end of Spooner and the Dodgers. In fact, it was the end of the fireworks for the Yanks.

Russ Meyer and Ed Roebuck blanked the Bombers on four hits the rest of the way. The winners got only eight hits in all, not one for extra bases except Skowron's.

But even more humiliating was the fate of the Dodger heavy artillery which had been making so much noise the three previous days.

Snider fanned in his only appearance. Roy Campanella was baffled completely by Ford's change of pace and never got more than a piece of the ball, although he walked once. He also fanned once.

Carl Furillo got one hit and one strikeout, while both Gil Hodges and Robinson were blanked.

Gilliam, Reese and Amoros, in addition to Furillo, collected hits but none was for more than one base.

The Dodgers scored their lone run in the fourth. Reese launched the inning with a single and Don Zimmer, batting for Snider, struck out. Campanella walked to place a man in scoring position and Furillo's single accomplished the job. But neither Hodges nor Robinson could sustain the rally.

Ford, in addition to his curve, fastball, changeup and control, had perfect support.

McDougald at third did a fine fielding job on four hard chances and Joe Collins, replacing Skowron at first when the Dodgers shifted to righthanded pitchers, made an outstanding play in the seventh when he gloved Reese's hard hit grounder and threw to second for a forceout. There were two on and two out at the time. If Collins had thrown to first, he would have been too late and Ford would have found the bags loaded.

Skowron's home run, incidentally, was the seventeenth in the Series, tieing the record. Each team fashioned a doubleplay, making a total of eighteen and another Series record. The Dodgers' twin killing was their eleventh, which stands as a Series record for one club.

Berra, catching his thirty-ninth Series game, broke a record held by Bill Dickey, now a Yankee coach, and Rizzuto tied Joe

DiMaggio's mark of fifty-one Series games. This is Phil's ninth Series. Joe played in ten.

Elston Howard may be setting some kind of a Yankee record, too. He fanned three times in four trips today, running his strike-out mark for the Series to eight.

With the Series going the full distance of seven games, all hands now can confidently look forward to a raise. The owners are in clover.

Once, when the Yanks wrapped it up in four, they were told at the victory banquet by General Manager George Weiss: "Don't dream of a raise—the Series finished too quickly."

THE MERCIFUL EXECUTIONER

By Al Cartwright

From The Wilmington (Del.) Journal-Every Evening, October 5, 1955

JOHNNY PODRES was a merciful executioner.

Three batters and 16 pitches in the bottom of the ninth, and the Yankees were dead.

It was a swift, neat end to a deliriously tense afternoon, one in which the world's championship had teetered on virtually every moving baseball.

And when Shortstop Pee Wee Reese flipped out Elston Howard, he flipped out with the last batter the most insidious whammy of all time—Yankees over Dodgers in the World Series—at the same time putting to rout the greatest frustration of 'em all. That would be Brooklyn's failure ever to win a world's title in seven other playoffs dating back to 1916.

The Brooks' magic number turned out to be eight.

Even the most bitter New York rooter in the jammed stands at Yankee Stadium yesterday had to feel a pinch of pleasure for the new champions, by this time going crazy with acrobatic joy down on the diamond as they reeled towards a clubhouse that was jumping for long afterward. Even the bleeding loser near the press rows, who came up with the best crack of the hour as he dragged himself out of his seat: "Wait 'til next year!"

If it is any consolation to the proud, classy Yankees, it can be truly said that they made 'em sweat. Seven games, and a 2 to 0 thriller in the very last one before they bowed to a Brooklyn opponent that they had owned over the years, like a man owns a pet. The Yankees, their second-line pitching a flop and with their most glamorous slugger, Mickey Mantle, of only token use, went down swinging.

Swinging is the right word, used either to describe their losing cuts at the pitches of the new boy wonder, Podres, or the way they finally dangled at the end of the World Series rope.

There must be police raids on crowded crap games that are more orderly than the scene in the whooping, milling Brooklyn bathhouse. As TV and movie cameras and bright lights and microphones took up every hunk of space that wasn't occupied by a

57

screaming ball player, a frothing announcer or a scribbling news-paper guy, the Dodgers finally made it to baseball's heavens.

We were more or less comfortable near Carl Furillo's diggings, shouting back and forth to this old Reading playmate, when Yogi Berra and Phil Rizzuto of the losers came in to pay their respects. The first Dodger they paid was their fellow Latin, Furillo.

"We finally beat you two unmentionables," roared Furillo, by this time wearing nothing but a cigarette. "What are you two guys going to do now—start raising mushrooms?"

There was warm small talk batted back and forth.

"Amoros plays me wrong," Berra is saying, without a tinge of defeat in him. "Everybody else give me all the left field I want. He has to be going the right way and makes a great catch."

"All right, so we play you stupid," laughs Furillo, crazily. "So we beat you. Hey, let's send that guy Billy Cox a wire and tell him to get lost in Harrisburg. Let's wire him that the boys didn't choke up."

Jackie Robinson pushes his way over to Berra and shakes his hand, saying, "I still say you're the only one of the whole lot we fear."

Yogi grins and asks Jackie, "What are you gonna do now, quit?"

Jackie whispers something in a Berra ear and they both laugh. Then a photographer grabs Yogi and Rizzuto and poses them with various Dodgers and pretty soon the two grand Yankees retire to comparative oblivion while the Dodgers and their well-wishers continue to make with the shake, rattle and roll.

Victory was a cold can of beer and a crazy derby on Duke Snider and a beaming Walt Alston and a happily cussing Jake Pitler and everybody trying to talk at once to a panting, jabbering, ecstatic Johnny Podres. V-Day, for the Brooklyn Dodgers.

When peace is restored sometime around the middle of December, they soberly will thank their stars that a 23-year-old left-handed pitcher named Podres was on their side.

The story of the Brooklyn ascension has got to be the New York State youngster who, started almost in desperation, pitched an 8-3 triumph that was the Dodgers' first in three games, then came back to shut out the unbeatable home club in the finals. Two starts, two nine-inning wins for a pitcher who hadn't completed a game since June, who had been relieved 13 straight times, who 10 days before the series was hurtin' so that he couldn't even throw.

It was the bottom of the fourth, Brooklyn ahead by 1-0 and Podres had just left Berra on second after Yogi had led off with that preposterous pop-fly double that Snider let fall. This was the third inning in a row that a Yankee had been marooned, and by this time it was apparent that Johnny still possessed all the tangible equipment—mostly the hard one, mixed with the letup ball that was his meal-ticket—that had so completely tamed New York over in Brooklyn. So we scratched on the scorebook, "Fourth inning, seems like Podres has it."

By "it" was meant the ball game, and that is the way things turned out. But not after Podres was put through the cruelest wringer that any pitcher has ever experienced. An eight-hit shutout is a shutout the hard way, and a 2-0 lead against the Yankees is no armchair. That was the backdrop of the Podres performance.

Those sixth and eighth innings of Podres' were sheer wonder, beautiful baseball. The Amoros catch on Berra, which doubled HcDougald off first base with nobody out and two on, saved his life, for if the ball had dropped the score would have been 2-2 and Labine would have been summoned. Podres was grateful. He needed no Red Cross in the eighth, with Rizzuto on third and McDougald on first, after a bad-hop single that should have meant the second out. Podres delivered three straight balls to Berra, got a strike and then his man, on a short fly to right. Danger still ahead, because Bauer was up. But Bauer was struck out, on a pitch that Podres later said "really had something on it. I doubt if Bauer saw the ball."

Finally, the tidy ninth—1-2-3, bang, and Podres and the Dodgers do it against the Yankees, four games to three. A sparring partner had flattened Marciano.

Other Baseball

BIG MAN FROM NICETOWN

By Dick Seamon

From Time, August 8, 1955

HIS LEGS are buckled into clumsy shin guards; his face is hidden by the metal grille of a heavy mask. Behind him, vague and impersonal, rises the roar of the crowd. His chest is covered with a corrugated protective pad, and his big mitt is thrust out as if to fend off destruction. Exactly 60 ft. 6 in. straight ahead of him, the pitcher looms preternaturally large on his mound of earth. As he crouches close to the ground, his field of vision gives him his own special view of the vast ballpark. The white foul lines stretch to the distant fences; the outfielders seem to be men without legs. Between him and the fly-catchers, from the far outfield grass to the brown base paths, the rest of the team twitches nervously in place. In a sense, the game belongs to him. He is the catcher.

The once-a-week ball fan may think of the catcher merely as a target for the pitcher to shoot at. Actually, the job is the most demanding in baseball. A good catcher must be able to take punishment. Foul tips batter his hands; the batter's big club swishes past his skull; base runners hit him with intent to maim as they slide for home. Through it all he must use his head, for he is baseball's tactical commander, its platoon leader. He must watch the signs according to the batter, the score, the inning. He must hide his own signals from the runner on second, check his fielders as they shift position, be ever alert for the hit-and-run—the dangerous play that can be stopped before it starts by a catcher calling for a pitch-out.

No active player in American baseball fills that formidable job better than a burly, bulging (5 ft. 9 in., 205 lbs.), cocoa-colored catcher named Roy Campanella, currently enjoying one of the best seasons of his long career on the best team in baseball.

On the bench, ruminating over a cud of tobacco, the Brooklyn

60

Dodgers' Catcher Campanella is the picture of tranquility. He never makes an unnecessary move. Take away the uniform, and he would look for all the world like a displaced Buddha in calm contemplation. But the fans sit up when he waddles to his place behind the plate. A remarkable transformation takes place: the somnolent bulk becomes a quick and agile athlete. After he has strapped on the "tools of ignorance," hunkered down in the close confines of the modern catcher's box, he is the heart of the team. The pitcher waits for his signals. (Earlier, team and manager have talked over opposing batters, come to some tentative conclusions about strategy.) Campy calls for the curve or the fast ball, the change-up or the slider. It is a rare event when the man on the mound shakes him off, i.e., refuses his signal. By now most Dodger pitchers, reveling this week in an unbeatable 13½-game lead in the National League, know that their catcher knows best.

Squeaking with enthusiasm, Campy keeps a chatter of encouragement flowing back to the pitcher. "Come on, roomie," he will holler at his road-trip roommate, Don Newcombe. "Hum that pea." Neither Newk nor anyone else is permitted a moment's carelessness. Once, when Don Newcombe crossed up his catcher with a slow curve after taking the signal for a fast ball, Roy promptly flipped off his mask and padded out to the mound. "How come you give me the local when I call for the express?" he demanded in singsong irritation. Campy believes that his chatter helps. Says he: "You shouldn't be a dead pants out there."

All the while, going through his acrobatic gyrations—lunging for bad pitches, darting like a great cat after well-dropped bunts, settling under pop fouls or wheeling and firing to pick a man off base—Campy keeps the good catcher's track of every aspect of the game. It takes a hog-wild pitcher to whip a ball out of Campanella's reach, or stick a pitch in the dirt that he cannot dig out. "I line up my body for the way it's coming in," he says, "and jump if it's too much outside. I do it all pre-advance. It might be easier just to stick out the glove like most of them, but you might get the wrong tendency. If you keep moving every day, you'll get in the right habit."

Never has a catcher kept moving as much as Campy. In 19 years of active play, he has caught nearly 3,000 games. For nearly six years he survived a man-killing, year-round schedule—Negro leagues in the summer, tropical ball in the winter. In rickety buses he rattled across the Midwest and the Central American mountains, playing for peanuts, but always playing well. During seven seasons as a Dodger regular he has cheerfully suffered an extraordinary collection of broken bones, beanballs and assorted bruises. He has learned his trade so well that today old-timers rank him with the best ever, with Bill Dickey and "Gabby" Hartnett, "Mickey" Cochrane and Roger Bresnahan.

Somewhere in their vast farm system, the Dodgers feel sure, they have a replacement for their tiring third baseman, Jackie Robinson, for their spry but elderly (36) captain and shortstop, Pee Wee Reese. When the time comes, they may even be able to turn up another outfielder almost as good as Duke Snider. But a substitute for Campy is a dream. To Dodger rooters, 1955 is the year of destiny, and destiny has the bulky shape of Roy Campanella.

Brooklyn teams have always had a special genius for blowing ball games in a thousand different ways. Brooklyn ball fans grew up with the Daffiness Boys and their bonehead base running of the '20s. They remember a rooter who turned murderer with rage over a loss to the Giants, a minister praying vainly for victory (1946— the Cardinals won the pennant) on the steps of Borough Hall, Catcher Mickey Owen dropping a third strike and losing a championship. With the inevitability of Greek tragedy, the beloved Bums were often contenders, sometimes won pennants and never won a World Series.

From the first, this year promised to be different. The Dodgers started so fast that the whole league has been chasing them hopelessly ever since. With a ten-game and an eleven-game winning streak, they racked up the big lead that they have been hanging on to steadily. They have been equal to all their troubles. Out of long experience, Manager Walter ("Smokey") Alston knew just how to discipline Big Don Newcombe when he kicked up a full about pitching batting practice; Big Newk has been pitching (18 won, 1 lost) and hitting (.376 at week's end) with astonishing skill ever since. With Pee Wee Reese, Junior Gilliam and Carl Furillo all doing their share, there is hardly a chance that the team can pick up its old habit of relaxing and folding in the stretch. Above all, Campy is back in shape. For two weeks the Dodgers fretted while he recovered from a loose bone spur in his knee; now he functions with his old, Buddha's efficiency. Last week he was back behind the plate to help a couple of rookie pitchers, Don Bessent and Roger Craig, hold off the opposition and give the Dodgers' sore-armed veterans a rest. At bat, he is once more teaming up with Centerfielder Duke Snider to make one of the toughest one-two hitting combinations since Ruth and Gehrig. Campy settles into the batter's box with sure confidence—legs spread, left foot in the bucket so that he is half facing the pitcher—and he rattles out base hits and moves with the swift authority that is the secret dream of youth. Roy Campanella has been nurturing that dream ever since he was 15, when he started playing baseball for pay in a North Philadelphia neighborhood known as Nicetown, where he was born 34 years ago. From his Sicilian father, piano-legged Roy inherited his proportions and a capacity for enjoying hard work. While he supported a wife and five hungry kids on the proceeds of a vegetable wagon, John Campanella still managed to save enough cash to chip in with his brothers and open a chain of neighborhood grocers. From his Negro mother, Roy learned piety. Although his father was a Roman Catholic, his mother took him to Baptist church, raised him on the precepts of the 23rd Psalm. Today, Campy sees nothing unusual in the fact that he sends his own eldest son to a Presbyterian Sunday School simply because it fields a smart "Little League" baseball team.

As a roly-poly youngster, Campy sold newspapers, cut grass, shined shoes. Mornings he got up at 2:30 to help his older brother Lawrence run a milk route. By 5:30 he was back in bed; at 8 he was on his way to school. Always, young Roy's income was turned over to his mother, and always, his allowance was spent on movies or a ball game. Shibe Park (now Connie Mack Stadium) was within walking distance of the Campanella home, and any afternoon there was a game, Roy was there, too. For a quarter a kid could get an unofficial bleachers seat on the roof of one of the houses adjoining the field.

Most kids on the narrow Nicetown streets played a form of stickball; not Roy Campanella. His big hands felt awkward on a slim broomstick. He played honest sand-lot baseball with the Nicetown Colored Athletic Club or the Nicetown Giants. Soon he was good enough for American Legion ball with Loudenslager Post No. 366.

Campy was not much of a hitter in those days, but he made the most of the gifts he had. In the spring of 1936, the baseball coach at Elizabeth Gillespie Junior High School put out a call for candidates. The best boys would be allowed to play for nearby Simon Gratz High School. Campy watched his buddies gather into separate groups, one for pitchers, one for infielders, one for outfielders.

No one moved to the catcher's circle. Then and there, he made up his mind. Why ask for competition? He would be a catcher.

Campy was only 15 when the owner of the Bacharach Giants, an all-Negro semi-pro team, offered Mrs. Campanella $35 a week for her son's services on Friday nights, Saturdays and Sundays. Mrs. Campanella boggled at the idea of Sabbath baseball, agreed only when the Bacharachs' owner promised that wherever the team was playing, he himself would take Roy to church on Sunday.

No sooner was Campy squared away with the Bacharach Giants than he was hired away by the Washington Elite Giants (which later became the Baltimore Elite Giants). One afternoon the Elite manager gave Campy a uniform to try on and whisked him off to a game in Norristown, Pa. Before long, Campy quit high school and went barnstorming with the Elites from New York to Kansas City, following the crazy, mixed-up schedules of the Negro leagues.

Before the major leagues started to siphon off their stars, the Negro circuits had enough good players to fill a Negro-American and National League. From May to October the "bus" leagues zigzagged across the U. S. Their buses were rolling dormitories: seats, aisles and luggage racks did double duty as beds. Often there was no time for a meal stop, and sometimes no restaurant would serve a colored team. Then the players would carve up a big bologna and make sandwiches as they rolled along. Eating money, when Campy started out, was 50¢ a day.

When he was not catching, Campy played the outfield or pitched; the trick was to stay in the line-up at any cost. "Since there was no trainer to tell us when we got hurt, a man kept playing as long as he could stand up," Campy remembers. "You had to. You got paid if you played. There were no averages kept in those days. You couldn't go up to the boss and say 'Look here, I'm hitting .350, so how about a raise?' All you could do was make sure you played every day."

For all their long season, the rough-and-ready Negro leagues could not keep Campy busy enough, and he took to spending his winters playing Caribbean baseball. Latin embellishments added much to the color, if not the caliber of the game. Puerto Rican fans passed the hat for him when he hit a pair of home runs; Campy returned the kindness by distributing a 100-lb. bag of potatoes in the slums. In Mexico he learned all the things that could happen to a baseball in thin mountain air. "You could hit a ball nine miles, but the running was awful. The pitchers couldn't curve the ball, either."

One night in Caracas, Campy remembers with glee, Pitcher Saul Rogovin (now with the Philadelphia Phillies) decided that he was not in the mood to work. His manager thought otherwise and sent him to the mound. To prove his point, Rogovin promptly walked the first four batters. Furious at this insubordination, the manager called the cops and Pitcher Rogovin was marched off to the local jail.

In those days, the Negro leagues had a standard gag: a report that a scout from a major-league club was in the stands. It was a bitter joke, because Negro players had not yet been accepted by the majors. One cold October day in 1945, after a team of Negro All-Stars had been whipped by a collection of big-leaguers, Dodger Coach Chuck Dressen cornered Campy outside Newark's Ruppert Stadium. He told Campanella that Branch Rickey, then the Dodgers' president, wanted to see him. Campy went along with what he thought must surely be a gag. But next day in the Dodgers' Brooklyn office he was scowled at, whispered to, thundered at, gently praised, scathingly questioned. "Mr. Rickey had me buffaloed," he recalls with awe. Asked about his weight, he answered that he was pushing about 215. "Judan priest!" Rickey roared. "You can't weigh that much and play ball!" Said Campy: "All I know is I've been doin' it every day for years."

Finally Rickey waved his unlit cigar and came to the point: How would Mr. Campanella like to join the Brooklyn organization? There was a rumor going around that Rickey was forming a Negro league, and Campy, wanting no part of the prospective Brown Dodgers, turned Rickey down cold. A few days later, he found himself in a gin rummy game with another Negro ballplayer named Jackie Robinson, 1938-40 topflight halfback for U.C.L.A. Robby came out with big news: he, too, had an offer from Rickey and he had signed—not for the Brown Dodgers, but to play with the Montreal Royals of the International League. He was about to become the first Negro to break into organized baseball. "I could have kicked my butt," says Campy now. But his own chance was to come.

In March 1946, in response to an urgent telegram from Rickey, Campy came home from the winter games in Venezuela and reported to Brooklyn. There were still a few Dodger farm-club managers who wanted no part of a Negro player. But that spring, while Jackie Robinson drew most of the attention and most of the attacks, Roy Campanella and a promising Negro pitcher named Don Newcombe quietly reported to the Dodgers' Class B ball club in Nashua, N. H. Their new manager: long-legged, schoolmaster-ish Walter Alston. They liked him on sight.

Before they left for Nashua, Campy and Newk got a long lecture from Rickey, filled with colorful descriptions of the insults they might get. As it turned out, there was little trouble: both Campy and Newk quickly became popular. The only ugly incident occurred when Manchester Catcher Sal Yvars (who later made a tour in the big leagues with the St. Louis Cards and N. Y. Giants) came to bat and tossed a handful of dirt in Campy's face. The usually mild-mannered Campy whipped off his mask and snarled, "Try that again, I'll beat you to a pulp." Yvars never tried it again.

Otherwise Campy was the politest of players. Claude Corbitt, Syracuse lead-off batter, found that Campy would begin each game by saying, "Good evening, Mr. Corbitt. How are you tonight?" Complained Corbitt: "The first time, I was so stunned that I could barely tap the ball back to the pitcher."

Campy, who began the 1946 season with an opening-day home run, became Nashua's big gun at the plate. He hit 13 homers in 113 games—a solid achievement at Nashua, where there was no outfield fence. A local farmer offered 100 chickens for every home run, and Campy sent his 1,300 prizes to his father, who raised them as a sideline to his vegetable business. By the end of the season, Campy was an almost unanimous choice for the league's all-star team and received its most-valuable-player award.

In 1948 Campy was called up to the majors, and the Dodgers' Manager Leo Durocher was dead set on using him as his catcher. General Manager Branch Rickey (a sociologist who is now having plain baseball trouble with his cellar-dwelling Pittsburgh Pirates) had other plans. Keep Campy on the bench, he ordered. Make it look as if he can't make the team. Having reaped the profits of opening the major leagues to Negroes, Rickey wanted the added rewards from sending Campy to the St. Paul Saints as the first Negro in the American Association. Dodger fans would never let him get away with it if they knew how good Campy was.

Durocher screamed havoc (a particular talent), but Campy went out to St. Paul. He stayed a month (and hit 13 home runs while he batted .325) before he got Rickey's O.K. to return. The Dodgers had slumped dismally into sixth place. When the beer-keg backstop walked purposefully into the Ebbets Field clubhouse, Durocher was facing a three-game series with the Giants. "Get dressed," he ordered. "You're catching tonight." With Campy's help, the Dodgers climbed back to third place.

Next year, under a new manager, gentle Bert Shotton, the Dodgers won a pennant. Jackie Robinson ran wild on the base-paths (he stole 37 bases), took the National League batting title (.342). Campy was still playing the relentless game he had learned in the Negro leagues. Beaned by a Pittsburgh pitcher's fast ball, he was carried to the hospital suffering from a severe concussion. Next day, nevertheless, he was back in uniform, ready to hit batting practice. Shotton stared at him. "You all right?" he asked in disbelief. "Sure," said Campy. "Then what's your left eye out of line for?" demanded Shotton.

That day the indestructible Campy consented to ride the bench while he got his left eye back in line. He was back in action the next afternoon.

For the next two years, the Dodgers came close—but never quite close enough—to another pennant. Campy, too, had good years and bad breaks. In September 1950 he grabbed at a foul tip and suffered a dislocation of his right thumb. That winter, the hot-water heater in his home blew up in his face. As the year wore on, Campy picked up a startling assortment of injuries: a split thumb from a foul ball hit by the Athletics' Eddie Joost in an exhibition game, a bruised hip (during a slide), a chipped elbow when Whitey Lockman of the Giants crashed into him. Still he played, and still he was the sparkplug of the team.

All through the third game of the memorable 1951 pennant play-off with the Giants, Campy kept ducking into the dugout toilet to pray for victory. When Bobby Thomson connected for his unbelievable, game-winning home run for the New York Giants, Campy swore at the soaring ball: "Sink, you devil, sink!" He kept muttering until the ball disappeared.

For Campy, 1952 was a slow year; he had a bad arm and his hitting was off. The Dodgers won the pennant, but once again they lost the World Series to the Yankees. In 1953, his arm healed, Campy went to town. He had the best hitting year for any catcher in the history of organized baseball. He caught 144 games (of 154 scheduled), got 162 hits, walloped 41 home runs, wound up with an average of .312 and the most-valuable-player award. Once more, the Yankees won the World Series.

Last season was Campy's worst ever. His left hand, hit by one of Yankee Allie Reynolds' World Series pitches, was badly bruised, and his batting average sank to .207. He wondered whether he would ever play again. After a while, the hand was partially paralyzed. This spring, after an operation, he was back. Two fingers of his left hand were still stiff, but, said he: "I can curl them around a bat handle, and that's what counts." At a gathering of baseball writers not long ago, the grand ballroom of New York's Waldorf-Astoria resounded with a special song in his honor (to the tune of *O Sole Mio*):

> Oh, Campanella, oh, he'sa my boy,
> Oh, what a fella, dat mighty Roy!

To the big, beaming man from Nicetown, life has become a lot nicer than it used to be in the old "bus-league" days. With his $45,000-a-year Dodger salary, plus $10,000 or so more from his Harlem liquor store and some extra folding money from cigarette endorsements, Campy can afford steak every day instead of bologna.

For his wife and six kids, Campy has bought a comfortable home in a prosperous section of St. Albans, L. I. He tends the backyard rose garden himself, officiates at the outdoor barbecue, is never too busy on afternoons at home to play catch with his three boys. Indoors, the large house is cramped with Campy's hobbies. A vast and valuable collection of toy trains clutters the attic; an entire wall of the basement den is covered with carefully tended aquariums of expensive tropical fish. Once the conversation swings around to the bright little creatures, Campy actively resents a change of topic—even to baseball.

For running around St. Albans, the Campanella family is happy to use a Willys jeep station wagon. For trips to the ballpark or the Harlem liquor store, there is a brand-new, copper-colored Cadillac. "When they see that car outside the store," says Campy, "they go around saying, 'Campy's here.'" Sales skyrocket as admirers flock in to shoot the breeze. "So long as they walk out of the store with a package, that's all I care." To Campy, the most fun of all is peddling "Campy's Old Peg," a house-branded bourbon named by Mrs. Campanella for her husband's famous throw to second.

Near his liquor store is a Y.M.C.A. where Campy spends almost every winter afternoon coaching youngsters in basketball and other sports. "You have to be a man to be a big-league ballplayer," he says, "but you have to have a lot of little boy in you, too."

In his wide-eyed, grinning way, Campy shows a lot of the boy. When he steams into second base, say, on a long double, he invariably hoists up his pants to his bulging waistline and stands on the base looking pleased as Punch. In almost every movement he seems to convey the idea that the world is treating him right. He never stops kidding with his roommate, Pitcher Newcombe. "Can I play the television tonight, big man?" Campy will ask, and Newk will snap back: "Maybe, Meat, if I say so." He hums to himself as he works his cap on the hat-stretcher in the dressing room (the gadget expands caps drawn tight by sweat). With a great gold World Series ring on his finger, and wearing a snazzy blue suit with plaid socks, he looks as sharp as he feels.

Unlike Jackie Robinson, Campy, a gradualist by instinct, does not feel that he has to crusade for the rights of his race—except by living right and always playing the best ball he can. Once, when Robinson was spoiling to get into an argument with an umpire, Campy quickly calmed him down with: "Come on, Jackie, don't be like that. Let's not take any chances. It's nice up here."

Baseball, and all it has brought to Campy, is a wonderful way of life. "I love this baseball," said Roy Campanella. "When you're a kid you play it and it starts going down into you when you're a child. Once that feeling leaves you, your will to play is gone. I saw a movie once showing Ted Williams running those bases, jumping like a kid. I don't care how old you are, you have to have that spirit. I know I've got it and I don't think I'll ever lose it. Baseball doesn't owe me anything, but I owe it plenty. Everything it's done for me has been good and nothin's been bad. The day they take that uniform off me, they'll have to rip it off. And when they do, they can bury me."

NO HITTER

By Edward Prell

From The Chicago Tribune, May 13, 1955

A NO HITTER always is a fantastic sight, but the one pitched yesterday afternoon in Wrigley field by the Cubs' Sam Jones had the extra thrill of becoming reality while three Pittsburgh Pirates were on the bases.

With two teammates warming up in the bullpen, the 29-year-old right hander suddenly became the only calm person in the park, striking out the next three Pirates to put a bizarre finish to the greatest pitching feat in Wrigley field since 1917. It seemed almost only co-incidental that the Cubs had a 4 to 0 victory as Jones, the rookie, became the man of the moment.

Thirty-eight years ago when the field was named Weeghman park, Jim (Hippo) Vaughn of the Cubs and Fred Toney of Cincinnati went into the 10th inning with a double no hitter. The Redlegs made two hits in the 10th to win, 1 to 0, but Vaughn's name went into the record books for his nine inning achievement.

Almost 3,000 games had been played in Wrigley field since that historic day and when Jones took the mound yesterday. Down the years it had become known as a jinx park for no hit feats. Hank Borowy, on Aug. 31, 1948, missed one when Gene Hermanski of the Dodgers singled in the second inning. The only one to reach base on Borowy, Gene was cut down trying to steal.

Yesterday's performance came on a day when rain threatened and held the crowd to 2,918, smallest of the year. The overcast sky was made for Jones and his fast ball. The Cubs made no errors, so there were no questionable decisions on batted balls, and until the ninth no Pirate had reached second base on Jones. When he went into the ninth inning, his defense had been forced to make only three difficult plays.

Randy Jackson made a one hand stab of a terrific liner off the bat of Frank Thomas in the fourth inning. In the seventh, Jones got his glove up just in time to slow up a bounder by Dick Groat. Gene Baker pounced on the ball and with a quick underhand flip nipped the runner. In the eighth, Eddie Miksis raced far back near the vines in center for George Freese's drive.

So, when Jones ambled to the mound at the start of the ninth he had walked four and fanned three. Manager Stan Hack sent Jim King to left field in place of Bob Speake for added defense.

Gene Freese was the first batter. On the first pitch he bunted foul out of Catcher Clyde McCullough's reach. The next four pitches were balls and Freese was on first base.

Preston Ward, an ex-Cub, was sent up to swing for Vern Law, the Pittsburgh pitcher. When the count was 2 and 2, Freese dashed to second on a wild pitch. On the next ball, Ward walked. A pinch runner, Roman Meijas, went in for Ward.

Jones next faced Tom Saffell, a rookie from the Pacific Coast league. The count was 3 and 1 when Big Sam missed the plate to fill the bases. The two Cubs in the bullpen started pitching faster. Manager Stan Hack came out and presided in a conference at the mound, and the fans cheered when Jones stayed.

Now it was not only a question if Jones would get a no hitter. The game itself was beginning to hang in the balance.

This is where Sam took charge. He spun three fast curves past Dick Groat, who didn't swing at a single one. That brought Roberto Clemente, rookie outfielder, to the plate. He missed in two terrific lunges at the ball, fouled off two, then went down swinging.

Jones curved his first pitch away from the bat of Thomas, then had the first ball called against him in 10 pitches. Thomas missed a high curve for the second strike, and the no hitter was there for all to applaud when the slugger took a third strike on Sam's 136th pitch of the game.

His teammates, led by Hack and McCullough, poured out of the dugout and went into a wild back slapping, hand clasping celebration. It was a modest moment of fame, too, for the 38 year old McCullough, who first came to the Cubs in 1940. Never before had he caught a no hitter.

This was the fourth victory in seven decisions for Jones, 6 foot 4 inch, 200 pounder who came to the Cubs last winter along with Outfielder Gale Wade and $60,000 from the Cleveland Indians for Ralph Kiner. Last year he won 15 and lost 8 for Indianapolis, champions of the American Association, and struck out 178, second all-time high in the A. A.

Until yesterday, Jones had beaten only Cincinnati in the National League. The second of his three victories over the Redlegs,

April 24 in Chicago, was in a two hit, 2 to 1 game. Ted Kluszewski doubled in the third and Ray Jablonski singled in the eighth for the only Redleg hits.

At the finish yesterday, Jones had added distinctions. He had become the first Negro ever to pitch a no hit game in the major leagues and he had taken over the National League's strikeout lead from the New York Giants' John Antonelli. Thomas was Sam's 46th strikeout victim in 53 innings. This was only the third complete game for Jones, who has been troubled by wildness.

In the first five innings, only one ball was hit to the outfield. Ted Tappe, later to hit his second Cub homer, ranged to his right in the first inning for a tall fly by Groat.

Dale Long walked with one out in the second inning, but was thrown out trying to steal by McCullough. Toby Atwell walked to lead off the third inning, but after Gene Freese popped out and Pinch Batter Felipe Montemayor fanned, Saffell forced the base runner with a tap to Dee Fondy.

Jones set down the Pirates in order in the fourth. Long led off the fifth with a walk, but Ernie Banks grabbed George Freese's grounder and turned it into a double play.

The no hit hero was perfect in the sixth and seventh, but at the start of the eighth he passed Long for the third time. Miksis sped back for George Freese's drive and Jackson caught Atwell's hot drive, throwing to Fondy to double Long. That was his pitching record until the long, long ninth.

O, yes, the Cubs had an offense. The ball fell safe almost every time they swung against Nelson King, the starter and loser, and Law. Their hit total reached 15, the Jones boy getting two of them.

Baker walked in the first inning and scored on Tappe's double to left after Speake's single. Fondy singled in the second, stole second, and came home on a line double past third by Miksis.

Jackson singled to center off Law at the start of the fifth and was forced by Tappe, who scored when Banks bounced a triple past Saffell. Tappe concluded the scoring in the seventh by knocking his homer into the left field seats.

Jones broke into organized baseball with Wilkes-Barre, Pa., of the Eastern league, in 1950, and his record of 17 victories and eight defeats, 20 complete games, and 169 strikeouts (a league record) won him a promotion to San Diego of the Pacific Coast league in 1951, where he fanned 246 for a league mark while winning 16 and losing 13.

Jones finished the 1951 season with Cleveland, reporting in September, and in two games with the Indians lost one and won none. He remained with the Indians at the start of the 1952 season, and compiled a 2-3 record while appearing in 14 games. He was optioned to Indianapolis in July, and was unbeaten while winning four in the remainder of the association campaign.

He yielded 160 hits in 187 innings, and had an earned run average of 3.32 in winning 10 and losing 12 for Indianapolis in 1953.

Jones, an air force veteran, is married and the father of two children, Sam Jr., 3, and Michael, 1. His wife, Mary, and the children will fly to Chicago from their home in Monongah, W. Va., arriving tonight to stay for several days.

Sam was born in Stewartsville, O., on Dec. 14, 1925.

THE SAGA OF 'DAVY' BERRA

By Jerry Mitchell

From The New York Post, May 27, 1955

Born on a hilltop in old St. Loo
A frontier town and a good one too
Played ball on the lots so's he'd know what to do,
An' hit his first homer at the age of two.

* * *

Yo-gi, Yogi Berra,
Hero of the Yankee club.

* * *

Ate pizza pie, morning, noon an' night.
Got so his belly was quite a sight.
But a boy must eat if he's gonna grow,
Yog asked for more of mama mia's dough.

* * *

Yo-gi, Yogi Berra,
Never a dinner-time sub.

* * *

Played some at soccer, an' some at pool,
Got good and strong but never cruel.
Played some football like all the rest,
But always liked his baseball best.

* * *

Yo-gi, Yogi Berra,
A boy-of-the-future, bub.

* * *

Caused so much talk with all his clouts,
The Berra house stayed full-a scouts,
They all bid high and made such talk,
But Yog said he'd only sign with New York.

Yo-gi, Yogi Berra,
Causing the scouts to rub.

* * *

In '43, when he was breakin' in,
With Norfolk's Tars, came an awful din,
The war involved us and that very fall,
Yogi answered his country's call.

* * *

Yo-gi, Yogi Berra,
Catcher for the Norfolk club.

* * *

He changed his suit for Navy wear,
With those tight little pants so hard to bear.
He scrubbed the decks with such a hard rub
That soon he was down in the depths in a sub.

* * *

Yo-gi, Yogi Berra,
Crewman in a Navy sub.

* * *

When he came home, his warring done,
Yog went back to baseball an' back to fun.
His submarine work had him so hard an' lean,
That he went right to Newark an' hit .314.

* * *

Yo-gi, Yogi Berra,
Home from the sea in a tub.

* * *

Up to the Yankees that very fall,
He who had answered his country's call.
Heard he'd go back if he didn't hit more.
So he upped his mark to .364.

* * *

Yo-gi, Yogi Berra
Rookie on the Yankee club.

Since that year Yogi's grown in size,
And increased in stature baseball wise.
He's copied Bill Dickey's catching style,
And slugs every ball a country mile.

*   *   *

Yo-gi, Yogi Berra,
Hero of the Yankee club.

*   *   *

In springs past Yog got started sad,
Bothered by colds, slumps an' everything bad.
But this seems a different spring indeed,
He's hitting so hard, he makes the ball bleed.

*   *   *

Yo-gi, Yogi Berra,
Hero of the Yankee club.

*   *   *

In yesterday's first he caught Johnny Kucks,
Helping the kid aim his swift an' his hooks.
Helping him too with his arm an' his bat,
Not to mention what's under his hat.

*   *   *

Yo-gi, Yogi Berra,
Hero of the Yankee club.

*   *   *

His work wasn't done with that 8-4 win,
He caught the next too, wearin' a grin.
His first-inning homer with two aboard
Was more'n Washington could afford.

*   *   *

Yo-gi, Yogi Berra,
Hero of the Yankee club.

PERILOUS PLIGHT OF THE PITCHER

By John Lardner

From The New York Times Magazine, September 18, 1955

THIRTY-FIVE years ago, as every serious student of baseball knows, the operators of the game committed themselves to a theory of entertainment which calls for the ball to be knocked over the fence as often as possible. Since then, to insure this end, they have been progressively stimulating the outbound genes of the ball—extraverting it, so to speak—and bringing the fences closer to the batter, until, today, in some baseball parks, false walls and synthetic trellises cast their shadows on the infield itself, and the ball will twitch if you look at it.

On the question of fence encroachment, Carl Erskine, an intelligent pitcher who works for the Brooklyn Dodgers, had a few bitter words to say recently. As happens every year at this time, a group of players was discussing the possibility of Babe Ruth's home-run record (sixty home runs in one season) being broken some day. Most of the players thought it unlikely. After all, the ball had already reached a state of great mobility in Ruth's time, and the Babe had unique gifts as a slugger. But Erskine made a sinister point.

"Suppose the owners fake it?" he said. "I mean, suppose they eventually make the fences so close and easy that Ruth's record has got to be broken?"

It was a melancholy, morbid conception. The reason for that is that pitchers today tend to be morbid, melancholy men. Their lives and minds have been warped, twisted and soured by the boom-boom, big-hit policy that now governs the game. It's natural for them to suspect almost everyone of plotting almost anything—from a cheapening of the home-run record to further invigoration of the pellet, or a new, tighter balk rule—that will make the pitcher's lot more miserable than it is already. The pitcher, like the guinea pig, sees experimentation from the negative side. To him baseball adjustments since 1920 represent, not so much a constructive plan to please the home-run-hungry public, as an effort to do for the breed of pitcher what the ruling classes barely failed to do for the

Indian, the buffalo and the whooping crane—i.e., wipe them out.

George Susce, a Boston Red Sox pitcher, is the son of an old ball player, now a coach, George Susce Sr. Another Red Sox pitcher is reported to have said one day this year: "The old man was a catcher, when he played ball. No pitcher would ever raise his child to pitch."

To my way of thinking, the saddest effect of the age of home-run baseball has been this harassing and harrowing of pitchers—the ordeal by shock it has brought to the men who throw the ball. As a class they are martyrs to concussion. (It's true that batters are hit by baseballs more often than pitchers are; but that is merely the measure of the pitchers' desperation.) The present-day pitcher is subject to severe occupational strains and stresses. One hundred and twenty times per game, on an average (if he lasts through the game, which has become increasingly improbable), the choice that faces him is between:

1. Throwing the ball, and seeing it exploded over the fence.
2. Holding on to it, and having it go off in his hand.

(The radioactivity of the ball is heightened at intervals, though the manufacturers deny this, without much conviction, by thinning its skin and tightening the yarn inside the casing.)

Before he throws the ball, or during that gloomy moment itself, the pitcher is restricted by a set of iron-maiden rules that give him as much freedom of movement on the mound as though he were pitching from a telephone booth. He is thus frustrated in his natural impulses of self-defense against base-runners, who have gotten on base by means of secondary explosions, or line drives. Recently—or so all pitchers suspect, and will tell you—the "strike zone" has been curtailed; umpires no longer call strikes on low pitches that cross the plate a few inches above the batter's knees. What with rules, frustrations, suspicions and exposure to blast, the modern pitcher has developed a number of curious patterns of performance and reaction, on and off the field. I give here a few case histories of pitching insecurity, taken from the pitching staffs of New York ball clubs in 1955, that illustrate some of these patterns:

A. Pitcher has become reluctant to win more than thirteen or fourteen games in a season. His announced reasoning is that if he has a big year, with twenty wins or more, he will get a big pay raise, and so expose himself to a big pay cut in some future, less successful year, with resulting problems of readjustment to the lower standard of living, when it comes. This reaction (the Billy Loes Block, so called) is very uncommon, but shows that even winning can intimidate a modern pitcher.

B. Pitcher is inclined to lose eighteen pounds in a nine-inning game, so grim is his task under present-day pressures. Generally speaking, this condition (known to science as Newcombe's Recession, or the Alice-in-Wonderland Dwindle) produces a fear of lasting nine innings, lest the pitcher finally disappear entirely, and be divorced for desertion, or declared legally dead after seven years.

C. Pitcher pitched a complete game in 1951, and was unable to do so again for almost four years, being done in at the last moment whenever he tried it. The predicament (Labine's Late Blight) has been known to cause pitchers who are suffering from it to leave railroad trains one station early, for fear of a train wreck on the last leg.

D. Pitcher has come to a period in his life when he is always scored on in the first inning, though things go well with him after that. Pitchers afflicted with this problem (Maglie's False Start) will go so far, in private life, as to get up at 11 in the morning, instead of the usual 10, to avoid catching colds, or cutting selves fatally with razors, between 10 and 11.

The neuroses listed above reach their fullest flower at Ebbets Field, Brooklyn, and the Polo Grounds, New York, where it is possible for a batter to clear the introvert fences merely by popping the extrovert ball into the air. Other notorious pitcher traps, or hotbeds of insecurity, exist in Boston, St. Louis, Philadelphia, Cincinnati and Kansas City. A pitcher whose mind has been scarred by his experiences in environments like those finds it hard to behave normally in his non-working hours. In crossing streets, he will not look to the right or left while in motion, for fear of a balk being called against him. He hesitates to answer the door, because it may be the manager coming to take him out. He is afraid to look over his shoulder, because he may see a relief pitcher warming up in the bullpen; or (this neurosis is subdivided) he may not see a relief pitcher warming up. He falls flat on his face when he hears backfires, because he thinks they are line drives.

It may be true, as the baseball operators believe, that most of the public prefer the loud game, the home-run game, to the pre-1920 game of tight defense and low scores. But there are many fans, including your correspondent, who do not. The pitcher commands our sympathy, not only because he suffers, but also because the conditions that have made him a martyr force him to be a craftsman and an artist as well in order to survive.

Ford C. Frick, the baseball commissioner, is among those who feel that the artist (the pitcher) deserves help in his struggle against the philistine, or apeman (the swinger). Several times in the last few years, Frick has come out in favor of re-legalizing the spitball, which was barred in 1920. The spitball would help pitchers greatly today, as it did in the past, because it is hard to hit and easy to throw. It was barred for that reason—and the baseball owners, who still like that reason, have ignored Frick's suggestion about the spitball. The fact is commissioners of baseball can commission only the kind of baseball that their employers, the club owners, want—which, in the case of Frick's employers, is home-run baseball.

When his spitball idea was cold-shouldered I asked the commissioner what else he could suggest in the way of prevention of cruelty to pitchers.

"Well," he said, hopefully, "they might add an inch to each side of the plate, to give the pitcher a wider strike zone. That would help." But they haven't and they almost certainly won't, in our lifetimes, or in the lifetimes of Ted Kluszewski, Willie Mays, Duke Snider, Ernie Banks and Mickey Mantle.

There are those who will tell you, with straight faces, that the balance of power is not as strongly against the pitcher nowadays as pitchers would like you to think it is. Last spring, when the revival of the spitball became an issue briefly (on paper), a poll was taken of many players, some of whom (not pitchers, but swingers, men of wrath) said, in effect: "What do the pitchers want with the spitball? They have the slider. That's enough."

The slider? It's possible that there is such a thing as the slider and, this being so, that it helps the pitcher. Or it may be that the slider is one of those national illusions that professional groups are sometimes able to foist off on the public, such as the idea that building all passenger automobiles in the shape of cockroaches represents artistic and mechanical progress. Not even its propagandists can agree on exactly what the slider is; striking an average from the stories, it seems to be a pitch that curves infinitesimally, a cross between a curve and a fast ball, or as the players say in their franker moments, a "nickel curve."

I can't help remembering that, a few years ago, strong baseball intellects like Casey Stengel were cynical about the slider, to the point of doubting its existence. Today, Stengel, like nearly everyone else in baseball, especially the hitters, vouches glibly for the reality of the slider. A representative interview with a ballplayer about the slider will run as follows:

Q. Well, what does it do? Slide?

A. Naw. Naw. That's the one thing it doesn't do, slide.

Q. Does it skim?

A. Yeah, it kind of skims. Or glides.

Whether it skims, glides, scrunches or merely obtrudes, the slider has this in common with every other kind of pitch now in use, that it is constantly being knocked out of sight. When a reporter asks a batter what kind of pitch it was that he pounced on for the winning home run, he gets one of four standard answers: "I hit a good fast ball." "I hit a good curve." "I hit a good change-up," or "I hit a good slider."

It should be noted that the hitter always describes the pitch as "good," in these circumstances, out of courtesy both to the pitcher and to himself. The pitcher, on the other hand, will sometimes contradict him and call it a bad or unlucky pitch—"it hung," or "it got away from me"—because he is unwilling for the moment to face the dismal fact that there is nothing whatever in his repertory, under present conditions, that can keep home runs from dropping over the fences, short and long, as steadily as rain in Assam.

Why, then, stubborn people ask occasionally, are there still a fair number of shutouts and low-hit games every year? As regards low-hit games, the record shows that these are not necessarily low-score, or successful, games—one big hit behind a couple of walks, or a walk and an error, can destroy the day's work, as it often does for Bob Turley of the Yankees, a consistent low-hit pitcher. As for shutouts: It's true today, as it always has been, that on certain days good pitchers have such good control that batters cannot find the ball at all—and even the modern radioactive ball, when missed entirely, will seldom recoil more than 200 feet.

However, anything short of perfect, day-long control on the pitcher's part is futile, as the cases of Carl Erskine and of Murry Dickson, a Philadelphia pitcher, demonstrate. Dickson and Erskine are two of the best control pitchers in baseball; but statistics prove that practically every one of their rare lapses produces a home run.

One factor in the modern game, and one only, works partly in the pitcher's favor. In the process of becoming apemen, or troglodytes, most batters, from tiny 150-pounders up, have formed the

habit of swinging at the ball from the heels, in a huge, swashbuckling arc. The all-out swing impairs timing and accuracy. It can
lead to strikes, strike-outs, and even shutouts. But—unless the
pitcher himself is perfectly accurate—it can lead to shellshock for
pitchers instead, and to home runs that sail into the next county,
pursued by press agents with tape-measures.

Loud baseball, and the hot ball, have wrecked pitchers' lives in
more ways than one. The classic case of shell-shock, of fatal (pro-
fessionally) concussion, was Ralph Branca's. The big Brooklyn
right-hander never recovered from the home run Bobby Thomson
hit off him in the playoff of 1951, though Branca was a young man
when it happened. To show its versatility, the lively ball deviled
another Brooklyn pitcher, Chris Van Cuyk, out of the big leagues
by its work at short range—the opposition took to bunting on
Chris, and the ball coughed and jerked in such violent spasms,
between his large feet, that it ended his usefulness to his team.

From the microcosm of the Brooklyn club, representing all modern baseball, we'll take one more example, the saddest. The condition that drove Rex Barney from the game forever, just a short
time ago, was chronic high-pitching. There is only one thing that
can keep a man, who has already proved he knows how, from ever
again throwing the ball low enough for a batter to hit it—an un-
conscious terror of what will happen if he does. Thus, the buoyant
ball and the sudden fences spooked Barney out of business.

There came a time, in spring training, when they tried the experiment of hobbling Barney with ropes, and channeling his aim
with a species of blinkers, to make him pitch in the groove. It didn't
work. It is a sordid picture, and we'll drop the curtain there.

ALL-STAR ACCOLADE

By Robert L. Burnes

From The St. Louis Globe-Democrat, July 13, 1955

STAN (THE MAN) MUSIAL wrote a brilliant new page into his book of glittering diamond achievements at County Stadium when he broke up the twenty-second annual major All-Star game with a tremendous home run that gave the National League a 12-inning 6-5 victory over the American League.

The second the ball left Stan's bat, some 45,314 fans, most of them wildly partisan National League fans, went berserk. Musial stroked the ball easily, the first pitch thrown by Frank Sullivan of the Red Sox in the inning, and there was no question that the ball was gone and the game was over.

As Musial reached home plate, his cheering mates, led by Manager Leo Durocher, Coach Fred Haney, Willie Mays, Ted Kluszewski and Red Schoendienst, mobbed him. There was a motion afoot to carry Stan off the field on their shoulders but Musial refused by the expedient of crawling several feet until they desisted. They settled instead for pounding him on the back.

This was Musial's twelfth All-Star game, one more than any other major leaguer has ever played. The second time he stepped to the plate he broke a record for times at bat in the series and his homer, his fourth in All-Star competition, broke a tie with Ralph Kiner and Ted Williams, each of whom has three.

For the National League, it was the ninth victory against 13 losses in the long series. It was a tremendous uphill battle and compares favorably with the Nationals' 4-3 victory in the 1950 game at Comiskey Park in Chicago.

In that one, the Nationals trailed, 3 to 2, in the ninth inning when Kiner tied it with a homer. Red Schoendienst finally won it with a homer off Detroit's Ted Gray in the fourteenth. Until today, that was the only overtime game in the history of the series.

For six innings today, the National League looked sadly outclassed.

To all intents and purposes, the American League won the game before a man was retired in the first inning. The Americans greeted

Robin Roberts of the Phils like an old friend and, considering this was Roberts' fifth start in the show (tying Lefty Gomez of the Yankees for such honors) that might have been a factor.

Harvey Kuehn of the Tigers and Nelson Fox of the White Sox delivered back-to-back singles. Kuehn scored when Roberts wild-pitched while in the process of walking Williams.

Then Mickey Mantle of the Yankees, batting left handed, powered a tremendous drive over the screen in dead center about 410 feet from home plate and the American League had four big runs.

But after that fast break, the American League bats were stilled, except for one mildly tainted run, the rest of the way. That run came off Harvey Haddix of the Cardinals in the sixth inning and was the only break in a creditable performance by the Red Bird southpaw.

With one out, Yogi Berra singled and Al Kaline got a double when his harsh-bounding ball smashed off Ed Mathews' knee and wrist into left center for a double. Berra scored on Mickey Vernon's soft grounder to Kluszewski on which the only possible play was at first.

That wound up American League scoring. Don Newcombe of the Dodgers cut them down for an inning, helped by a tremendous leaping catch by Willie Mays of a drive by Williams against the fence in right center.

Sam Jones of the Cubs came on in the eighth, hit one batter and walked two with two out and Joe Nuxhall of the Reds was summoned in a hurry to strike out Whitey Ford. Nuxhall hurled steady shutout ball for three more innings, handed over the job to Gene Conley of the Braves at the top of the twelfth.

The six-foot, eight-inch Braves right hander, using his motion deftly in the deepening shadows, wound up the National League hurling with a flourish, striking out the side in the twelfth just before Musial won it. Thus the victory went to Conley, squaring accounts for him. He was the loser last year at Cleveland.

Against starter Billy Pierce of the White Sox, the Nationals didn't have a chance as the stylish southpaw hurled three superb innings. Schoendienst singled but was cut down trying to advance when a ball dropped away from Berra. Pierce struck out three of the remaining eight batters he faced and four popped on the infield.

Early Wynn of the Indians also blanked the Nationals, although not as convincingly as Pierce, for three innings. Then the Nationals broke through against the Yanks' Whitey Ford.

After the game, Manager Leo Durocher, making himself heard above the mighty din in the National League clubhouse, paid tribute to his team. "They were like a bunch of college kids," he said, "whooping it up on the bench. Even when they were five runs behind they kept saying they knew they were going to win."

The unquenchable Mays, like Musial a non-starter, finally broke it open. He led off the seventh with a single against Ford, languished on first while two outs were accomplished. Hank Aaron drew a pass and Johnny Logan (both of the Braves) blooped a single to right to admit Mays. Stan Lopata smashed a ground ball to Chico Carrasquel at short and he kicked it as Aaron scored.

That reduced the margin to 5-2 but there were only two innings left and the outlook wasn't much brighter as Schoendienst and Musial went out in the eighth.

Mays then singled. Kluszewski drove him to third with a single. Ransom Jackson of the Cubs kept it alive with a single to right, scoring Mays and when Kaline's throw bounced past Al Rosen, Kluszewski scored. The Red Sox' Sullivan then came in, was tagged for a single by Aaron to drive Jackson home with the tying run. Logan almost won the game then with a shot over second but Carrasquel, whose error provided a run in the previous inning, made a brilliant stop and throw.

From then on it was muxhall and Conley against Sullivan. Each side threatened enough to keep the fans on edge.

That set it up for Musial and his clincher. As Stan raced happily around the bases, loser Sullivan trudged slowly to the clubhouse, a tough luck loser. But he had learned a lesson that National League pitchers know—you can't throw the fast ball by Musial.

That's what it was, Musial said, a letter high fast ball on the outside. "Funny thing," Stan said in the clubhouse. "I was going for the bundle the two previous times up. This time, as leadoff man, I was just trying to get on base. I just met the ball." He said he knew it was a homer, too, the moment it left.

FARM BOSS WITH A GREEN THUMB

By Harold Rosenthal

From Elks Magazine, December, 1955

A HALF-DOZEN years ago word seeped through to a national magazine that not all baseball front-office men were bumbling, inarticulate dopes whose conversational gambits were limited to, "All we
have left are a couple of seats behind a pole," or "we needed that
seventh game in the World Series to break even."

There was a fellow, they were advised, Fresco Thompson, whose
wit and witticisms were wafting through the major leagues—at
training camps, at dreary doubleheaders, and in smoky convention
halls—like some tingling ocean breeze.

An able young man was put on the job immediately; was told to
leave no stone unturned to catch Fresco in print. "Go as far," he
was advised, "as to actually live in Brooklyn if you think it's necessary." Fresco had just been elevated to the directorship of the
Dodgers' far-flung farm system.

The young man buttonholed hundreds of people, in and out of
baseball. He carefully filled several notebooks with anecdotal material on Thompson, on Fresco the player, the manager and the
front-office man. The end product looked, and read, like something
vaudevillans used to buy on the installment plan from some central
gag agency when they knew the act was in desperate need of a
paint job but there wasn't enough money to hire a first-class gag
writer to help save the act.

For Thompson the end product was a source of acute irritation
from the third word of the title, "Baseball's Mr. Wisecrack," down
to the last bit of Thompsoniana, the one about Brooklyn being so
well equipped with mechanical devices in spring training—mechanical pitchers and mechanical ball retrievers—that "maybe (and here
Fresco could be visualized as giving his straw skimmer a real saucy
twirl) yessir, maybe next year we can have mechanical batters and
then we'll be able to dispense entirely with the ball players!"

"That article," declared Lafayette Fresco Thompson, vice-president of the Dodgers, his wide scholarly-appearing brow wrinkling

reflectively in a slight frown below his wavy greying hair, "made me out to be something of a clown. That I'm not."

That is a sentiment to which the New York Yankees, humbled by the first World championship Dodger team in history, will subscribe one hundred per cent. Two victories by Johnny Podres murdered them—the young lefthander is a Thompson product. So are the other young pitchers who worked in the Series—the Karl Spooners, the Roger Craigs, the Don Bessents.

The Clem Labine who pitched such effective relief was brought up from St. Paul in 1951 because Thompson thought the sinker-ball ace was ready. The Sandy Amoros who made that amazing catch to start the ruinous (for the Yankees) double-play in the seventh game is also a Thompson production. The tiny Cuban wanted $1,000 to sign off a rough island equivalent of one of our own sandlots.

"Give it to him," ordered Fresco in a decisive telephone conversation with Brooklyn's on-the-spot Caribbean scout, Al Campanis.

Fresco Thompson, originally out of Centreville, Alabama, by the way of Chicago, St. Louis, and the Washington Heights section of New York City, is now a solid burgher of Freeport, Long Island. At 53 he has held on to his sense of humor. He's even an excellent listener.

Thompson has managed to laugh in situations, too, where other men would have let grandma have it right in the shins. He has also managed to survive several changes of top management in the Dodger set-up, which makes him a kind of a Dr. Karl Menninger able to quote the baseball rules book backward.

Humorous? Yes. Clown? No. Clowns don't wind up as chief architects of world championship baseball teams.

A Fresco-and-the-Dodgers history is pretty much a chronicle of the rise of Brooklyn from the status of a pre-war sports-page joke to the strongest team in baseball today. Fresco has been a part of the whole Wagnerian epic in Brooklyn.

He played second base for the Dodgers in 1931 under the famed Uncle Wilbert Robinson. The Robins (out of honor to Uncle Robbie) suffered from a painful attack of the shorts in two vital categories—finances and players. Also, sometimes they'd change presidents of the club without advising the manager.

Fresco managed in the Brooklyn organization under the brilliant but unpredictable head man, Larry MacPhail. He was the manager of the Reading, Pennsylvania, club which MacPhail bought from a disgusted absentee Maryland chicken farmer for $5,000. Included in the purchase price were 40 uniforms, 20 players and a 20-passenger bus still doing service today somewhere in the Dodger organization. So is one of the 40 players. You might have seen him on TV last October—Carl Furillo.

MacPhail went off to war and Branch Rickey took over as the No. 1 man in Brooklyn. Thompson managed in the upper echelons of the minors for the Mahatma. When Walter O'Malley, current panjandrum of the Brooklyn shooting preserve, bought out Rickey for a million dollars after the 1950 season Fresco stayed, although he was commonly regarded as a Rickey man. Moreover, in each succeeding switchover of power Thompson has always moved up a notch or two.

The last boost moved him to vice-president in charge of farm operations and scouting. That is a job in baseball second only to the one occupied by the man who has to go ask the bank for additional cash.

Depending on the viewpoint, there could have been an even bigger boost for Fresco Thompson just a few months after his 50th birthday. When the time for Charley Dressen to leave after the '53 World Series, O'Malley's choice for field boss was Thompson. Thompson's choice was to continue as talent boss. So, O'Malley turned to the candidates within the organization, and that's why the picture of Walter Alston is adorning magazine covers this winter rather than Fresco Thompson's.

Why did Thompson turn down the job of piloting the most colorful club in baseball at what would probably have been a juicy boost to an already ample salary? It goes back to a decision made in the late years of World War II while leading a bunch of re-treads and 4Fs through the motions as the New Orleans entry in the Southern Association.

At the end of 1945, Thompson surveyed what had been seven or eight entertaining years of managing in the minors, from way down in Williamsport, Pennsylvania, up through Montreal. Fun? Yes, but fun's only fun. It was time to think of the future.

"I sat down and wrote Branch Rickey a letter," recalled Fresco, "and when I look back it was a pretty important one. I wrote him that I wanted to get somewhere in baseball where my own efforts produced the results, not where everything depended on a man who I had no control over, hitting the ball or making the right throw."

It was the big decision in Fresco Thompson's life. The sharpest brain in the business, whether it belongs to Casey Stengel, Alston, Mayo Smith, Marty Marion or Mike Higgins, to name some of 1955's more successful pilots, must go for naught if the hand of the man clutching the bat in that vital situation trembles at the crucial moment.

The minors, thought Fresco, had been fun, but now he was big-city minded. When there was a sudden desperate need for personnel in a place like Thomasville or Newport News, Fresco thought it would be nice if he was on the listening end instead of the beseeching one for a change, too.

Rickey also thought it a good idea. Thompson moved pronto into the more than slightly-frenzied atmosphere on the fourth floor of 215 Montague Street in downtown Brooklyn and has been there since.

Yes, the minors had been fun and there had been plenty of situations like those which had been used to point up the wise-cracking abilities of Fresco's in that previously-mentioned article. There was the time when a leading doctor-fan had been "riding" Fresco all season. Fresco maneuvered the tables on the medico in drastic fashion.

"I had a good boy pitching a two-hitter," smiled Fresco. "He had a two-run lead, but he gave up a single and a walk. I went out there to take him out. As I came out of the dugout this doctor, in a front row box, called 'Another mistake, Thompson?'

"I stopped right there. 'A mistake, doctor? Well, at least MY mistake will be able to work tomorrow.'"

Fresco thought back over the years. "You know that guy tried to get my job just for that crack. Claimed I was picking on him."

Then there was that triple play in Montreal. An eminent stockholder in the club was on hand and witnessed his first triple killing. The stockholder was a big man in the dry-goods business; in baseball he didn't know the difference between a fungo and a foul tip.

That didn't stop him. Next morning he was in the Royals' office bright and early. "Fresco," he offered sagaciously . . . "thees play I see las' night. . . . The one that gets trois hommes . . . beg par'on, t'ree men. A verr' good play. Yes! We can have lots more of them, oui?"

Enough of the past lest Fresco hurl that "clown" charge again. Clowns aren't charged with the dispersal of roughly eighteen per cent of every revenue dollar taken in by a major league ball club (double that if player bonus payments are included.) Clowns don't make decisions where not only the current financial health but the future personnel welfare of a major-league ball club is concerned.

Somewhere along the World Series trail in September you thrilled to the double-barreled victory performances of youthful Johnny Podres. There was a long chain of events which led to the pale-eyed lefthander's getting the Yankees one-two-three in the ninth inning of the seventh and final game of the World Series.

The chain had to start somewhere. It started with the decision to give the young man a thousand-dollar bonus to sign, and to throw in a small cash consideration for his father, who had been a high school pitcher before him for the same iron-mining community up in Northern New York.

Who made the decision? Put a couple of check marks alongside the name of Lafayette Fresco Thompson.

The name is legit, all the way, although the "Lafayette" has virtually disappeared. Once when Fresco was sold by Pittsburgh to Buffalo some acerbic Pittsburgh scribe scribbled, "Lafayette Fresco Thompson and all his names were released outright to Buffalo today."

The name has figured on the sports pages in one way or another for more than a quarter of a century. It started when he was named to the all-scholastic New York City team while playing for George Washington High School. It rings a bell in such places as Grand Island, Nebraska, Kansas City, Omaha, and such National League cities as New York, Brooklyn, Pittsburgh and Philadelphia. It's a name most people couple with a sharp and ready wit. In retrospect a lot of people now pushing fifty or having traveled beyond that milepost are apt to say, "he had to be slick-talking; he wasn't much with that bat."

A base and base-less canard! Thompson, judged by today's standard, was an ample hitter. With the Phillies in four years his lowest mark was .282. How many teams today would turn down a .282-hitting second baseman who also knows what to do with a glove? Even in Fresco's last full year in the majors under Uncle Robbie in Brooklyn he hit .265.

Fresco's trouble was that he played with what was probably the heaviest-hitting second-division club in major-league history in Philadelphia.

"I hit .324 one year and I wound up as the sixth or seventh-place hitter on the club," he recalled. "They wouldn't even let me take batting practice. I wasn't allowed to speak to guys like Lefty O'Doul and Chuck Klein."

In Philadelphia, Fresco was named team captain, got an extra $500 for additional duties like carrying the line-up card out to the umpires. In later years he described his captain duties as something akin to being foreman of a WPA leaf-raking detail. And if this comparison means anything to you, you're starting to get up there in the years, too.

Fresco helped slice no World Series melons with the Phillies but he had fun. There were things like four-game series with the Pirates in which *both teams* scored in double figures in *every game!* There was also an opportunity to coach at third.

Fresco loved to coach, especially when they were playing Cincinnati and a large lefthander named Eppa Rixey was pitching. Rixey compiled a tremendous record for the Reds; he won more games than any other lefthander in National League history and some day he will grace the Hall of Fame. For Thompson, however, he was a sitting duck.

Rixey's trouble was that he was still fighting the Battle of Shiloh, almost three-quarters of a century after the final results were in. College man, too.

So one college man, Thompson (Columbia) went to work on another (U. of Virginia) and it was an awesome job Fresco did. Just by whistling. He whistled one tune over and over as Rixey sought to catch the corners of the plate. It wasn't even a new tune, just an old war ditty, "Marching Through Georgia." It drove Rixey into a positive frenzy and it didn't cool him any, either, to learn that the fellow doing the whistling was a native Alabaman.

It was through his Alabama connections that Fresco got his first job managing, just as he had used a rather close connection—his father—to get a job playing with Grand Island in the Nebraska State League.

Actually, Fresco had first obtained a job as an infielder with Cedar Rapids in the Mississippi Valley League. Got it, $150 a month and all, all by himself, just by writing and enclosing some of his all-scholastic clippings.

Fresco's father, a shoe buyer for J. C. Penney, however, had been at a convention at Atlantic City, had gotten to chatting about his son who, he boasted, was a professional baseball player. One of his listeners was the manager of the J. C. Penney store in Grand Island. He perked up his ears. He was also the president of the

Grand Island ball club. "I'll take him," he said, with one eye on the talent aspect of the deal, the other on how it might help his business career.

How did the young man work his release from Cedar Rapids? Merely by writing and asking for funds to get there. His unconditional release came in the return mail.

The family angle bobbed up again in Fresco's first managerial job. In Birmingham he had an uncle who was a judge. The then-owner of the ball club was a lawyer. The judge's recommendations carried a lot of weight.

After Birmingham it was way stations like Hartford, Williamsport, into Brooklyn to help in the front office preparations for the 1941 World Series, then out to Reading where young Lee MacPhail, now farm director for the Yankees, had been installed as general manager by his father ("go down there as manager, Fresco, and help the boy out.")

More bouncing around on busses and always the conviction that his destiny didn't lie in the spiked-shoe department but in the front office. "I'd go to the winter meetings each year," observed Fresco, "and I'd see maybe fifty or sixty fellows who had managed the season before now standing around in the lobby looking for jobs. There'd be only one or two front-office fellows in the same spot. And they didn't have that desperate look, either."

Now the onset of World War II started taking its toll of baseball talent. In 1942, one week before the Dodgers' minor league training camp at Staunton, Virginia, broke up, Al Treadway, the manager of the Johnston, Pennsylvania, club in the Class C Middle Atlantic League, was drafted. MacPhail promptly drafted Fresco for the role. He spent the first couple of months worrying more about gas coupons and flat tires than about the club's won-and-lost record.

On Decoration Day that year Fresco wired MacPhail thusly: "Not having heard from you I'm going to pick a new manager from a hat and am coming home." That had results. A couple of days later MacPhail sent a relief and Fresco came back to Brooklyn.

Over the years Fresco has been on the receiving end of some pretty poignant wires himself. The Wisconsin State League is now extinct but the Dodgers once ran Sheboygan there when their farm system numbered as high as thirty under Branch Rickey.

The manager there was en route to his first pennant and was beginning to get a little nervous about it. He wired Thompson for a hard-hitting outfielder and a good righthanded pitcher. The records in the Brooklyn office showed the club was in first place by 11 games, had only 9 to play.

Fresco's return wire read: "Outfielder? Pitcher? What for? You can go fishing for the rest of the year and still win the pennant." He also treasures the memory of another plea for help which read, "temporarily in first place by five games but need help badly."

Life in Montague Street, together with flying trips to such outposts as Montreal, Mobile, St. Paul and Newport News to check on the progress of the local procurators, isn't one long laugh for Thompson. A comedian and nothing more would have laughed himself out of the job many years ago. Last September when the Dodgers were making merry in celebration of their pennant clinching in Milwaukee Fresco was just about as far away as a Dodger official could be. He was at Mobile on a trouble-shooting deal. Was he successful? Well, Mobile managed to finish fourth in the regular Southern Association season, came on to win the playoffs and then came through as the Dixie Series champion.

Running a baseball farm system, even after it's been cut from almost thirty to fourteen clubs, can be compared to something like handling the control tower at Chicago's Midway Airport with one hand. The other is playing a xylophone solo, of course. It ain't easy.

In Brooklyn it's especially difficult because there are *two* main objectives in the Dodgers' operation. If that reads like faulty grammatical construction, put the blame on Walter O'Malley's desk, not here. He's the head man.

One main objective is to develop players who will win pennants and world series championships for the Dodgers. That's fine and highly commendable, of course. The other main objective is to develop players of such excellence as to convince other clubs to part with large sums of money for them in the hope that they will help win pennants and World Series in their new surroundings.

Between these two goals Fresco Thompson does a daily tight-rope stint. Isn't it easier because there are only half the number of clubs, half the number of players, there were to worry about four or five years ago? No, if anything it's tougher. Production on the top level has to be just as high.

Brooklyn, under O'Malley, has made no secret of the fact that its farm system must produce a surplus of players for sale to support the continued operation of the farm system to produce more players for further sales, etc., and here we go around again, boys.

The gimmick is, of course, for the Dodgers to skim the cream off the top with the Don Zimmers, the Don Hoaks, the Podreses, the Amoroses, the Spooners and the Craigs. And always there have to be the Irv Norens, the Chico Carrasquels, the Billy Hunters, the Sam Jethroes, and the Danny O'Connells available for sale to other clubs at large sums.

Brooklyn, according to O'Malley, is consigned to the have-not category until it gets a new stadium capable of holding those big 60,000 Sunday and holiday crowds. (Ebbets Field holds about 35,000 with the fire department looking the other way). Until that time, and perhaps after that, too, Fresco Thompson will have to keep those "two main objectives" in his sights constantly.

Lesser objectives consist of worrying about 39 scouts, 20 of them full-time employees, and what they're doing at the moment, whether they're in Mexico City or Mexico, Mo., in Caracas or in Carthage, Ill. Scouting isn't just the business of signing talented young men; just as important is the business of *not* signing talented prospects.

"If you sign every good-looking kid who comes along you have to go broke," declared Fresco. "If you miss enough you'll wind up in last place. This is the only business in the world where a young man is paid large sums of money before he proves his ability. You've got to learn to live within a cockeyed economic framework.

"Talent hunting, however, has its compensations. You go to camp in the spring and you see a kid you signed yourself or told some scout to go ahead and sign. He's grown a couple of inches and he can do things after a year or two he couldn't do when you first signed him. He's doing now what you thought he might eventually be able to do.

"It's a big kick. You see a boy who everyone else passed up and now he shows unmistakeable signs of coming stardom and you feel pretty good. And then you see a boy who you paid $10,000 to and he's no better than he was when you signed him. And you know he isn't going to improve, either."

Brooklyn has to depend more on careful scouting than upon a fat checkbook for a fairly obvious reason. This doesn't cast a shadow on the abilities of non-Dodger scouts. Having the power to give a red-hot young prospect $75,000-$100,000 makes a scout's job tougher, not easier. You give away "x" number of $100,000 checks to kids who turn out to be duds and pretty soon the man upstairs goes and gets someone else to look the kids over. In the final analysis the business of knowing who *not* to sign shares equal billing with the ability of knowing who to sign.

Intangibles further complicate Thompson's job, along with that of every other farm director. Every letter, no matter how impossibly nutty it sounds, is subjected to careful scrutiny and investigation if it refers to talent. Every kid who asks for a "look" gets some kind of a test.

Why? Because while the $100,000 bonus boys grab the headlines the facts remain, and will continue to remain, that the bulk of the major league players still sign for nothing or almost nothing.

Fresco has his nose planted too deeply into reports, box scores, rules, draft lists, waiver lists, options and airplane and railroad schedules these days to get much of a chance to see many ball games. If he sees a hundred a year it's a lot. The minor-league encounters he witnesses on rutty infields under deficient lighting systems probably outnumber the major-league games three to one. His job is not to watch the major leaguers, however. He has to come up with the kids who will be playing on the major-league diamonds four or five years from now.

Baseball has been good to Fresco Thompson and Fresco has been good for baseball. In choosing it as his life's work, however, he was aware that he'd be at home far less than most people—like people, for instance, engaged in making penicillin, perusing gas meters or penning TV commercials.

It's had its compensations, though—Florida every spring, the President's box at the World Series, and enough money to send his only daughter, Ann, abroad last summer for a vacation.

Ann visited several places in Germany. She liked Heidelberg best, and the ecstatic post card she sent Daddy emphasized that there were 40,000 American GIs stationed there.

"Heidelberg! GIs!" snorted Fresco. "If it's GIs she wanted she could have taken the bus down to Fort Dix."

WHO'S EXCITED?

By Howard Preston

From The Cleveland News, August 30, 1955

Copyright, 1955, The Cleveland News

(Portrait of a man who resolved this season not to become upset no matter what happened to the Indians.)

IT ISN'T hard to swear off following the Indians. Let's see—this makes the third time. I swore off after the 1940 season when they lost out by one game. I swore off in 1949, the year after they won a pennant. It is easier to swear off in years following pennants. It's tough to do so when they have a chance to win for the first time in several years. First thing you know you are losing a little weight and you have gas. You seem to have knots in your stomach.

It's silly to get so excited about such a little thing as a baseball game. A man should be able to take baseball or leave it because it makes no difference in his life who wins. You know that the players are hired and they come from all around the country. You have no reason to care, really.

A fellow I know had to quit listening to baseball games on radio because he got too excited. His doctor lets him listen to a resume or final scores but not to the actual game. This man would get excited and wouldn't eat his dinner. If it was a night game, he wouldn't get to sleep until it was finished and if the team lost, he couldn't go to sleep. Here was a man who didn't see a game because possibly it was in Washington or Chicago but he would re-play the game in his mind. Couldn't get to sleep at all.

So, who cares what they do? Oh, good luck to them, naturally, but no more staying up for those late night games in the West. If they're going to play, why not play ball at a decent hour? But then it doesn't matter. No getting excited this year.

Why should adult people care whether Rosen hits home runs or Doby leads the league in runs batted in or if Feller pitches or not? Actually it is a little silly, isn't it? And you take some guys, when they're working out in the yard. They have the radio on the window sill and they turn it up so that they can hear it over the noise of a lawn-mower. That's going too far, all right. My gosh, you'd think a man could cut the grass without baseball, wouldn't you?

It is a relief not to bother with the team this year because a man can find a lot of other things to do—even find things to worry about if he wants to. What's more important, a man's health or baseball? Naturally his health.

The way to do is to adjust a sense of values so that everything is in its place. It doesn't matter what the Indians do so you ignore them and if they blow a close game in the late season you don't even read about them. The main thing is not to let the baseball bug get you and just be calm like I am and please pardon these finger-nails, but how did the Indians do today?

WHY DO BUNTS ROLL FOUL IN CLEVELAND

By Hal Lebovitz

From Collier's, April 1, 1955

Copyright, 1955, Hal Lebovitz

LET'S SAY you have just become the manager of a last-place club for a brand-new American League franchise. What's your first move? Study the records of your personnel? Make some trades? Buy players? Hire new coaches? Revamp the farm system?

Not Lou Boudreau. When he was named manager of the Kansas City Athletics a few months ago, his first move was to call the Bossard family in Cleveland. He offered Harold, the eldest Bossard son, the job as head groundskeeper of the Kansas City ball park. "Write your own ticket," he told Harold.

Boudreau isn't crazy. Once upon a time he managed and played shortstop for the Cleveland Indians. Emil Bossard was groundskeeper, aided by sons Harold and Marshall. "Emil was the tenth man in our lineup," Boudreau says. "I wouldn't be surprised if he helped us win as many as ten games a year."

That same touch is still helping the Indians, as general manager Hank Greenberg admits. "A good groundskeeper," he says, "can win his share of games, and the Bossards are the best."

The Indian infielders are so delighted with the condition of their diamond that you might say they literally worship the ground they walk on. When shortstop George Strickland came over from the National League in 1952, the greatest change he found was under his feet. "I can't say enough about the difference," he observed. "When you make an error in Cleveland it's seldom because of a bad hop. Best infield I ever played on."

Strickland's high opinion of the sixty-four-year-old Bossard is reflected all around the league. Just before the Yankees met the Brooklyn Dodgers in the World Series of 1953, the American Leaguers put in a call to Hank Greenberg. Would he consent to send Bossard to Yankee Stadium to give some professional advice? That the haughty Yankees should come seeking help was the highest possible compliment. Bossard went, and advised them how to turn their diseased grass into a healthy green and how to repair their infield. He was paid handsomely.

98

Last summer Greenberg received a call from the Detroit Tigers. The once-lush Briggs Stadium diamond was falling into disrepair. The Tiger ballplayers were moaning about bad hops and bumpy ground. Bossard was dispatched to the rescue. The biggest trouble, it turned out, was caking of the dirt strip around the infield. Bossard told the Detroit groundskeepers of a new rolling process he had developed. It softened the skin area of the diamond perfectly, according to the Tiger infielders. Bossard received a check and a testimonial letter from Jess Walls, the Briggs Stadium manager— plus a tremendous tribute in the Detroit Times.

The numerous job offers received by the younger members of the family are further proof that the Bossards are recognized as groundskeeping geniuses. It would be unethical (and useless) to try to hire Emil away, so the other teams try his sons. Each year at least one major-league club makes the attempt. Only one has ever succeeded. Son Gene was enticed away by the Chicago White Sox in 1940 and he's been head groundskeeper at Comiskey Park ever since.

Harold, of course, refused Lou Boudreau's recent offer. The younger Bossards—both of whom are in their forties—have comfortable salaries and fine homes in Cleveland and enjoy being with Pop. One of Harold's sons is a full-time member of the Cleveland ground crew and another son, along with a boy of Marshall's, is a part-time worker.

Although the Bossards are renowned throughout the league, few of the fans in Cleveland's huge lake-front stadium realize the importance of the three groundskeepers to the Indians. To the fans, the reason for a high hop, a bunt rolling fair or foul, a base hit through the infield, a runner safe or out by a wink, is good luck or tough luck, depending on how they're rooting.

Chances are, luck has less to do with it than the Bossards. In Cleveland, when a ball takes an unusual hop, it's often planned. Diamond doctoring isn't a Cleveland exclusive, of course. It's attempted throughout the majors. But Emil Bossard, it is unanimously agreed, is a diamond doctor *summa cum laude*.

The art of doctoring diamonds to give the home club the greatest advantage was first propounded by the great Giant manager John McGraw, and it's been done ever since. Ordering these invisible booby traps is much easier than making them, however, and it was not until Emil Bossard arrived on the baseball scene that a diamond became fully custom-built for the talents of the home nine. The

Bossards speed up the field one day, slow it down the next, tilt the foul lines to control the direction of bunts and engage in all manner of tricky—but strictly legitimate—maneuvers.

The Cleveland players think so much of the Bossards, as a result, that last season they voted them a three-fourths World Series cut, totaling $5,034.45.

Cleveland manager Al Lopez, who says the Bossards "helped us win the pennant," counts heavily on them for day-to-day assistance. Although he may discuss strategy in general terms, Lopez says he never directly advises Emil or gives him specific instructions concerning diamond manipulations.

"I leave it up to him," grins Lopez. "He never second-guesses my managing and I never second-guess his groundskeeping."

The Bossards, like Lopez, are profound believers in percentage baseball. They study the Indians from the day spring training opens. Emil, in fact, goes to spring training each year. How many pull hitters on the club? How many ground-ball hitters? In which direction do they hit? Is it a fast club? How many good bunters?

Similarly, they study the pitchers and rival hitters. They have daily conferences. Harold, a former minor-leaguer, is a particularly keen baseball student.

Then, for each home game they custom-build the infield to give the Indians the edge percentage-wise.

"Oh, we know a trick or two," admits Emil and the wrinkles around his eyes fan out on his smiling weather-beaten face. "This is a game of inches. An inch is often the difference between a base hit and an out. We try to have the inches go our way."

The Bossards won't divulge their master plan for the present season, but they do reveal what they did last year when the Indians won 111 games for an all-time American League high.

"We figured it this way," says Harold. "We have three guys who could pull the ball down to left field—Al Rosen, Bobby Avila and Al Smith. That's one third of the offense. So we decided to speed up the field down third base."

The key to diamond doctoring, according to the Bossards, is the first bounce. "If the first bounce is quick and sharp the ball has a better chance of going through the infield," explains Emil. "So we work on the area where the ball first hits. That's usually in the dirt circle between home plate and the infield grass." To speed up the ground along the third-base line, says Harold, "we rolled it plenty and didn't give it much water before games, especially when we played the weaker clubs, who couldn't pull." Last summer, Rosen, Avila and Smith shot a number of hits over or past opposition third basemen, and many Cleveland wins were traced directly to a hardened third-base line.

Of course, the speedy infield worked both ways: Rosen, who is slow afoot, also had to field on it. "But since he knew what we had done," says Emil, "he was able to play deeper. With the ground around the plate so hard, he didn't have to worry about bunts. They'd roll out to him faster."

Wherever possible, however, the Bossards try to tailor the infield to suit the fielders. Second baseman Bobby Avila used to like a fast field around second because it made the balls bounce higher instead of hugging the ground. Now he feels he gets a better start on the ball if it comes at him medium to slow. At first base last summer, the groundskeepers had a problem: Vic Wertz had never played that position before. Without telling him what they planned ("He had enough to think about," says Marshall), the Bossards kept the ground soft around first early in the season so the balls wouldn't come to Vic too hard, and made it faster later as he became more adept.

The '54 diamond was concrete-hard in comparison to the one fashioned by the Bossards for the 1948 World Champions managed by Boudreau. That year's infield quartet—Ken Keltner at third, Boudreau at short, Joe Gordon at second and Eddie Robinson at first—was slow-moving, "so we made the skin part of the diamond so soft they must have felt as though they were playing in rocking chairs."

For the current campaign, a safe prediction would be that the successful '54 formula will be maintained, especially with the advent of Ralph Kiner, another right-handed pull hitter.

But whenever Bob Lemon pitches, the ground goes soft. "Lemon," explains Harold, "has a sinker. The batters hit it on the ground."

Bob Feller also gets the soft-ground treatment these days. "He's come up with a sinker, too," is the Bossard explanation. "But in the old days we made the ground as hard as we could for Feller. When Bob had his fast ball, he'd strike out as many as 15 batters every game. That's 15 guys a hard infield couldn't help. On the other hand, only three or four of our guys would strike out. It's all percentage."

Diamond tempering (or tampering, if you will) is as legal as the knuckle ball, as long as the dimensional regulations of the rulebook are followed. And like the knuckle ball, it doesn't always work.

Take the last World Series (which Cleveland lost, of course). In the fourth and final game the Giants' Willie Mays hit one of Lemon's sinkers into the dirt. It took a kangaroo hop over Rosen's outstretched glove for a clutch double, reminiscent of some Rosen had hit during the season. Later in the game, Smith hit a similar bounder—except that Hank Thompson at third base stabbed it.

Said Joe DiMaggio, covering the game from the press box, "First time I ever saw that happen to the Bossards. It calls for a Congressional investigation."

The Bossards know the answer. Says Harold, "With Lemon pitching, we tried to make the ground very soft. But we were afraid to soak it too much; there isn't much sun in October to dry the excess water, and the ground might have become too muddy. So we didn't use enough water and the ground got too hard."

Away from home the Indians are on their own. The first time the Indians appeared in Comiskey Park last season, coach Tony Cuccinello called to each Cleveland player as he entered the batting cage. "Look at the third-base foul line." It was sticking up like a Dutch dike, leaning inward, making it virtually impossible for a bunt to roll foul. The doctoring was so obvious the Indians could adapt their strategy to it.

"The secret," declares Emil as if lecturing his son Gene, the White Sox groundskeeper, by remote control, "is to keep your tricks hidden."

Papa Bossard unhappily chalked up a victory for Gene, however, in Comiskey Park one afternoon last May. That day, the speedy Sox ran Cleveland's Mike Garcia off the mound by stealing five bases in less than four innings against the veteran hurler.

This incident caused radio broadcaster Van Patrick to challenge Emil. "I'll bet the next time the White Sox come to Cleveland for a series they'll steal at least two bases."

"A buck," said Bossard emphatically, "says they don't steal any."

"I knew when I shook hands with Emil," said Patrick later, "that I had just lost a dollar."

He was so right. Bossard halted the Go-Go Sox without a single theft. "All we did," says Emil, "was loosen up the soil about an inch deep so their spikes wouldn't grip. They had to stay close to the bag or get picked off."

One of the Bossards' biggest boosters is the Yankees' Phil Rizzuto. "He calls us the greatest," says Emil proudly, "but he doesn't trust us." Rizzuto learned quickly about the Bossards. On his rookie appearance in Cleveland, the Yankee Scooter beat out three bunts. The next day he bunted again. Each time he tried, the ball rolled foul. Until last year, the third-base foul line always was slanted outward when the Yankees came to town. But after Rizzuto lost his status as a regular, the lines were beveled inward to give Avila the edge.

"Last year," reveals Harold, "we generally slanted 'em out only for the White Sox and Senators."

Lou Boudreau, knowing Bossard's skill, thoroughly tests the ground before each game by hitting grounders to his infielders. "I see you've got a well at third base," he'll shout to Bossard if the balls slow down.

Visiting teams don't often complain about diamond doctoring. But Bossard admits he isn't infallible and on rare occasions he gets complaints from his own tepee. Once in a while a player in a slump will protest that he isn't hitting past the infield because the ground is too soft. Emil always tries to co-operate. "The worst thing on a club is a guy in a slump," he observes.

Al Rosen, a keen baseball student, often talks over ground problems with the Bossards. "We listen to him," says Harold. "He has some good ideas."

Rosen's advice on groundskeeping helped set the stage for the Tribe's greatest day last season. The Yanks were coming in for a double-header on Sunday, September 12th. It was their last stand, and they had to win or drop out of the race. But the Indians were crippled. Rosen had a bad leg and there were other injuries.

"Make the field as slow as you possibly can," he urged the Bossards. "That might equalize our speeds."

"We intended to make it slow anyhow, because Lemon was pitching the first game, but after Rosen talked to us we went all out. We made the infield slower than ever before," says Harold. "The Yanks didn't have a chance to test it in advance because it was only a one-day stay."

The Indians won the first game 4-1 and the second 3-2 before 86,563 people, the largest regular-season crowd in baseball history. But not until the unsuspecting fans who were there see this will they realize why so many Yankees grounded out that day when the Indians, for all practical purposes, won the pennant.

For Rosen the Bossards also custom-build the batter's box. He requests an elevation of about an inch at the spot where he plants his right heel to give him a more comfortable stance against tough pitchers.

"When Ray Boone was with us, we had a problem," says Harold. "He liked a lower box. Finally he told us, 'Rosen is the better hitter. Make it right for him.' "

The Bossards build most of their own groundskeeping equipment and are constantly inventing new tools.

Emil's prize device is his drag—42 inches long, 16 inches wide and containing 1,000 tenpenny nails. "Other groundskeepers use rakes," Emil points out. "But everybody rakes differently. Our drag does away with rakes and all the soil gets the same touch."

Another of his pet possessions is the Bossard Tarp, made of spun glass and weighing half as much as the standard infield cover. Since it cannot absorb moisture it does not gain weight, nor does it require drying after a rain. Furthermore, it cannot rip. Bossard predicts all major-league clubs will be using spun-glass tarpaulins eventually.

Including himself, his two sons and grandson, Bossard has a year-round crew of 12. During the summer he adds about 25 high-school boys. Then there's the gang from Wellington, Ohio, a town about 40 miles from Cleveland. For each night and Sunday game, about a dozen citizens from Wellington journey to the stadium at their own expense, put on groundskeeper uniforms which they purchased themselves and sit with Bossard in his special box along the left-field line. If it rains, they help him with the tarp. They get no pay, only free entrance into the park. In this unique group are a doctor, the Wellington chief of police, several businessmen and a newspaper reporter. "They're crazy about baseball," explains Emil, "and it's a break for us to have them."

As an extra aid, Bossard keeps in close touch with the Weather Bureau. Throughout each game he makes periodic checks and notifies Manager Lopez of approaching rains. Needless to say, rain warnings affect Lopez' strategy. More than once last season, the Indians protected an early lead by making sure 4½ innings were played before the rains came.

A few years ago, Cleveland was beating the Red Sox in the last of the fourth, 5-1, with two men on and one out when the skies opened up. It rained hard for 63 minutes, and when it finally stopped, the outfield was thoroughly flooded. The infield was dry because Bossard's gang had spread the canvas in less than four minutes, but it didn't seem that the game could resume—and unless it went five innings, it wouldn't count.

Joe Cronin, who was then the Red Sox manager, walked out to umpire Bill Summers and said hopefully, "There isn't a chance in the world to finish the game." Summers agreed, and turned to Bossard for confirmation.

"Just give me 25 minutes," said Emil, "and the field will be playable."

"I'll give you exactly 30 minutes," said the astonished umpire.

Emil had his men dig huge holes in the outfield. As the water drained into these pits, the Bossards hauled it out with pails and poured it into wheelbarrows and literally pushed the puddles off the field. In 25 minutes the field was ready, the game was resumed and the Indians won.

That night Bill Veeck, the Cleveland president, phoned Bossard, thanked him for the victory and gave him a $500 gift. "That," says Emil, "was the biggest thrill of my life." Last Christmas, the Bossards got bonuses from the grateful Greenberg.

Bossard and his sons are probably the highest-paid grounds-keepers in the game. In addition to working for the Indians, they also are on the Cleveland Browns' payroll for taking care of the stadium during the football season. Bossard employs no unusual turf tricks for the Browns. "Give us a dry, fast field" is coach Paul Brown's orders, "and we'll take our chances."

"When the Cleveland Rams were here," reveals Emil, "it was just the opposite. Their coach, Adam Walsh, wanted the slowest field he could get."

Because football cleats somehow deaden the soil, Bossard has to install a new infield after each grid season. For this, he mixes his ingredients as carefully as the most meticulous chef. He scouts around Greater Cleveland until he finds a clay that satisfies him. To this he adds strained builders' sand to attain the desired consistency.

Bossard takes pride in building the best pitcher's mound in base-ball. In 1946 a committee of pitchers, in an effort to make all mounds uniform, polled the league's hurlers. It was unanimously agreed, "Copy the one in Cleveland."

He also is fiercely proud of the thick green carpet in the stadium outfield. The stadium grass is a mixture, mostly creeping bent, with a little Kentucky blue and clover added. "It takes 50 per cent more work, but it's 50 per cent better," he says. "The secret of good grass is to feed it. Give it plenty of fertilizer. We use over two tons a year."

Emil says quietly, "I guess fixing fields is the job I was intended for, just like I suppose an artist is born with a special talent."

Emil might not have discovered his special talent if hard times hadn't hit St. Paul, Minnesota, in 1911. Emil was working at his father's hardware store, but business was so slow that year he began looking around for something else. "I heard they were doing some building at the St. Paul ball park so I went there and they put me to work carrying lumber. I'd never seen a baseball diamond before."

Within three weeks Bossard was asked to give the grounds-keeper a hand. When the snow melted he learned how to manicure a diamond. On opening day, the head groundskeeper took sick. "He stayed sick so they made me head groundskeeper at $80 a month," Emil recalls. He listened to the ballplayers, got good and bad advice and learned by his mistakes. Soon he became so proficient that other American Association owners prevailed upon him to rehabilitate their diamonds.

Then, in 1936, Cy Slapnicka, just appointed general manager of the Cleveland Indians, fired the groundskeeper he had inherited. "Recommend another," he said to his manager, Steve O'Neill. Not long before, O'Neill had been in the American Association, where he had piloted the Toledo Mud Hens. "The best in the business," said O'Neill, "is Emil Bossard at St. Paul."

Slapnicka offered Emil a two-year contract, and Emil accepted. Not once has he regretted the move. In Cleveland he soon made enough money to buy an eight-suite apartment which provided him a supplementary income. His sons became tenants.

A few months ago he sold the apartment at a 100-per-cent profit and bought a large home in a Cleveland suburb. His sons did likewise.

"You watch," promises Emil Bossard. "We'll have the best lawn in town. You know why? Mama will take care of it."

Football

FLIPPIN FLIPPED IT

By Stanley Woodward

From The Newark (N. J.) Star-Ledger, November 13, 1955

Copyright, 1955, The Newark (N. J.) Star-Ledger

RISING TO THE occasion with furious opportunism, the Princeton football team beat Yale, 13-0, before a jammed crowd of 46,000 in Palmer Stadium this afternoon.

After staving off the whipping Yale T attack in the first half, the Tigers struck for seven points in the third period and added a clinching, if unnecessary, touchdown on a pass-interception in the second-last minute of the game.

As if guided by a script written by a fanciful Hollywood long-hair, the Tigers did it in a manner so dramatic as to stretch verisimilitude to its uttermost limits.

Royce Flippin, captain and potential All-America tailback from Montclair who had been benched with injuries for all but three plays during previous games, was the leading Yale executioner.

He fired a pass which set up the tie-cracking touchdown, then scored it himself with a bull-like charge over Yale's right tackle.

A right end named Joe DiRenzo played second lead in the implausible Tiger production. He recovered two critical Yale fumbles, one of which set the situation for Flippin's touchdown.

He scored the second Princeton touchdown, intercepting a wild pass by Yale's quarterback, Dean Loucks, in the left flat less than two minutes from the end.

This was the game in which the Tigers held on by their finger nails in a wild first period when the Yale attack, moving with horrid speed, threatened to engulf them.

As a matter of fact Loucks, running the T option, actually went over the Tiger goal line on Yale's apparently unstoppable assault from the opening kickoff. Unfortunately, however, he no longer possessed the ball when he hit the end zone. Smacked on the two-

yard line he dropped it and a character from Orange named Ben
Spinelli recovered it.

Having taken the force of Yale's opening burst, during which
Dennis McGill and Al Ward, the alien halfbacks, ran like dervishes
and Loucks both passed and ran, the Tigers settled down and
contained the Elis. There were other Yale threats but Princeton
rose to every occasion and the Elis contributed certain self-destroy-
ing fumbles.

As the result of the victory Princeton is now the hot favorite
for the Ivy League championship. All the Tigers have to do to
clinch it is to beat Dartmouth in Palmer Stadium next Saturday.
Despite their muddy 7-6 defeat by Harvard at Boston last week,
the Tigers are now odds on.

The denouement which came today was set up by hell-roaring
games between Princeton and Yale last year and the year before.
Yale won in the last minute in 1953; Princeton did the same at
New Haven last year.

These events provided a natural ballyhoo for yesterday's event
and Ken Fairman, the Nassau athletic poobah, was virtually
drenched with ticket applications. All seats were gone at the close
of applications on Oct. 27 and late blooming Tigers and Elis were
shut out by the thousand.

The place probably could have been sold out twice over and it
may be honestly said that the show, and also the weather, justified
the avidity of the clients.

The game was fierce and the outcome uncertain until the virtual
close. The weather was sunny and warm causing a general emer-
gence from overcoats. The bands marched and played bravely and
Miss Margaret Truman, escorted by our trenchant Governor
Meyner, smiled graciously and bravely into the eyes of 50 lenses.

The pair arrived five minutes before the start and the photographers still were working them over when Princeton delivered the
opening kickoff to Yale.

Yale came whipping down the field for three successive first
downs and it looked as if the Elis—who had beaten Army the
previous Saturday—were going to make a shambles of the Tiger
defenses.

They arrived at the Princeton's 16 after chewing off chunks of
ground apparently at will. There Loucks, a good option runner,
slammed over Princeton's right tackle and went the rest of the

way, even though he carelessly left the ball on the one-and-a-half yard line for Spinelli to recover.

Yale was back again in a few minutes. This time Ward actually ran over the goal-line, after taking an option flip from Loucks. Unfortunately Yale was offside and his 28-yard run was nullified.

Then Yale took a 15-yard holding penalty and Bill Agnew put Princeton in the game by intercepting a pass on his 23.

The Tigers marched purposefully, capitalizing on the weak side of a heavily overshifted Yale line. They got across midfield before the first period was over and kept on after the teams had changed goals.

Flippin made his first appearance on the second-last play of the first period and remained to fire a pass to Agnew in the second for a first down on the Yale 18.

The Tigers could not get the rest of the way. A Statue of Liberty play with Agnew carrying failed to fool the Elis and they took the ball on downs on their 12.

Yale had the edge for the balance of the half though neither got a close-up shot at the goal line.

Flippin returned for a few plays but went out when Princeton lost the ball. Princeton received the second-half kickoff but stalled after one first down and punted to the Yale 22 where Don Mayer, guard, stopped Ward in his tracks with a savage tackle.

On the third down play with six to go, Ward fumbled and the opportunistic DiRenzo recovered on the Yale 22.

Flippin came back in the game and fired a bullet pass over center to Agnew for eight yards. Dick Martin ripped through a trap hole on a spinner for a first down on the Yale seven.

The Tigers moved only three yards in two downs but on the next play, launched from a left single-wing formation, Flippin summoned fierce impetus and smashed over left tackle into the end-zone.

The Tiger cheering section went into schizophrenia and the ululations trebled when Martin, whose miss in the Harvard imbroglio resulted in a 7-6 defeat for Nassau, successfully place-kicked the extra point.

Late in the third period a dangerous situation developed for the Tigers. Curtis Coker, Yale fullback, intercepted a jump pass just over midfield and started down the north sideline with a blocker ahead of him and no one in sight to stop him. John

Thompson, Princeton center, however, cut across and threw himself under both carrier and blocker, knocking Coker over the sideline.

On the second-last play of the period a weird play occurred. Ward punted for Yale and the ball rolled into the end-zone, then hopped back out, settling on the Princeton one-foot line.

Most people insisted it was a touchback, but the referee ruled the ball was dead where it settled, which put Princeton in a precarious position when the final period began.

They got out of it by furious defense and DiRenzo's persistent opportunism. McGill ran Princeton's punt to the 34 and the Elis came storming in. Loucks passed to McGill and Ward ran an option pitchout to a first down on the 17. In two plays Yale was on the nine where Loucks ran another option to the right.

Johnny Sapoch, Princeton quarterback and backer-up, slammed into Loucks, dislodging the ball. DiRenzo was there to smother it.

After that there was only one bad situation for the Tigers. They tried to run the ball on fourth down near midfield and didn't make it. Yale gave it back, however, also on downs.

A Princeton punt then immersed Yale in its own territory and Loucks started throwing passes in an effort to redeem the lowering situation. He fired a juicy one wide to his own right.

DiRenzo picked it off and galloped 18 yards for the touchdown without being tagged. The Princeton end was so ecstatic following this development that he missed the extra point.

The game ended after the next kickoff and the Tigers moved uptown to begin a celebration which apparently is going to go on for two or three days.

ODD FELLOWS THESE COACHES

By Maury White

From The Des Moines Sunday Register, September 11, 1955

LAST FOOTBALL SEASON as the wife of a well-known coach was performing her morning bed making a mouse sauntered from beneath a blanket, stared her in the eye and scooted away. She was disturbed. Women do not like to have a mouse around the house. Human mouses, maybe, but mousy mouses—never!

The coach came home for dinner. His wife had worked up a case of indignation. She was violently anti-mouse and expected her husband to vote the same.

"Really? Was there really a mouse in the bed?" asked the coach in pleased, almost gleeful tones.

A happy home almost went up in smoke.

Fortunately the coach had an explanation—a good one.

"I woke up twice last night," he told his wife. "Each time I felt a crawling sensation on my legs.

"But when I threw the covers back, nothing was there. I figured my nerves were shot.

"If you hadn't found that mouse, I'd have quit coaching," he solemnly assured her.

The wife is still anti-mouse, but at least she's not anti-husband.

Being a coach's wife, accustomed to the strange and strained life of in-season troubles, she didn't even think the incident was too unusual.

His nerves COULD have been shot.

Football coaches, as a breed, are about 110 per cent absorbed in their jobs. Occasionally they humor someone and talk about something else, but they're really thinking football.

The season is a 12-week period of constant worry and little delight.

It is located between the sweet talk of recruiting and the smothered belches of the banquet season.

It can be, and most often is, a tortuous time. Coaches lose sleep, weight, hair and—if they don't win enough—friends.

Prosperity is no mental tonic. Good coaches, like good generals, always plot enemy strength against their weaknesses. The boss of an undefeated team takes many imaginary beatings on the blackboard.

They are always planning. A few years ago, after playing at Maryland on Saturday, Missouri's Don Faurot had a Sunday morning breakfast date with President Harry Truman.

Faurot, who dropped into a restaurant for an early cup of coffee, became so absorbed in revamping his defense that he forgot about Harry.

"He'll understand," Faurot later soothed horrified friends. "The president must be a busy man, too."

This type of intenseness (ulcers simply flourish on it) is the trademark of the coach in season. They live the game they coach.

Players, like wives, sometimes operate on small doses of sympathy. Take the time, before the school dropped football, when the St. Louis University quarterback broke his nose three weeks in a row.

The third week, as he trotted off the field in disgust, Coach Dukes Duford came over to console him. His intentions were good.

But St. Louis started moving ahead on the field. As it did, Duford started getting excited. Eyes glued to the action, Dukes put his arm around the injured player and asked:

"Is it the same one you broke last week?"

Aware that they drive themselves too harshly, some coaches try to relax. Iowa's Forest Evashevski bought an organ and learned to play it. Oklahoma's Bud Wilkinson "untightens" in a steam bath.

Matty Bell, former Southern Methodist coach and now athletic director there, liked to listen to jokes the morning of a game. Old jokes, not new ones.

One of Bell's friends, a talented story teller, would sit around with Matty all morning. "Tell the one about . . ." the coach would request. The friend would comply. Then Matty would laugh.

The strain of trying to get 11 people working as a mechanical unit in the face of intense emotion—and in front of rabid crowds—is what turns coaches gray. They need a long working day.

When Herman Hickman was coaching at Yale, he established 7 a.m. as the time for all coaches to assemble. He would, he said, accept no excuses for tardiness, except sickness or death.

Then he caught the eye of Stu Clancy, an assistant who doubled as an embalmer in a nearby suburb.

"I mean private," Hickman said sternly, "not professional deaths."

So it's a hectic time. But the coach, at the end of a season, is like a small boy who has just lost an aching molar.

He's glad the pain is gone—and already anxious to look at the replacement.

FOOTBALL'S BIGGEST SHOW

By Harry T. Paxton

From The Saturday Evening Post, November 26, 1955

IN THE WHOLE crowded calendar of American athletics, there are a select few events that mean something to people everywhere, including many who ordinarily pay no attention to sports. In baseball it is the World Series. Horse racing has its Kentucky Derby, and golf its National Open. In college football there is no exact parallel. However, there is one game that stands apart. This is the star-spangled finale between the Army and the Navy, now about to take the stage for the fifty-sixth time this Saturday at the Philadelphia Municipal Stadium.

Unlike the big annual fixtures in other sports, the Army-Navy football game seldom has championship significance. But there are many who consider it the greatest spectacle of them all. Whether the game turns out to be a nonstop thriller, like last year's 27-20 Navy victory—or inept and uninteresting, as must happen occasionally—this is always a show with a unique flavor and emotional wallop.

If it is true that football is the sport most closely resembling military combat, then it is at the Army-Navy game that football has the perfect setting. Here the alumni are men who wear the uniform—and have elected to wear it for life. They sit together by graduating classes, except for those who bring parties of guests. One of the most warming sights of the afternoon is the reunions that go on between old classmates who haven't seen each other in years—the one serving perhaps in Europe and way stations, the other in the Far East.

Insignia of high rank are commonplace. This is the top sports affair in attendance by military and governmental officials, including Presidents—Teddy Roosevelt was the first in 1901.

Then there are the young gentlemen and officers-to-be of the brigade of midshipmen and the corps of cadets. You don't need to be any passionate admirer of the military way of things to respond to this feature of the afternoon. When those erect, disciplined

114

ranks come swinging in turn onto the field, it is a scene that does something to the normal American pulse.

After the football teams take over the premises, many in the stands will have sobering thoughts of certain former players who will never get back to an Army-Navy game. On the West Point side, at least twenty football men have lost their lives in wars, from Paul Bunker, a 1901-02 All-American, who died in a Japanese prison camp in World War II, to Tom Lombardo, the 1944 captain, and John Trent, the 1949 captain, both of whom were killed in Korea.

At Annapolis, the list of known war fatalities among football players is even higher. There were thirteen from the 1935 squad alone. The 1915 squad, to give a random additional example, produced Rear Adm. Henry Mullinix, whose ship was torpedoed by the Japanese in 1943. From the class of 1930 came a halfback named Harold Bauer, who was posthumously awarded the Medal of Honor after being shot down while leading a marine fighter-plane squadron at Guadalcanal in 1942, and an end named Dudley Morton, whose submarine, the Wahoo, was lost in 1943.

These honor rolls are a part of the special atmosphere that surrounds this game. There are older football classics than Army-Navy. In many college stadiums you will see more elaborate band shows and cheering-section stunts. Each region has traditional contests of deeper local appeal. In any season there may be some title-deciding game which generates greater country-wide excitement. But the Army-Navy rivalry has the broadest base of all. These are national schools. Their meeting is college football's one truly national attraction.

Of the 100,000 who see the game, more than half—at a conservative estimate—come to Philadelphia from other parts of the country. There probably is no other annual one-day event that draws such a multiplicity of advance preparations.

In the Philadelphia area this week various Federal and local agencies have issued emergency directives. Without special clearance, no aircraft may fly within three miles of Municipal Stadium the afternoon of the game. All drawbridges must stay down, so as not to impede the flow of traffic. Certain factories in New Jersey whose smoke sometimes drifts across the Delaware River to the stadium will suspend operations. Philadelphia firemen are hosing down nearby city dumps to suppress any fumes.

Authorities are surveying the playing field to determine whether some spots need touching up with green dye. The concessionaires, Nilon Brothers, are ready with everything from 150,000 hot dogs to 10,000 chrysanthemums raised especially for this date. The Pennsylvania and B & O railroads have worked out the complex logistics of bringing as many as forty special round-trip trains with 25,000-30,000 passengers to the stadium from New York and Washington within a period of less than two hours. Philadelphia hotels are preparing to fit 8,000-10,000 visitors into a total of 6,500 rooms.

This diverse multitude is turning out for a football game which is always a war. It is generally close—in only eleven of the fifty-five Army-Navy games has the margin been more than fourteen points. And as a long line of upsets has demonstrated, you never know in advance who's going to win.

Shortly before one recent Army-Navy game, a cadet player was chatting with a friend. "I'm worried about the number of green linesmen we have this year," he confided. "They don't realize what it's going to be like. You don't know what shock action is until you've played in an Army-Navy game."

It has been that way from the beginning. No football series was ever such a complete "natural" as this competition between the two service academies. At military outposts all around the world Army and Navy men have arranged parties to hear the game broadcast on Saturday, whether it comes on a breakfast time, as in Hawaii; in the evening, as in Europe; or at three o'clock in the morning, as in the Far East.

This sort of thing has been going on for years. As early as 1926 telegraphic accounts of the game were being relayed to the fleet by short-wave radio. Game broadcasts were beamed to all overseas areas during World War II. Col. Russell P. (Red) Reeder (Ret.), a former Army player and assistant coach who is now an assistant graduate manager of athletics at West Point, tells about hearing a broadcast of the 1942 game about 200 yards from the front lines on Guadalcanal.

This year the Armed Forces Radio Service will send its own live broadcast of the game over the facilities of the Voice of America, whose six powerful shortwave transmitters in New York sweep from Thule in the north down across Europe and south to the Caribbean.

Ships and military installations in the Pacific will get the regular commercial radio broadcast of the Mutual Broadcasting System, which has added Hawaiian and Latin-American outlets to a 576-station domestic hookup. At bases in this country Army and Navy men can see the game on television over a 160-station National Broadcasting Company network.

Some of the country's most eminent citizens are rabid Army-Navy football fans. General of the Army Douglas MacArthur was student manager of the 1902 West Point football team—he was also a varsity baseball player. MacArthur's interest has never diminished—he still gets intensive briefings on Army football affairs from Coach Earl (Red) Blaik. As superintendent of the Military Academy from 1919 to 1922, MacArthur promoted football and athletics generally. When the first of Army's great Blanchard-and-Davis teams snapped a five-year losing streak against Navy in 1944, he raidoed from his headquarters as supreme commander in the Southwest Pacific:

THE GREATEST OF ALL ARMY TEAMS STOP WE HAVE STOPPED THE WAR TO CELEBRATE YOUR MAGNIFICENT SUCCESS

MACARTHUR

A potent Navy enthusiast was President Franklin D. Roosevelt, who had been Assistant Secretary of the Navy during World War I. FDR never attended the game during his twelve years in the White House, probably because his physical condition made it impossible for him to observe the custom of changing sides at half-time. This custom was dropped during the regime of President Truman, who turned out almost every year. In any event, Roosevelt was a strong armchair rooter for Navy. He consistently bet sizable sums on the game with his military aide, Maj. Gen. Edwin (Pa) Watson.

Several years before Roosevelt's first term, Army and Navy stopped playing for two seasons—1928 and 1929—in a dispute over player eligibility. Annapolis had adopted the prevailing rule which limits a boy to three years of college football. West Point insisted on its right to field any bona fide cadet, even if—like such Army stars of that era as Light Horse Harry Wilson and Christian (Red) Cagle—he had already played four full years at a civilian college before entering the Military Academy.

In 1930, with the depression setting in, President Hoover

ordered an Army-Navy game played to raise money for charity.
In 1931 the same thing happened, so in 1932 the academies decided
that they might as well resume relations on their own. The difference of opinion on eligibility remained, though, until a day in 1938
when President Roosevelt abruptly invoked his authority as commander in chief to settle the issue in Navy's favor. FDR handed
Pa Watson a note for delivery to the Military Academy: "From
now on West Point will abide by the three-year rule."

Although the Army-Navy game steams up alumni and well-
wishers everywhere, it is at the schools themselves that things come
to full boil. There are football rallies every week at both Annapolis
and West Point, but for the climax game everything is magnified.

Signs go up on the buildings expressing the "Beat Army!" or
"Beat Navy!" theme. The big Thursday-night rallies may feature
"name" speakers. At West Point one year Ike Eisenhower—still
a general then—addressed the cadets by telephone from Washington saying, "The Army and the Navy are the best friends in the
world 364½ days a year, but on this one Saturday afternoon we're
the worst of enemies!"

At Annapolis, war paint has been applied to Tecumseh, bronze
replica of a wooden figurehead from the old warship Delaware.
Tecumseh is a talisman to whom generations of midshipmen have
made obeisance in appealing for favors—a passing mark in an
exam, a victory over Army. Meanwhile West Pointers are awaiting the outcome of the annual Goats-Engineers game—a contest
between teams drawn from the lowest-ranking and highest-ranking
students. A victory for the Goats is always perversely regarded as
a good omen for Army against Navy.

Friday morning the teams leave for Philadelphia—"If only to
get them away from the bedlam around here!" says Capt. C. E.
Loughlin, Navy's director of athletics. The same day, tractor
trailers depart with the displays the middies and cadets have rigged
up for pregame and half-time stunts.

One year the cadets constructed a giant wooden cannon from
which they intended to shoot a dummy sailor. They test-fired it
first on their parade-ground, which was fortunate, because the
dummy sailed about 500 yards through the air—enough to carry
him far out of the stadium in Philadelphia.

The powder charge was reduced to proper proportions and the
cannon was sent off to the stadium. It never got inside. It was too
big to pass under even the largest entrance gate. The cadets still

didn't give up on it. They took the cannon back to West Point, rebuilt it on a smaller scale and brought it back to use the following year.

Many students center around the Navy goat, Bill XIV, and the Army mules, Hannibal and Pancho. The Navy goat came onto the field one year in a float designed to resemble a perfume bottle. Another time he emerged from a Trojan wooden horse. The mules last year, billed as "Army's Answer to Atomic Warfare," rode in together on a trailer truck. To Navy's delight, the truck subsequently got stuck in the mud near one of the end zones.

Once the middies and cadets take their seats, they supplement their organized cheering and singing by holding up signs ribbing each other. Several years ago, for instance, when Army was being criticized for a light schedule, the Navy came up with this parody of the West Point song, On, Brave Old Army Team:

> We don't play Notre Dame,
> We don't play Tulane,
> But we play Davidson,
> For that's the fearless Army team.

Sometimes there are extracurricular pranks. The weekend before the 1946 game some midshipmen slipped into West Point in the dark of night and daubed the streets and statues with bright red paint. They were ordered back after the game to scrub it off.

Then there was the successful "goatnapping" of Bill XIV by a group of cadets in 1953. Professing deep regret, the West Point authorities sent the goat back to Annapolis with an escort commanded by a colonel, who issued this statement upon arrival: "They say in the Army that there are four general classes of officers—aides, aviators, asses or adjutants. I am adjutant at West Point, have been playing aide to a goat all day, and feel like a bit of an ass."

If Navy wins on Saturday, relays of midshipmen will keep two bells at Annapolis ringing for twenty-four hours. One victory bell was brought from Japan by Commodore Perry and presented to the Naval Academy in 1858. The other came from the bridge of World War II aircraft carrier Enterprise.

If Army wins, the team will be met, when it returns to West Point on Sunday afternoon, by cadets with the victory wagon. The players will be loaded into this venerable conveyance and hauled up the hill into the grounds. As many cadets as can get a hand in will pull the wagon by a long rope—the "2400-Mule Team," this is called.

On Monday you could tell who lost just by watching the boys get up in the morning at either academy. Many of the lads at the losing school will be shivering in their underwear—cadets and midshipmen are in the habit of wagering their bathrobes on the game.

The superintendents of both institutions—Lt. Gen. Blackshear M. Bryan at the Military Academy, Rear Adm. Walter F. Boone at the Naval Academy—think of the Army-Navy game as a high point in their programs of athletic training for all students. Both place stress on physical-contact sports such as football. The superintendents also value the game as an esprit builder and as an outlet for blowing off steam.

They further regard the Army-Navy as good institutional advertising. In particular, they think it helps to get boys interested in the service academies. They like to see as many candidates as possible applying for West Point or Annapolis appointments each year. It was this publicity angle, incidentally, which led Navy to accept a Sugar Bowl bid last season.

Finally, the Army-Navy game is a financial must at both schools. Congressional appropriations for the service academies make no provision for intercollegiate sports. For years their athletic programs—twenty varsity sports at Navy, seventeen at Army—have been supported by independent agencies, the Naval Academy Athletic Association and the Army Athletic Association, respectively.

The associations get some of their money from membership dues and from other sports. But about 90 per cent of their total revenue comes from football, and the Army-Navy game is by far the largest item. It constitutes the difference between profit and loss.

At Annapolis last year the Naval Academy Athletic Association took in $911,000. Of this, football produced $805,000, with the Army-Navy game accounting for $395,000—Navy's half the gross. The situation at West Point was comparable.

These figures explain why the Army and the Navy prefer to play at Philadelphia Municipal Stadium, which has been the scene of the game since 1936, except for a three-year interlude during World War II. The Philadelphia site has a number of assets. It is conveniently located about halfway between the two academies, and convenient also for the Washington dignitaries who like to attend.

But the most compelling advantages are financial. This stadium seats more people—about 100,000—than any other on the Eastern seaboard. The city of Philadelphia charges Army and Navy only a token rental, hands them the concessions and other extra-profit sources, and provides various services free.

And it doesn't cost the schools much to send the 2500 cadets and 3700 midshipmen to a Philadelphia game. They put them on trains Saturday morning, give them lunch; then turn them loose after the game until midnight, when the trains start back. The total expense is about $35,000.

This last item is the biggest single reason why the service schools always resist proposals to move the game to another part of the country, as they did recently when Chicago made a pitch for the 1956 game. Athletic officials at the Naval Academy—which will be the "host" school in 1956—estimated that transportation alone for taking more than 6000 cadets and midshipmen to Chicago would cost nearly $700,000. Extra expenses for meals and hotel accommodations would run the bill up to more than $900,000. The schools obviously couldn't pay this themselves, and it was questionable whether Chicago would want to pick up the tab—as it did back in 1926, when Army and Navy were brought out to dedicate Soldiers Field in the only non-Eastern game of the entire series. Anyway, the Defense Department recently turned Chicago down.

Since World War II, the Army-Navy game has often been the artistic as well as the financial salvation of Navy's football season. Navy had a great collection of players during the war, although they couldn't quite match the West Point squads featuring Doc Blanchard and Glenn Davis. But in 1946, with the war over, several of the Naval Academy stars promptly went back to civilian schools, and Navy headed into a losing cycle that was to last for six years.

The 1946 Navy team won only a single game. Meanwhile Army, with Blanchard and Davis still on hand, was going through its third straight undefeated season. The Army-Navy game that year shaped up as no contest, and it started out that way, with Army running up a 21-6 half-time lead.

In the second half, events took an amazing turn. Navy pulled the score up to 21-12, then to 21-18. Midway in the final quarter they started one last drive from their thirty-three-yard line. With Municipal Stadium a madhouse, and frenzied spectators pouring down from the stands along the sidelines, the clock ran out with

Navy in possession on the Army four. That night Navy rooters were as exuberant as if they had won.

In 1948, Navy had lost every game on its schedule, while Army had lost none. The middies proceeded to battle the cadets to a rousing 21-21 tie. Then, in 1950, came perhaps the biggest of Army-Navy upsets. By this time the West Pointers had gone through twenty-eight games without a loss. Navy's record for the season was two wins and six defeats. Yet the lads from Annapolis pounded out a convincing 14-2 triumph.

Army leads in the all-time series standings with twenty-eight victories to the Navy's twenty-three. There have been four ties. The cadets also have pulled their share of surprises over the years. Coach Earl Blaik, who took over at West Point when Army football was at low ebb in 1941, thinks honors have been about even in the upset department during his tenure.

Blaik has had an over-all record of ninety-five wins, twenty-five losses and eight ties during the past fourteen years at Army. His log against Navy, however, has been only six-seven-one. As Blaik analyzes it, Army lost in 1941-42-43 to superior Navy squads. The 1944 and 1945 games, which Army won, were battles between two even teams.

"In 1946," Blaik continues, "we started out to annihilate them, then just staved them off. When we took them in 1947, they were expecting to beat us. Before that 1948 tie, practically our entire squad was weakened by nausea from some tainted turkey on Thanksgiving Day. In 1949 we trounced Navy. When Navy beat us in 1950, I guess you could call that an upset. But it was no upset when they won in 1951 and 1952. Our 1953 victory was an upset for Army. So that makes two upsets for us and one for them."

Blaik thinks the game means even more to the Navy than it does to the Army. "There is tremendous pressure in the Navy from the top on down for victory over the Army," he declares.

Each school always has an open date the Saturday before the Army-Navy game, which allows two weeks to get ready. Aside from this mixed blessing, Blaik declares that Army's preparations for Navy are basically the same as for every other game on the schedule. "We play our games one at a time," he says.

The Navy coach, Eddie Erdelatz, says the same thing. Like Blaik at West Point, he took over at Annapolis when football had hit bottom. Until last season, when Navy had its first standout team in years, his chief success was in the Army game. Going into this season, Erdelatz had won twenty-three, lost nineteen and tied four in his five years at Annapolis. Against Army, however, he had won four out of five.

Erdelatz at this point won't talk much about the Army-Navy games he has coached. He doesn't want to appear to be claiming that the victories were due to his masterminding. He mentions tactical innovations he has put in for certain Army games, but is at pains to add that the big thing was the tremendous spirit of the players and the entire Naval Academy.

The spirit on both sides has been fabulous from the first Army-Navy game in 1890. Football was already an established thing then at many colleges, following the pioneering example of Princeton and Rutgers in 1869. The Naval Academy had played its first outside opponent in 1879. At the Military Academy, on the other hand, the policy-setting academic board had opposed sports competition as a frivolous distraction, and had never authorized the formation of a football team.

It was an enterprising cadet named Dennis Mahan Michie who was most responsible for breaking through this barrier. Michie knew and loved football, having played it at Lawrenceville Academy. More important, his father happened to be the biggest wheel on the Academic Board. When the Annapolis team challenged West Point to football combat in 1890—a challenge young Michie is believed to have instigated—he talked his influential father into getting official sanction for the game.

So the Army-Navy series opened on the parade grounds at West Point on November 29, 1890. Along with the 270-man corps of cadets, the audience included, according to the New York Sun, a delegation from New York City consisting of "about 150 officers of the Navy, the Army, and the naval reserve, with not a few ladies." Chairs were found for the ladies. Everybody else stood.

Dennis Michie—who later died in action in the Spanish-American War, and in whose honor the modern West Point stadium is named—had organized a robust fifteen-man Army squad, featuring a "line of giants." However, this original Army team couldn't match the skill in such maneuvers as the V wedge of the more experienced Navy players, who had come through a six-game schedule with four wins, one loss and one tie. The Navy captain, Charley Emrich, became the first high-scoring hero of the series, going over for four touchdowns—worth four points apiece at that time—in a 24-0 Navy victory.

There is legend that another first was established that day when the Navy squad, marching up the hill from the ferry station to the West Point grounds, appropriated a goat from somebody's front yard and brought it along for good luck. According to an Annapolis inquiry on this point, the goat didn't make his debut as a Navy mascot until 1893; the Army mule entered the picture in 1900.

But if it took a few years for all the trimmings to evolve, the central element of intense interest was established immediately. A contemporary account reports that at the conclusion of the first game, "The Annapolis men went wild over their victory. When the score reached Annapolis last night the naval cadets"—they weren't "midshipmen" then—"were so delighted with the victory of their team that they fired twenty-four guns and then paraded the streets with horns."

Similarly, when the news of a 52-16 Army victory at Annapolis the next year was wired back to West Point, "the pent-up enthusiasm of the corps broke forth. The cadets marched around the post. The superintendent extended his congratulations, the band played, guns were fired (eleven, one for each member of the team), bonfires were lighted with fine effect."

The heat over those early games flamed up to the point where the highest authorities in Washington cracked down. In the 1893 game at Annapolis, where 10,000 watched the Navy win by 6-4, there was plenty of rough stuff on the field and some even more violent outbursts in the crowd. One row between a brigadier general and an admiral wound up in a challenge to a duel. Whether the duel ever came off is not definitely known, but this episode led to suspension of the series. President Grover Cleveland's Cabinet accomplished this by the device of having the Secretary of the Navy order the respective schools to play football only on their home grounds. The game didn't resume until 1899.

This was the first—and longest—of four interruptions in the series. The 1909 meeting washed out when Army canceled the balance of its schedule, when a cadet player, Eugene A. Byrne, was fatally injured in a midseason game against Harvard. During World War I the 1917 and 1918 games were called off. The final break was the aforementioned dispute of 1928-29.

It would take a book to do full justice to all the great games and players of the Army-Navy series. There was Charley Daly, the dynamic little Army quarterback at the turn of the century, who later became a successful West Point coach. There was Navy's "Three-to-Nothing" Jack Dalton, who kicked field goals to beat Army by 3-0 scores both in 1910 and 1911. There was Baby Brown, who kicked two field goals for a 6-0 Navy win in 1912.

One of the all-time superathletes at West Point was Elmer Oliphant. In his first appearance against Navy in 1915 he scored every point as Army won, 14-0. The next year the orders of the day at Annapolis read like this the morning of the game: "6:00 A.M.—Rise; Stop Oliphant; 7:00 A.M.—Breakfast; Stop Oliphant!" Navy just couldn't do it. Oliphant starred again in a 15-7 Army victory.

A top thriller was the seesaw 1922 game which Army won with a last-minute touchdown, 17-14. But the No. 1 classic is generally considered to be the 1926 game before 110,000 at Soldiers Field in Chicago. Navy was unbeaten that year. Army had been stopped only by Notre Dame, 7-0. The middies jumped off to a 14-0 lead. Then the cadets caught up and went ahead. In the fourth quarter Navy got its third touchdown—and third extra point by Tom Hamilton—to finsh in a 21-21 tie.

That was as close as Navy came to winning from 1922 until 1934—the longest time either team has gone without a victory. There were two tie games during that stretch, and two years when they didn't play.

In 1934 Navy finally broke through with a 3-0 victory on a field goal by Slade Cutter and a great all-around performance by Fred (Buzz) Borries, the quarterback and safety man. Says Navy's assistant director of athletics, E. E. (Rip) Miller, "Borries made about ten last-man tackles in that game."

Since then the balance of power has been shifting back and forth, with the five-straight Navy streak from 1939 through 1943 the lengthiest period of dominance on either side. The first three of these wins came under Coach Emery (Swede) Larson, who never lost to Army as player or coach. In 1939 Larson had a big sign put up over the main entrance to Bancroft Hall at Annapolis: IT CAN, IT SHALL BE DONE. BEAT ARMY.

Year after year, the Army-Navy game is staged before one of the biggest of all sports crowds. Tickets often are as hard to find as uranium. Although 102,000 is generally given as the attendance figure for the games at Philadelphia Municipal Stadium—this includes everybody inside the park, the more than 6000 cadets and midshipmen, the 1600 Pinkerton guards, the 400 city policemen, the 1500 program and concession vendors, the nearly 500 representatives of the press and broadcasting.

The schools actually have between 91,000 and 92,000 tickets to sell. They offer them first to members of their athletic associations. The Army Athletic Association and the Naval Academy Athletic Association each have membership of about 15,000, consisting primarily of alumni, plus such added starters as congressmen, all of whom automatically qualify. Members can order personal-use tickets at five dollars apiece, and additional ones at six dollars.

The members always take most of the tickets, and sometimes all. From 1945 through 1950 none were left over for public sale. In 1951, when the so-called cribbing scandal at West Point practically wiped out the varsity football squad, there was a ticket surplus. But things are back to the point where you have little chance of getting a ticket unless you have an Army or Navy friend to order it for you. A few tickets always wind up in the hands of scalpers, of course, and generally there are a couple of hundred late turnbacks in Philadelphia on the day of the game.

Both West Point and Annapolis recruit boys with football ability. The day is long gone when Army and Navy—or anybody else—could stay in big-time competition without recruiting. And the predominant view at both schools is that it is important to their standing with the public to make a good showing in the big red-blooded American sport of football. West Point and Annapolis authorities will assure you, however, that football players are treated just like any other students, and must meet the same standards for getting in—and staying in.

The 1951 cribbing at West Point revolved around the fact that the same examination would be given to different groups on different days. Some cadets tipped off others on what questions to bone up on; for still others the offense simply was being aware that this was going on. Says General Bryan, the West Point superintendent, "I wasn't here when it happened. I can tell you that West Point today is sound. Our boys are cadets first and football players second.

Last year Army star Don Holleder was kept out of the first two games as the result of punishment for a disciplinary infraction.

This year halfback Mike Ziegler similarly was disqualified for the entire season. Ziegler and fifty others got out of the doghouse early, however, when Prince Albert of Belgium came to the Military Academy on October fourth. An ancient West Point custom provides that visiting royalty can request amnesty for all cadets undergoing punishment.

How do Army and Navy football players compare with the other students by such yardsticks as percentage staying in the service and advancement in rank? No precise figures are available, but it is the belief of officials that the football men do just as well, if not better. The number who have been decorated for heroism is high.

As of 1950, there were eighty former Navy players who had become admirals, including William F. (Bull) Halsey, Jonas Ingram and Richard Evelyn Byrd; and ninety-eight Army players who had become generals, including Omar Bradley, Joe Stilwell, James Van Fleet and Dwight D. Eisenhower. Ike never got in a Navy game, though. He made the first team as a halfback in his second year, but suffered a knee injury two weeks before the finish of the season which ended his West Point football career.

A few years from now service-academy football will become a three-way affair. The new Air Force Academy expects to start playing Army and Navy as early as 1958. Football men won't be surprised if the ambitious younger institution makes trouble for the older ones straight off. It is apt to be a long time, though, before Air Force vs. Navy or Air Force vs. Army acquires the special significance of an Army-Navy game. This one has a large niche all its own.

THEY EVEN CHEERED GENERALS

By Frank Yeutter

From The Philadelphia Bulletin

TALK ALL you want to about "shining hours" and "tumultuous celebrations," no outburst in Army football ever equaled the uninhibited bellowing in the West Point dressing room after the Cadets licked Navy 14-6.

And it wasn't only cadets and their friends and relatives who shouted and cheered. No sooner had the Cadet team raced and pranced up the concrete stairs in the northwest corner of the Stadium than General Maxwell Taylor, Chief of Staff and former superintendent of the Academy, accompanied by Lieutenant General Blackshear M. Bryan, present "supe" trotted up back of them.

Although the dressing room doors were closed the boisterous, emotional cheers could be heard outside. As the two generals entered even they got a cheer from the joyous Cadets.

The celebration reached such a point that one Cadet, clad in immaculate gray uniform, charged out of the dressing room. His uniform was not entirely regulation, however. He wore a high silk hat to which was pinned a large button reading, "Beat Navy."

The first cadet player to arrive was reserve back Glenn Allen. Right on his heels were Ed Szvetecz, who played a whale of a game at center, and Dick Fadel, a guard. They had their arms over each others shoulders and shrieked like a couple of banshees. Then came Dick Warner and Dave Bourland, also yelling, with two-point kicker Ralph Chesnauskas pushing them up the stairs.

Dick Murtland, sweat and grime pouring off his face, was with Dick Stephenson, the great right tackle. Murtland next to team captain Pat Uebel was Army's most gainfully employed runner. Stephenson's face showed the rigors of his line battle. He was scratched and torn on the cheek and plastered with dried blood.

As Don Holleder struggled to the bath house several friends called "great game" to him and his tired, taut face brightened with a happy smile. The last to arrive was Army's biggest gun—Uebel— who later was tapped for "greatest player" by Coach Red Blaik.

128

Bob Kyasky, the cadet who was to have been Blaik's "ace in the hole," was a study in disappointment and happiness. His tricky knee went back on him midway in the game and he hobbled off the field under support of two training aides. Attired in sweat clothes when the team came off, most of the players clapped him on the back and made him their "mascot" of the great victory.

The winning players trumpeting voices roared for at least 10 minutes before Coach Blaik opened the dressing room door so the writers could get his version of what happened.

All this week Blaik has been in a sly, good mood, his almost smug attitude openly predicting victory.

"But I didn't predict victory at any time," he insisted. "I knew our team was intensely anxious to win. So I had no worries about how they'd play."

It was pointed out to Red that the Cadet team was "naval" in the first half, in that they were "all at sea" trying to combat Navy's great George Welsh and Ron Beagle.

"Navy did two things we didn't expect," Blaik explained. "They used a six-man line on defense. Ordinarily they used uneven lines, either five or seven men and 'slant charged.' We hadn't seen any of their maneuvers with a six-man line so our running offense was thrown out of gear.

"Then on offense they threw that double flanker play at us. We weren't prepared for that, either. So there was little we could do either on offense or defense until we made the adjustments at half time."

As soon as he mentioned half time several writers were ready with the question why Holleder didn't throw a pass when Army reached Navy's three-yard line and "stop the clock." It was at this point that Army made it to Navy's one just as the half ended.

"We had used our five legal times out," Blaik explained, "so calling for an extra time would have cost us five yards. I'm not going to criticize Holleder. He did what he thought was best. We had sent in word to use a pass play to stop the clock but he thought his call was better."

After the Blaik explanation, Holleder was asked why he ignored the order from the bench and resorted to a running play.

"It was one of those things," he said. "The coach said to use 'Right 14 pass' but I called for the running play. So we didn't score. That's all there was to it."

Then Blaik was asked how he prepared defenses against Welsh's dangerous passing.

The little Navy quarterback passed from any position on the field with either Beagle or Navy's right end, Jim Owen, as targets.

"We were pretty well aware of Navy's pass offense," Blaik admitted, "and I want to impress everyone with my opinion that Welsh is a truly great passer. But we decided to let him have his short and screened passes and defend against his deep throws. Then, too, we sent the middle of the line in to rush him and keep him from getting set to pick his receivers. That defense worked quite well, although we weren't very familiar with his screened attack. He got away with two or three but none of them actually hurt us."

Then Blaik was asked how it was possible for Uebel and Dick Murtland to run so consistently through Navy's line.

"That, too, was an offense especially planned for Navy's slanting line charge. There were times that we waited for Navy linemen to commit themselves then got the delayed run under way."

Blaik was asked about the one or two "innovations" he said he had for this game.

"We didn't get a chance to use them," he said. "Each of the new plays were pass plays with Kyasky throwing. We couldn't use them after Kyasky was hurt for Murtland, although a splendid runner, can't pass. Everything in that 'new play' department depended on Kyasky having a good day."

Blaik couldn't veer away from his opinion of Welsh as a passer and Uebel as a runner and the magnificent comeback of the Army team after the first half which ended 6-0 for Navy.

"Welsh is really marvelous," Red insisted. "I think Navy's passing was superior to that of last year when they beat us. And Uebel was a truly great runner. Stan Slater at left guard made an important recovery for us. Holleder played well. There was some question about why I took Holleder out in the second period. I wanted to tell him what we had learned about Navy's new defenses. There was no implied criticism of his play calling. I thought he did very well on some of the 'roll-outs.'

"But I couldn't pick out any one player as a star. It was a team effort and a great one. We stayed with a running attack because we could gain with it. There were several teams this year that resorted to running rather than passing and were successful.

But try to imagine how a team feels when it encounters the trouble we did in the first half then comes back and wins the way we did. Weathering a storm of that sort shows the mettle of a team. Ours was wonderful."

THE WILL TO WIN

By Dick Peebles

From The San Antonio Express, November 25, 1955

WAKE THE TOWN and tell the people—Texas 21, Texas A&M 6.

Scaling dizzy heights of greatness that even their staunchest admirers deemed impossible, the fired-up Longhorns upended the strongly favored Aggies in the 62nd renewal of their bitter rivalry this dull, gray Thanksgiving afternoon in Kyle Field.

There wasn't a thing about this traditional battle that went according to form. Texas, a 10-point underdog, outplayed the Aggies so badly in all departments that there was no doubt which was the better team today.

The vicious Longhorn defense allowed the Aggies just 30 yards rushing and 67 more passing and gave up just three first downs. All the first downs came on the Aggies' 80 yard touchdown drive in the second period. The remainder of the chilly afternoon, the Aggies were slammed down at every turn by the alert Longhorns.

The Aggies dedicated the traditional meeting with Texas to James (Sonny) Sarran, Brownsville sophomore. Sarran was critically injured Tuesday night guarding the Aggie bonfire pile. In receiving his injuries, Sarran saved two Aggiemates from the onrushing car that struck him near the bonfire pile. He is in St. Joseph Hospital, Bryan.

The Texas offense, more potent and imaginative than any Longhorn team of recent vintage, piled up 16 first downs in grinding out 295 yards on the ground and picking up 96 more in the air.

If there had to be a Texas hero, it had to be Walter Fondren, the 19-year-old sophomore halfback from Houston. But this was a team victory if ever there was one.

However, Fondren who scored the second Texas touchdown on a bull-like smash of seven yards, was the leading ground gainer on the field, picking up 98 yards in 20 carries. He also booted two points after touchdown.

But the 165 pound sophomore had to share the spotlight with junior Halfback Ed Hawkins and senior Fullback Delano Womack and senior Quarterback Charley Brewer.

Hawkins got the final Longhorn score on a two yard smash and also gained 81 yards in 14 carries. Womack gained 91 yards in 18 carries.

Brewer, who had his finest day in a Longhorn uniform, completed two of three passes for 10 yards, but he called a terrific game and was tremendous on defense.

Texas' loudest aerial bomb on the eventful afternoon was fired in the final 10 seconds of the first half. It was a 25 yard shot to End Menan Schriewer of New Braunfels who made a jumping fingertip catch in coffin corner.

It was this touchdown pass and Johnny Elam's conversion that enabled the Longhorns to hold a 7-6 halftime lead. Then they broke the game wide open with two touchdowns in the fourth quarter.

The defeat was only the second of the season for the surprising Aggies of Coach Paul Bryant and their first in conference competition.

Their only hope of sharing the title now is for Southern Methodist to upset TCU on Saturday.

Texas A&M hasn't beaten Texas since 1939, and the Aggies were expected to do it today. But the Longhorns didn't come here to lose. That was evident early to the capacity crowd of 41,800 and the millions of nation-wide television viewers.

The Longhorns suffered two heart-breaking setbacks that would have killed off a less determined team before they finally got up a full head of steam. Then there was no stopping them.

The Aggies had their bad moments, too. But they couldn't come bouncing back.

It looked like it was going to be a glorious day for the Cadets when Fondren fumbled on the first play of the game and Bobby Joe Conrad recovered for A&M on the Texas 19 yard line.

After three plays the Aggies were back on the 24 and they lost the ball on downs on the 13 following an 11 yard pass from Jimmy Wright to John Crow.

A few minutes later, Crow, a terrific halfback, raced 37 yards to the Texas 19 yard line only to see the effort wiped out by a clipping penalty.

Then it was Texas' turn to get kicked in the britches by lady luck. The Longhorns, with Fondren passing and running and Womack bucking the line, smashed 65 yards to the Aggie one foot line only to lose the ball on downs.

All of this happened in the first quarter. And before the teams were finally to unlock the scoring gates, the Longhorns got another jolt.

Fondren burst through a hole at right tackle and scooted 29 yards down the sidelines before being bounced out on the three.

The Aggies were penalized to the one for piling on Fondren but on the first play, Brewer tried a sneak. Aggie Fullback Jack Pardee stole the ball from him and downed it in the end zone for an automatic touchback.

That was the end of the wheel-spinning. The boys got serious after that.

Crow, who was the leading Aggie ball carrier with 18 yards in seven carries, touched off an Aggie drive by roaring up the middle for 12 yards and the Cadets' first down of the game.

Wright then connected on three out of four passes. The final one was a 34 yard heave down the middle to Crow on the Texas one where Hawkins lowered the boom on him.

When Wright sneaked across on the first play, there was just a minute and 45 seconds to play in the half. Crow's extra point effort was wide.

A short kickoff that Schriewer returned 10 yards to midfield set the stage for Texas' first touchdown.

With time running out, the Steers sent in Clements, their home run hitter, to bring home the bacon. He didn't fail. He passed 28 yards to Hawkins. Then he hit Womack on a screen pass that lost six back to the 25. Then he arched a 25 yarder that Schriewer made a leaping catch of, immediately in front of the Aggies' End Dudley.

Elam's conversion put the Longhorns in front 7-6 and they stayed there the rest of the day.

Neither team threatened in the third period, but things started to happen on the second play of he final quarter when Wright fumbled and Garland Kennon recovered for Texas on the Aggie 46.

Nine running plays later, the Longhorns were on the Aggie seven. They gave the ball to Fondren over right tackle. Five or six Aggies had a shot at him, but he wasn't stopping. When he bolted into the end zone and teammates pounded him on his back and head there was 10:40 still to play. Fondren kicked the point that made the score, 14-6.

There was nothing left for the Aggies to do now but take to the air. This they did to their sorrow.

Johnny Tatum, who was one of the standouts in the great Texas line, along with Gray, Schriewer and Gerald Petterson, intercepted Wright's second attempt on the Aggie 35.

Hawkins on a pitchout roared down the east sidelines to the five before Gene Stallings bounced him out of bounds.

Fondren and Womack carried the ball to the two and on the third play, Hawkins went over right tackle for the score. There still was 8:17 to play when Fondren made the score 21-6.

That's the way she ended with Longhorn fans deliriously happy pouring out onto the field to kiss and hug their victorious warriors.

There's an old football theory that you have to have the football to score touchdowns. The Aggies couldn't keep it long enough today. They ran only 44 plays to Texas' 77.

The Longhorns, who had won only four of their previous nine games, thus turned a dismal season into a great one. They came here with the desire to win. And they did in as convincing a fashion as this old rivalry has ever seen.

COLLEGE FOOTBALL'S GREATEST FOLLY

By Tim Cohane

From Look

THE DRAMATICS of the head-knocking scheduled this month at the Los Angeles Coliseum—the U.C.L.A.-Southern California football game—may well swirl around the handsome head and wide shoulders of the storied U.C.L.A. tailback, Ronnie Knox. Or perhaps not. In either case, the mere presence of Knox in the crosstown quarrel will provide thoughtful followers of big-time college football once again with this sharp reminder: The game continues to be the victim of abuses in recruiting and subsidizing largely because of the attitude of the men presumably responsible for everything that goes on within their institutions—the presidents. They are men who display, in their approach to the problem, the logic and valor of the ostrich.

The Pacific Coast Conference happened to provide the locale for the Ronnie Knox case. But the dereliction of duty it pointed up can be found in almost any section where the high-pressure game abounds.

Before he has played his last game for U.C.L.A. next season, 20-year-old Ronnie Knox may rank as one of the finest all-around halfbacks in history. Personally, he is a quiet, modest, thoroughly worth-while boy who lingers longest under his postgame shower in hope that he can escape more interviews and publicity. And he is a diligent, satisfactory student in U.C.L.A.'s theater-arts course. Aside from the $70 a week he earns as a part-time film cutter in the Allied Artists Studio, he apparently receives no other help toward his school expenses.

There is no evidence that he himself has ever violated a single Pacific Coast Conference rule on subsidizing or recruiting. Yet Ronnie respresents big-time football's most notorious documented example in recent times of rampant recruiting. Long before he drew a uniform from Coach Red Sanders in September, 1954, as a sophomore transfer from the University of California, Berkeley, he had received more publicity than a two-time All American.

Most of it traced to the activities of his spectacular step-father,

136

Harvey Knox, now 46, who was once described—by a coach at one of the three high schools through which Harvey steered Ronnie—as an over-aggressive football fanatic.

To sketch briefly the story of the Knoxes is like trying to translate Homer's Odyssey on the back of a Lilliputian postage stamp. It began 12 years ago when Harvey married a pretty divorcee named Marjorie Simpson. She had a girl, Patricia, 10, and a boy, Ronnie, 8. A friend once asked Mrs. Knox if her new husband showed any interest in her children. Mrs. Knox's smiling reply, "Yes, indeed!" constituted the understatement of the century.

From the start, a deep attachment sprang up and prospered between his new-found kids and Harvey.

On Harvey's side, it stemmed in part from his own childhood in a Monticello, Ark., orphanage. When he was 13, Harvey won a Carnegie medal for heroism for helping to rescue 35 boys from a fire that destroyed the orphanage.

Later, at Ouachita Baptist College, where he toyed briefly with going into the ministry, and at the University of Arkansas, Harvey played end.

He arrived in California in 1928 and was successively a service-station attendant, private detective, Las Vegas night-club operator and, for eleven years, a haberdasher in Beverly Hills to the elite of filmdom. In 1948, he overexpanded and went broke. Since that time, he has made it his full-time job to steer the careers of his stepchildren.

To push Patricia (film name: Eleanor Todd), Harvey harassed studio officials, hired good dramatic teachers and hatched nimble promotional plots. Patricia's reddish-blonde hair and fair skin photographed exotically, but her career has lagged behind Ronnie's thus far.

Now that Ronnie is ensconced at U.C.L.A. under a competent coach, of whom Harvey disapproves only briefly on an infrequent losing Saturday, Harvey may, in Patricia's behalf, set about shaking the pillars of the temples of Hollywood like a Sunset Strip Samson.

Harvey gave Ronnie his first passing and punting lessons, when the boy was 8 or 9, at Roxbury Park in Beverly Hills. They attended professional games and studied the master T-quarterback, Otto Graham of the Cleveland Browns.

As a sophomore at Beverly Hills High in 1950, Ronnie missed five weeks after suffering a concussion the second day of practice.

"A stupid thing to do with a T-quarterback," Harvey stormed, "letting him tee off in a scrimmage against those big tackles and guards." Ronnie played the last six games and passed for 42 points. But Beverly Hills was outclassed in its league.

Neighboring Inglewood had a more successful team. So to Inglewood Harvey moved the Knox family. As Inglewood quarterback in '51, Ronnie completed 59 per cent of his passes and threw for 19 touchdowns. Inglewood lost only one game, to Santa Monica, 26-12, after Ronnie's passes built a 12-0 lead. Harvey blamed the Inglewood coach for calling signals from the bench, and moved the family to Santa Monica.

As Santa Monica quarterback in '52, Ronnie completed 64 per cent of his passes, threw for 27 touchdowns, was voted California Inter-scholastic Federation's player of the year and outstanding player in both Los Angeles and Memphis high-school All-Star games. Santa Monica's successful coach, Jim Sutherland, did much to polish Ronnie's playing techniques. Sutherland, Harvey believes, is football's best passing coach.

Twenty-seven drooling colleges entered bids for Ronnie. Harvey jotted them down in a little black book and weighed them with the boy. High among the bidders was the University of California at Berkeley. Coach Pappy Waldorf envisioned Ronnie as ultimate successor to his star T-passer-quarterback, Paul Larson. The Knoxes leaned toward Cal because it was the most successful Coast T team, and in high school Ronnie had always operated from the T formation.

Cal's offer, on the surface, was legitimate. Ronnie was promised, according to Harvey, newspaper, radio and TV jobs around Berkeley to help meet his living expenses. Meanwhile, Cal had hired Jim Sutherland as a sort of special passing coach. This violated no letter of any Conference rule.

But behind scenes, there was heavy hanky-panky. The "Southern Seas," a California "rushing" (Coast lingo for recruiting) group in the Los Angeles area, hired Harvey for $400 a month. His sole job was to scout and screen desirable athletes for Berkeley. He was employed, beginning in March, 1953, for 16 months. This, of course, violated all concepts, if not the exact language, of Conference regulations on recruiting. California officials were to say they knew nothing about the "Southern Seas" arrangement with Harvey.

Ronnie entered Cal in September, '53, and starred on the freshman team. He completed his year in June, '54. Soon after, Ronnie and Harvey showed up in Red Sanders's office. They said they had left Cal and wanted to transfer to U.C.L.A. Harvey began explaining why. "I'm not interested in any reasons why you left Cal," interrupted Sanders. He then phoned Waldorf and Vic Schmidt, Conference commissioner, and informed them of the Knox intention.

The reason for the transfer, Harvey said in a public announcement later, was the failure of Cal to make good on the promise of jobs for Ronnie. Perhaps whoever made those promises felt Harvey's job with the "Southern Seas" ought to more than take care of Ronnie's obligations. This contretemps of itself would not have been enough to cause the transfer, however, had California's varsity been winning. "We're used to winning," Harvey informed Waldorf one day, "and we've joined a failure." Steppappy Knox further endeared himself to Pappy Waldorf by describing Cal's '54 spring practice as "the worst I ever saw."

It was natural enough for Harvey Knox to choose U.C.L.A., for Sanders had organized the Bruins into the dominant power on the Coast. U.C.L.A. had been one of the original 27 colleges interested in Ronnie, but rival "rushing" groups had argued successfully with the Knoxes that the Sanders single wing would not properly exploit Ronnie's passing talents. In a sense, the arrival of the Knoxes in his office seeking a transfer left Sanders in the strategic situation all coaches endorse—position as well as possession.

The transfer, Harvey maintains, could have been made in relative quiet and dignity, if Cal authorities had not publicly implied that the reason for it was the unwillingness of the Knoxes to play second string to Larson in '54. A well-publicized Berkeley comment went: "We can now go back to being the University of California instead of Knox College."

Such barbs were unwise. They set Harvey to cranking a 24-hour siren. He gave out the story of his job with the "Southern Seas," and showed a check to prove it. He then began scattering his fire. He said the University of Southern California had an even bigger bankroll for athletes than California had. He bestowed accolades of exalted purity on both U.C.L.A. and Stanford, whereupon it is said that Coaches Red Sanders and Chuck Taylor were badgered continually with bids from leading manufacturers of wings, halos and harps.

Harvey sought to justify his actions as a "crusade for youth," to prevent boys like Ronnie from being duped by the hollow promises of fast-talking alumni. Of course, Harvey's own attitude toward the Conference rules emerged in less than a pure light. And, furthermore, only after Ronnie left Cal had Harvey cranked the siren. But these were ethical areas Harvey side-stepped.

As the siren screamed on, school and Conference authorities removed wadding from their ears only long enough to dictate oblique, if dignified, replies. Nobody talked back to Harvey very loud or very long; the "Southern Seas," normally a turbulent body, was reduced to the quiescence of "Peaceful Lagoons."

At their spring meeting in Portland, Ore., last May, the Conference fathers rightfully cleared Ronnie of any violations and outlawed the "Southern Seas." There was nothing they could do about Harvey himself except to wish him on another planet. Somebody mentioned Saturn.

But why blame Harvey Knox and the "Southern Seas" for the unethical behavior that gave big-time college football a rainbowed eyes? This kind of thing could never happen if college presidents would face the facts, acknowledge what is an abuse and what isn't, and then concentrate on policing abuses. Harvey's "Southern Seas" job was just one kind of abuse by the alumni. There are also advance cash payments to players; others get automobiles, wardrobes, paid-up insurance policies due on graduation or guarantees of postgraduate professional-school scholarships. It goes on all the time with seldom an exposure, because documentary evidence can't be secured until a Harvey Knox happens along.

Further chicanery is practised after a player matriculates, because of the utterly unrealistic, unfair and ridiculous rules imposed by the Pacific Coast Conference. Private schools, like Southern California and Stanford, can give a boy a tuition grant and a job. The job is restricted to 50 hours a month and $1.50 an hour, if payment is derived from athletic funds. If funds are realized from some source other than athletics, a boy can work more hours and earn more, but such jobs are few. At a state school, like Cal or U.C.L.A. the tuition grant is not allowed. The only legal help a boy can get is from his job.

As a result, here's what happens: In most cases, a player can't make his living expenses, which vary from roughly $150 to $200 a month depending on the tuition differential, without getting help from outside. Since such help violates Conference rules, it is arranged by zealous alumni, and thus does not appear on the books of the college. It is done this way in practically every big-time football college. In short, they travel by a sham route. But Commissioner Schmidt can't prove it.

Fed up with the whole deal, the "rushing" groups themselves held a meeting at San Francisco back in the fall of 1951 to call for an amnesty, and a wholesale ethical scrubbing. All schools were represented: Southern California by the "Trojan Club," U.C.L.A. by the "Bruin Bench," California by the "Southern Seas," Oregon by the "Duck Club," and so on. They appointed the Pacific Coast Conference Alumni Athletic Committee, henceforth referred to as the PCCAAC. The PCCAAC drew up the following program:

1. An athlete who maintained minimum requirements as a student, and could prove need, would be given a bona fide job to meet minimum living standards—meaning tuition, board, room and books—as they were on each campus.

2. If the job did not return him enough to meet the living standards the difference could be raised through the work of the "rushing" groups. The difference, however, would be turned over to the university for disbursement through administrative channels.

3. No athlete would receive any further aid from any source whatsoever, and no inducements of any kind whatsoever would be offered him or anybody else to get him to attend a certain school.

4. The alumni "rushing" groups would voluntarily turn over all proselyting direction to the presidents or the faculty representatives of the presidents.

5. The offices of the presidents and the "rushing" groups would work together as a police force and would levy really stiff fines against groups and schools.

The program was first mailed to the presidents. Only one replied. It was then submitted to the December, 1951, meeting of Conference faculty representatives, athletic directors and coaches, which referred it for study and discussion to a committee headed by Wilbur Johns, U.C.L.A. athletic director. Johns reported favorably on the main points of the program to the Conference then turned it over to the college presidents.

That was almost three years ago. In that time, all the presidents have done is request the various "rushing" groups to turn over their books. The response from each was: "We'll turn over ours when everybody else turns over theirs." It would seem the presidents might have suggested a meeting at which all groups would turn over their books at one time. But nothing more was done.

Instead, the presidents have gone on concerning themselves with pointless restrictions that have no bearing at all on the real abuses. They have limited the appearance of a team in the Rose Bowl to once every two years. They threatened for a time to eliminate spring practise. They have countenanced the enforcing of the hypocritical $75-a-month job limitation. If they had adopted the PCCAAC plan, they could have prevented the affair of Harvey Knox and the "Southern Seas." Failure of presidents generally to adopt such a program constitutes college football's greatest folly.

Meanwhile, Ronnie Knox has given promise of becoming even as great a player as Harvey says he is. He spent his 1954 season of ineligibility (due to his transfer) as a member of the Red Shirts or Jayvees. His task was to simulate the role of the upcoming opponent's star back in violent scrimmages with U.C.L.A.'s 1954 national-championship team. The day Ronnie came up from defensive safety, hurled aside a blocker and held All America fullback Bob Davenport to a two-yard gain, Sanders knew he had a player whose defensive skills transcend, if possible, his offensive brilliance.

The campaign of Sanders to keep pressure off the boy by playing him down in the preseason this fall was like trying to deny the existence of atomic power. Photographers and writers sought out Ronnie. In the opening 21-0 victory over the Texas Aggies, Ronnie threw passes for all three touchdowns, ran hard and punted long and accurately.

Afterwards, Harvey held court and predicted Ronnie would pulverize Maryland the same way next week. Actually, Ronnie did kick beautifully against the Terrapins, and his passing sparked the Bruins into a first-half drive that was frustrated on the goal line by a fullback fumble. Later, Maryland's superior fire power from tackle to tackle took over and won a 7-0 victory.

Harvey sat in the stands, frowning, talking and taking notes. At least, he is interested.

Which is more than you can say for the college presidents.

THUNDER IN LOS ANGELES

By David Condon

From The Chicago Tribune, November 27, 1955

SOUTHERN California this afternoon shook down the thunder on old Notre Dame.

When the last bolt of lightning had struck, the scoreboard at the east end of Los Angeles's cavernous Memorial Coliseum read: USC, 42; Notre Dame, 20.

Jon Arnett scored 23 of those points in etching his name onto the list of men who have made the Trojans great in football. Jon scored three touchdowns and kicked five extra points as Irish partisans among the assembled 94,892 shook their heads first in disbelief, then in dismay.

Southern California's total was the greatest number of points rolled up on the Irish since the war time season of 1945, when Army scored a 48 to 0 triumph. The inspired Trojans of today might have conquered those 1945 Irish, 100 to 0. Notre Dame today played some good football and whittled the Trojan's edge to 21 to 20. Southern California played great football and fired back with 21 stunning fourth quarter points when Notre Dame envisioned a winning rally.

The Trojans outplayed, out-thought, and outcharged a foe that had been beaten only by Michigan State in nine previous games this season. The memorable victory makes the 1955 campaign a successful one for Southern California, which was staggering under four defeats in nine games at kickoff time on this warm afternoon.

This was Southern California's eighth victory in the intersectional series that began when the late Howard Jones first matched his Trojans against the late Knute Rockne's Irish 'way back in 1926. And it was the most decisive Trojan victory, bettering the 27 to 14 decision marked up in 1928.

It was perhaps the most stirring, surpassing the 1931 battle when Johnny Baker's field goal sealed a 16 to 14 conquest after Notre Dame entered the fourth quarter with a 14 to 0 bulge.

At half time this afternoon Notre Dame presented the Coliseum

143

with a plaque of Rockne. Southern California made presentation of a plaque of Jones.

No better date would have been chosen for presentation of these plaques, which will be mounted in prominent spots in the arena.

This was a game that would have delighted both Rockne and Jones. It was one of those old-time Southern Cal.-N.D. thrillers.

Southern California's 42 points are not the most ever scored by one team in this series. Notre Dame holds that mark . . . but why detail Notre Dame's history? This was the Trojans' afternoon.

And first to admit that was Terry Brennan, 27 year old Notre Dame coach. In the sombreness of the Irish dressing room Brennan paid tribute to the conquerors:

"Southern California has as good a football team as we have played all year. I would not rate them better than Michigan State, but they certainly were the Spartans' equal off today's performance."

Terry said "our kids gave all they had. They played the best they knew how."

The best Notre Dame knew was not good enough, and this was obvious almost from the opening kickoff when Southern California marched 68 yards on 11 plays to take a 7 to 0 lead.

The opening Southern California touchdown, scored on a 1 yard plunge by Ellsworth Kissinger, shocked the Irish into the best retaliation they could make all day.

Notre Dame needed only 12 plays to grind out the 67 yards to the Trojan goal. Paul Hornung, brilliant junior quarterback, covered the final 8 by a last second decision to run after he failed to spot a pass receiver. Hornung then booted the extra point and it was 7 to 7 after 10:52 minutes of play.

Now fans settled back for the action they sensed as impending. None realized that most of the action would be supplied by the Gold and Red clad warriors of Troy.

Only seven seconds had elapsed in the second quarter when the Trojans again were in command, this time for good. The 14 to 7 edge was supplied by Fullback C. R. Roberts, who sprinted 15 yards down the sideline after taking a pitchout. Arnett kicked the extra point.

Three minutes and 10 seconds later South California had a 21 to 7 bulge when Arnett scampered around his right end to score, with Bob Isaacson adding the point.

That touchdown declared Southern California's confidence in its superiority. The key play was a bit of trickery catching Notre Dame flat footed.

This came when the Irish had contained the Trojans on the Notre Dame 17, with fourth down and 6 yards to go. Southern California sent in a substitute, obviously one who brought in a play. They then lined up with Isaacson prepared to kick a field goal, Kissinger holding. They didn't kick.

Kissinger leaped up to grab the pass from center and rifled a first down aerial to Arnett on the 10. Arnett failed to gain on the next play, then followed with his scoring hike.

Any thoughts that the Trojans were home free ended two minutes before half time when Receiver Jim Morse and Passer Hornung collaborated on a 78 yard touchdown play. Hornung dropped back from the Notre Dame 22, calmly permitted Morse time to get down field, and lofted the ball. Jim gathered it in at full speed, near the Southern California 45, and raced away from Trojan defenders to cross the goal. Hornung's kick was wide and the Trojans led, 21 to 13, at half time.

The third period was scoreless, tho each team made deep thrusts into opposing territory and Notre Dame had the ball on Southern California's 3, with first down, at the finish of the period.

Fullback Don Schaefer carried on the first play of the action packed final quarter. He fumbled near the goal and Halfback Ron Brown of Southern California recovered in the end zone.

Southern California could not advance and quick kicked to the Irish 34. Notre Dame immediately sprung another Hornung to Morse pass play that carried to the USC 6. Hornung plunged 1 yard to score four plays later. His kick was good, Southern California's edge had been whittled to 21 to 20, and it appeared that everything would break loose.

It did. Southern California broke it loose! The Trojans scored at 4:42 of the fourth on a Jim Contratto to Arnett pass that covered 36 yards and the score became 28 to 20. They scored again (35 to 20) at 7:34 when Don McFarland ran across carrying the pigskin that Contratto had pitched from the Notre Dame 13; they added the final marker (42 to 20) at 12:52 with Arnett slicing 7 yards thru the left side of Notre Dame's line.

Southern California's third touchdown was set up when Notre

Dame's Dick Firzgerald fumbled on the Irish 21 on the first running play after a Trojan kickoff. The sixth Trojan score followed a pass interception by Bing Bordier on the USC 49. The final was set up when McFarland grabbed a desperate Hornung aerial on the Notre Dame 36.

THE RAVING

By Blackie Sherrod

From The Fort Worth Press, November 13, 1955

ONCE UPON an interview, while I searched for something new,
From an old and canny coach of football men
While I questioned, rather neatly, suddenly and so completely,
He became so indiscreetly, indiscreetly and even more.
He must be kidding, I muttered, thinking I'm a sophomore,
    Thinking I don't know the score.

Yes, distinctly I remember, it was in the cold November
When the coach brought honesty to the fore.
"Why yes, I know we'll beat them, we'll cook them and we'll eat
  them,
And if we have to cheat them, well, we'll cheat them," he swore.
"To hell with building character, that's something I ignore.
    You got to win, and nothing more."

"Our boys are much, much stronger; our wind is even longer
They got guys who train at the package store.
Our ends are tall and quicker; theirs couldn't be sicker.
Their coach is full of likker, a bum that I abhor.
If we can win by 100 points, then that'll be the score.
    That much and maybe more."

"They have a soft spot on the right, their guard's a neophyte,
We'll run through that hole for 90 yards or more.
This ain't scuttlebutt, he hasn't got a gut.
Won't bother with that nut, not a blocker on that chore.
Our trap play should work, from here to Singapore.
    Better than ever before."

"Their feller at right half, he's lovesick like a calf
All that he can think of is his blond paramour
You should see his pass defense, it would even make you wince
We'll tear him up like chintz, his zone's an open door.

That pass alone should make three touchdowns or four
    At least that, and maybe more."

"They have a favorite play, when the left half comes this way
On which they've made their yardage heretofore.
They don't know we know it, but he will always show it
Just before they blow it, he might as well yell 'Fore.'
We'll be there to meet him, like Marines upon the shore.
    We'll flatten him on the floor.

"Don't give their team a glance, they haven't got a chance,"
The coach spoke frankly, like a knight of yore.
While he talked, eyes a-snapping, suddenly there came a rapping
As of some one loudly rapping, rapping like a maddened boar.
Two men in white, they entered, and took the old coach o'er
    And led him out the door.

ALL IS CONFUSION

By Leo Fischer

From The Chicago American, November 20, 1955

OHIO GOT THE championship, Michigan State the Rose Bowl and Michigan the heartbreak.

That's the way the conference race wound up this gray November afternoon as the Buckeyes whipped Michigan, 17-0, in a wild battle that almost finished in a free-for-all.

When the gun sounded to bring this key game of the Big Ten season to its bitter end, hundreds of fans were on the field, one of the goal-posts had been missing for more than two minutes, the customers were pelting the athletes with snowballs, and the players had apparently become more interested in fisticuffs than in football.

It was a scene of confusion that seldom has been equalled on a Big Ten field. In the various melees, All-American Ron Kramer of Michigan was banished, while his team sustained six penalties in the last 90 seconds—one of them making it possible for Ohio to score its final tally.

"Michigan went down fighting," some wag commented—and that may be about all the consolation the Wolverines can get out of a nightmare finish in which they saw both the Big Ten title and the Pasadena trip vanish under the combined efforts of a great Ohio defense and a young man named Howard "Hopalong" Cassady.

The victory was the first scored by Ohio at Ann Arbor since 1937 and one of the most emphatic in the half-century these two clubs have been playing each other. It enabled the Buckeyes to finish the season with a 6-0 conference record, their second straight undefeated Big Ten season.

Michigan's defeat made the Wolverine windup 5-2 and dropped them to third place.

Michigan State, which finished its conference card a week ago with a 5-1 record, moved into the runner-up spot and thus becomes the Big Ten choice for the Rose Bowl, inasmuch as the champions are ineligible to return.

This will be the second time a second-place club has gone to the

149

New Year's Day classic. The other was Northwestern in 1949, when Michigan won its second straight title.

So much for the historical end of a weird contest in which so much happened that much of it escaped the huge 97,369 crowd that braved cold and snow to set a new mark for a college-owned stadium.

Regardless of what they may have missed, however, they all saw Hoppy wind up his collegiate career with one of his greatest exhibitions.

The 5-foot 10-inch All-American carried the ball 26 times for 146 yards, returned three punts for 40 yards, ran back one kickoff for 36 more and added seven yards on a pass interception early in the game when the issue was still in doubt.

When you add that tremendous offensive pressure to Ohio's amazing defensive display, you'll readily agree with joyful Coach Woody Hayes, who shouted over the din in his locker-room:

"We beat 'em all the way—all 60 minutes of it. When you figure they didn't get into our territory for 14 minutes, that we didn't make a fumble until near the end and that we didn't have a penalty until the boys got a little excited towards the finish, you've got to admit that it's perfection football."

Among those who got into the Ohio dressing room to extend congratulations was President Harlan Hatcher of Michigan.

Over on the other side, Bennie Oosterbaan was still trying to put the pieces together. His team was a favorite at kickoff time, and few around here didn't think that the day would end with the title and the trip to California in its grasp. Bennie sighed as he said:

"I guess they were just too good for us. They had a great team out there today. Michigan State will make a fine representative for the Big Ten in the Rose Bowl."

Michigan's 14-7 victory was the only setback sustained by the Spartans this season.

Asked about the players battling at the windup, Bennie declared:

"Well, it was an exciting game. Too exciting, maybe. And perhaps they did get a little out of hand at the end."

Actually, it was scarcely a desire on Michigan's part to "play dirty" that brought about the wild finish. It was just the culmination of an afternoon of frustration that began in the second period when the Buckeyes won the title, so far as the final score was concerned, on a billiard shot good for three points.

Both teams had battled back and forth without much decision, like a couple of fighters feeling each other out in a title match. Then the Buckeyes came up with their first sustained drive, which bogged down after they had gone 70 yards in 15 plays.

It was fourth down on the Michigan seven when Fred Kriss booted the ball. It hit the right upright, caromed over the crossbar and thus started off the afternoon on a fantastic note.

Officially the field goal goes into the book as 17 yards. Actually it was kicked from the 14 and traveled 24, but the scoring rules allow credit for only the distance from the original line of scrimmage, plus 10 yards.

Michigan never came close after that. The three points lasted as Ohio's lead until the fourth quarter when the Buckeyes added two touchdowns and a safety for some unnecessary emphasis on their superiority this afternoon.

The figures show how completely Michigan was throttled. The Wolverines made only five first downs to Ohio's 20, and gained a scant 95 yards from rushing to the Buckeyes' 333.

Passing was almost non-existent. The loser completed three out of nine for 14 yards and Ohio one out of three for four yards.

Here, too, was part of the fantastic story. One of Michigan's pass completions in the fourth quarter wound up behind the goal-line for a safety and two Ohio points. And as far as the Buckeyes were concerned that single completion was their first in three winning games—one of the many items that were more fitted for Ripley's "Believe It or Not" than a Big Ten championship football game.

Ohio's first touchdown came shortly after the start of the fourth quarter following a previous drive on which Michigan rallied to stop the Bucks on the four when Don Vicic was held for downs.

Michigan gambled as it started down the field with a 25-yard gallop by Terry Barr, the one play accounting for almost one-fourth of the day's yardage. The situation finally got to where it was fourth down, a yard to go on the Wolverines' 34. They didn't make it.

Ohio took over, and after an exchange of punts wound up in midfield with a 20-yard Cassady return. From there they pounded over, winding up with the score when Hoppy leaped into the end zone. He fumbled as he hit the ground and Michigan recovered, but the score was already official.

The crowd booed a little, but it really didn't make any difference.

Michigan completed two of its three passes after the kickoff, but a third was intercepted by Vicic, who returned 20 yards to midfield. Again the Bucks battered their way into scoring territory, but were halted on the 13 in the Wolverines' dying gasp.

Then the game began to fall apart. A punt gave the ball to Michigan on its 6, from where Jim Maddock passed to Barr, who caught the ball in his end zone and was immediately tackled.

As soon as the two points were chalked up, Michigan had to kick. It was an onside attempt which squirted off Kramer's foot for only a yard or two and was nabbed by the Buckeyes on Michigan's 21.

The fireworks began about here. The crowd had swarmed down to the field and while all this was going on at the south goal, had actually taken down the north posts. It was no mean job, since they are constructed of 4-inch steel pipe, but evidently some of the confident Ohios had come equipped with hack saws and perhaps acetylene torches.

Ohio got the ball to the 1-foot line with only one play, a 6-yard gain by Cassady, for his final effort of his four spectacular years. The rest was given them on penalties, one of which was the personal foul which resulted in Kramer's ouster.

From there, scoring a touchdown was an easy matter.

It wasn't so easy to chase the hundreds of customers off the field who rushed out, thinking the game was over. Finally the kickoff was staged, after which each play carried a penalty for one side or the other until the final gun mercifully put an end to what Ohio fans had hoped for and Michigan followers had never expected would happen.

HE WOULDN'T HARM A FLY

By Jack Gallagher

From The Houston Post, August 16, 1955

THE SOFT morning sun filtered through the elms of the tiny college town in Southeastern Ohio. The bells pealed the hour of 10 and a summer student, thick brown notebook under arm, strode purposefully past the window where Paul Brown sat.

"Bobby," Brown cupped his hands and raised his voice a treble. Bobby Freeman, a quarterback from Auburn for whom the Browns took a battle for his services with the Winnipeg club to the court room, continued blithely on his way.

Throughout the morning the telephone had rung for him, with calls from Alabama to Canada.

"Bobby," Brown said a little louder, and this time Freeman heard and stepped up his pace toward the window. "Bobby, don't accept any out of town phone calls. You hear me, don't accept any out of town phone calls." Freeman nodded thoughtfully.

Head down and arms flailing in a wide arc, Brown swung across the room, sat in a straight-back chair wedged between the dresser and the bed in the room of a girls' dormitory and picked up a blue fly-swatter. He leaned back and parked a foot on the bed.

"I never accept an out of town phone call from a newspaperman unless I know him. I've been nipped too often. I try to cooperate and then get misquoted. I have more trouble with Los Angeles writers than others. If you find a quote from me in a Los Angeles paper now it's usually gotten the illegitimate way—by not talking to me.

"The reaction of a small town boy from Massillon, who still backs off from city slickers? No. But I'll admit it's easy for people to get the wrong impression of me.

"Beginning two or three days before a ball game away from home I live with my club. They go to a movie and I go with them. They go back to the hotel, I go back to the hotel. I'm not available for radio and television appearances. Neither are my players. Maybe I've made enemies that way, but it's the way I operate."

When a question was asked about the large number of Negroes

on the Browns, Brown bit his fingernails, ran his hands past the skin on top of his head, and tugged at his belt.

"I wouldn't say I'm unusually lucky where Negro players are concerned. The Cardinals, I believe, have more Negroes than the Browns. Maybe we've been successful because the colored boys figure when they come here they get an even shake. They talk about me as a champion of the race. 'The Branch Rickey of Football.' Baloney. I take colored boys because I think they can win for me. I ask only that they play football the way I want it played.

"I've been asked by Negro groups to speak at banquets. They tell me I've done a lot for their race. I turn every one down. What I'm doing for them I'd do for anyone. Everyone gets treated alike in this camp."

Brown paused a moment and swatted a fly.

"We have had one and one-half hours of scrimmage this summer. Scrimmage, I believe, is merely a way of covering up coaching deficiencies.

"No coach—high school, college or pro—has to scrimmage. I used to scrimmage in the spring at Ohio State, that's all. None in the fall. We have individual contact work that serves us just as well as scrimmage. In one-on-one work we accomplish scrimmaging purposes without injuring anyone.

"You have a scrimmage, there's a big pileup, a leg is exposed, somebody falls on it and you've got a broken leg on your hands."

Brown calls every Brown play from the bench. He was asked if the occasion ever had arisen in which he was unable to call plays, perhaps because of illness. Brown reached over and rapped the wood of a desk in a large room on the campus of Hiram College.

"I wasn't able to send in my own plays at Ohio State because of college substitution rules.

"So I'd get a ball and go out on the field with my quarterback. I'd put the ball down on a spot on the field and say, 'It's third and 10 on your own 38. What are you going to call?' Then I'd say, 'All right, you gained five. What will it be?' Up and down the field we'd go, me firing the questions and him answering them.

"Gradually I got my quarterbacks adjusted to my thinking. Pretty soon they were thinking just like me. They can pass a lot of legislation against college coaches, but they can't stop them from walking up and down the field with their quarterback."

Brown has a reputation of being a disciplinarian. He runs his camp like a drill sergeant.

"We have George Ratterman, a young man given to capricious-
ness and pranks. When he came to the Browns people wondered,
'How is he going to get along with Paul Brown?' I'm supposed to
be a taskmaster, you know.

"Well, we get along fine. He keeps the camp loose. And I hasten
to add that George Ratterman is more than an adequate quarterback."

This is considered the roughest, toughest company in sports.
Yet Paul Brown rarely raises his voice around his players. He
never curses in their presence—the strongest word he uses is
"divil"—although privately he can uncover earthy phrases.

Hal Herring, a former Brown guard employed at Auburn the
past three years as assistant coach, had come up from Alabama
to sit at the feet of The Master. In telling a story, Herring cursed
softly.

"Excuse me, coach," he grinned sheepishly.

"You don't have to apologize, Hal," Brown barked back.

"The most disheartening part of this business is the draft. We
get wonderful reports on boys, and we draft them high and they
don't turn out to be what we want.

"And you know who's the most disappointed? Brown."

Brown pounced to the floor and as deftly as Ratterman unloading a pass, flicked his wrist and a fly was dead.

"Last night we had a discussion, my staff and myself, that lasted
into this morning. We were debating whether to call a defense we
use occasionally a four-four or a floating six. Just a matter of
terminology, understand.

"At any rate, that discussion prayed on my mind all night. I
slept well and didn't dream of it, but all the time I was conscious
of it. It dominated my thoughts."

A fly buzzed around Brown's head and he took a swipe at it.
The fly absorbed the blow, dipped his wings for a moment, and
was off. He buzzed back. This time Brown cracked him with the
swatter. He hit the floor, flailed his wings, regained his bearings
and flew away.

Back he came again. Brown pinned him against the screen. For
the third time the fly went down. He scrambled along, wobbled,
and sought desperately to right himself. When he did, he limped
to a corner. Brown put down his swatter.

"There's a fighter, that fly. I'm not going to kill him because
I admire him."

Boxing

UP FROM THE FLOOR

By Shirley Povich

From The Washington Post Times-Herald, September 22, 1955

Copyright, 1955, Washington Post and Times Herald

ROCKY MARCIANO arose from the humiliation of a second-round knockdown tonight and beat Challenger Archie Moore into a helpless mass to preserve his heavyweight championship of the world by a ninth-round knockout.

In the toughest fight of his career, with 55,000 persons in Yankee Stadium tensed to the primitive combat, Marciano saved his title by unloading an incessant hail of punches that put Moore on the floor four times before he could make it stick.

Put on warning that he was in with a dangerous foe when Moore sneaked a right hand to the chin that put the champion down for a four-count in round two, Rocky was swinging for the knockout in every round thereafter.

The bell saved Moore temporarily from further pitiless assaults by Rocky in the eighth round. The light heavyweight champion, down for the fourth time in the battling, was struggling only feebly to get his feet under him again when at the count of six the round ended.

In the ninth, Rocky resumed his flailing with a fury seldom witnessed in any ring. Catching Moore in the challenger's own corner, which was one of his favorite refuges tonight, Rocky landed a right hand in a wide arc and the evening began to draw to an end for Moore.

The challenger, numbed, started down. Rocky followed with a left hook that merely brushed the chin, but that blow was unnecessary. Like a wet sack, Moore descended into his own corner, his hair on end like a fright wig, the expression on his face as vacant as a rimless zero.

From the farthest corner, Rocky could see now for certain that he was rid of this man who had given him the hardest time in the 49 bouts of his career.

Moore took the full count of Referee Harry Kessler while in a sort of ludicrous heap, his rump full on the canvas, his legs askew in different directions, his left hand gripping the second strand of ropes and his bid to win Rocky's title as dead as his own reflexes.

There had been a sort of gesture by Moore at the count of nine to get up as he had done four times before, but this time his mind was making a command that his body couldn't keep.

It was Marciano himself, coming across the ring at the 10-count, who helped Moore's handlers get him back on to a corner stool and in some improved state of dignity.

Now it was over, and Rocky from mid-ring was blowing kisses to Mrs. Marciano, who was returning them eagerly from beyond the press row. And Papa Marchiegano from Brockton, Mass., was being helped into the ring to pose happily with his famed son, an unbeaten boxer who was adding No. 49 to his list of victims tonight.

But it had been a near-thing for Rocky. This was a fight that condition won for him, just as it was assumed that Rocky's always superb conditioning would be a factor. He needed all of it, too, to get off his neck this amazing man named Moore, who at 38, was an incredible athlete so full of fight that the 1-to-4 odds on Rocky appeared at times to be a ridiculous quotation.

One hundred and forty-four fights were in the record book for Moore, but in none of them had he ever become entangled with anything like the man who opposed him tonight at equal weights of 188 pounds.

It is almost safe to say that never were so many punches thrown in nine rounds by one man as were unloaded by Marciano tonight and Moore had reason to wonder what magic source of reserves the champ was calling on to keep his arms pumping as if they were hitched to some secret motor.

This was a night to be scored heavily in favor of Marciano, but Moore earned a solid claim on the memory of it, too, because until knockdowns began to pile up, he was the superior artist in the ring. Few fight crowds have been treated to as pure an exhibition of boxing's defensive skills as Moore gave tonight, and he wasn't lacking in punch, either.

But Moore couldn't make come true tonight the reputation he had emphasized for himself with his claims that he would know how to finish Marciano off when he got him in trouble. He had the Rock in trouble, deep, grave trouble in that second round, and he let him get away.

The troubles began to pile up early for Marciano. Warming up faster than usual, Rocky began to unload from the opening bell and he won the first round handily although Moore danced easily away from Marciano's best blockbusters.

And then in the first minute of round two, Yankee Stadium and probably the theater television screens around the nation were in an uproar. Rocky was on the floor. Moore had put him there.

Marciano, hooking a left to Moore's head, had been cracked with a short right-hand counter properly on the chin. He dropped as if struck by some giant hammer. His knees went to the floor and his eyes went into a senseless stare at the assembled ringsiders. His gloves were touching the floor.

There was pride in Archie's manner as he retreated into a neutral corner to wait it out, but at four Rocky was back on his feet, willing to continue. The recovery of the champ was so fast that Moore had to be beckoned to by Referee Kessler to resume the battling.

That's when Rocky got away from Moore, the self-styled finishing artist. Rocky waded inside, gave Moore little punching room, and began to fight himself out of his fog. His mad-bull lunges served to keep Moore too busy to measure him and Rocky lasted the round out smartly.

But it wasn't looking good for Rocky. Only his recuperative powers had saved him. Moore had demonstrated that he had a punch that could put the champ down, the same sneak right that Rocky's camp had talked about, and Archie had landed it. Besides that, there was blood trickling from Rocky's nostrils and from a cut above the left eye, too.

It was looking good for Moore on two counts—his ability to put Rocky down, and cut him up. But the blood disappeared in the ministrations in the champ's corner and it must have been a competent job by his handlers because blood didn't bother him again during the fight.

Obvious was Rocky's design when Round Three began. He wanted to get rid of this dangerous fellow quick, and he resorted to his most primitive flailing. But Archie, the canny old fellow, rebuked him for such crude tactics by planting two stiff lefts on his nose. Rock won the round by slipping in a left hand uppercut that tore at Archie's head just before the bell.

It seemed that Marciano must punch himself out in a furious fourth round. Moore, with new respect now for the bottomless energy of the champ, attempted to back out of range only to run into trouble on the ropes near Rocky's corner.

From there is was a solid one-minute hail of punches of every description by the over-eager Marciano, and still he couldn't wound Moore seriously. With a style and a guile that had served him so well in 19 years in the prize ring, Moore went into a rock-and-roll act that presented little besides his elbows and shoulders as a target for Rocky's belts, and he even fought himself out of trouble at the round's end.

The fourth round didn't end at the bell. Rocky was late with a left hand to the head, and Moore was even later with a solid right to Rocky's head, before the referee broke them.

Moore, who had won the second round, also had a margin in a dull fifth. But in the sixth he couldn't get untangled from the renewed fury of Marciano.

On the ropes near Archie's corner when he was to apply the finisher three rounds later, the champ caught Moore in distress again. A hard straight right to Archie's head, a bit high, staggered the challenger, and then a brutal, hammer-like right put Moore down for the first time. The count reached four when Archie bounced up, still full of fight.

But the fight began to empty from the challenger when Rocky moved back to the attack near those same ropes. Archie covered up smartly, let his elbows and his shoulders soak up most of Rocky's wild swings.

For a moment he even took the play away from Rocky with sharp counters, but at last he bobbed in the wrong direction, left his head exposed near Rocky's right side and an arcing right hand from above crashed against Archie's chin.

This time, there was less bounce in Moore, but at eight he was up getting his glove brushed off, and with some bravado advancing toward Rocky with his guard lowered in a show of confidence in his ability to protect himself. He lasted the round out but had the clock as an ally because only ten seconds remained after the knockdown.

Moore, of course, was sensing his approaching doom unless he could reach Rocky's chin with a punch that he could make stick. So in the seventh he unleashed one of his best bursts of the fight. He did hurt Rocky with a left-right combination to the chin and for a moment there was terror among Rocky's supporters, but the champ shook it off and belted Moore into some more of his defensive postures.

Near the end of that seventh Archie went down for a count of two, but this time it was a palpable slip. When he arose, though, Rocky was back at him with more of those ceaseless volleys, but elbows and arms and shoulders were all that he could find.

Now the guards that Moore set up for himself were feebler, and Rocky needed merely to wade through them to get into punching range. Late in the eighth he had Moore pinioned with punches in the same rope area in Archie's corner where much of the fighting was done, and then at last came the clean shot Rocky had sought.

It was a straight overhand right this time that caught Archie falling in toward the champ. Three punches later, two of them ponderous rights, Archie was on his way down. There was no definite sign, either, that Archie would be on his way up when the count reach six and the bell became his ally. He was saved at that point, but only for final destruction a round later, in 1:19 of the ninth.

YOUNG FIGHTER

By W. C. Heinz

From Esquire, July, 1955

IT WAS ABOUT an hour before the fight, and we were alone in the dressing room. It was warm in the room, and the fighter had stripped and then put on just his ring socks and shoes, and now he was lying on his back on the rubbing table with just a towel across his middle, staring up at the ceiling.

"You know something?" he said after a while.

His voice startled me. I had been sitting there listening to the sounds and the small talk of the preliminary fighters, and occasionally turning my head to watch them beyond the opening at the end of the black shower curtain with the pink flowers on it that hung between them and us.

"What?" I said.

"I feel different tonight," he said slowly, still looking up at the ceiling. "I don't know why, but I do."

"That's sometimes a good sign," I said. "You may fight your best fight."

It was his youth and his lack of experience talking. After he has fought a lot of fights he won't talk like that any more.

"I don't know," he said. "I never felt like this before."

Why do they do it? In this country last year there were about 3000 professional prize fighters. By the end of the year two of them had lost their lives in the ring, and only about two dozen had profited by as much as $10,000. The rest fought in the small clubs or populated the preliminaries in the bigger clubs, and Billy McNeece, now lying on his back in the small, musty dressing room at the Eastern Parkway in Brooklyn, is one of these.

"Just before they go into the ring," I said, "most fighters feel tired."

I had been watching, beyond the curtain, a preliminary boy named Andy Viserto. He had been moving around with his robe on, shadow-boxing and trying to loosen his shoulders, and while he had been doing this he had been yawning. He must have yawned five or six times in the thirty seconds or so that I watched him.

"I don't feel tired," McNeece said now. "I don't know how I feel."

I came to know McNeece through Jimmy August. We were standing together one day in Stillman's, watching the sparring in the two rings, when Jimmy said, "I've got a kid for you. If you're looking for a kid that's typical of the kind that comes into boxing, I've got one—wild, absolutely fearless, makes every fight a war, but a real nice kid with it all."

I have known Jimmy now for close to ten years and respect him as one of the few capable trainers, teachers and handlers of fighters still in the business. He is a short, stocky, bald man with brown eyes, who quit studying pharmaceutical chemistry at Columbia University thirty years ago to work with fighters, and he is particularly good with the young ones, since he is patient and painstaking and somewhat of an amateur psychologist.

"This kid was sent to me about six years ago," Jimmy said, "by a fighter I used to have, Dennis Deegan, who was a welter, back around 1936-'38. You may remember him. He had about forty pro fights, and topped the Ridgewood and the Jamaica Arena."

"Deegan?" I said. "What did he look like?"

"A good left hand," Jimmy said.

"I don't recall him," I said.

"He works as a track foreman on the Independent Subway and he's friendly with the family of this kid," Jimmy said. "One day he come up to me here and told me he had a kid he wanted me to make a fighter of. Then he brings the kid up, and when I got through working with the other kids I started to teach him, believe me, from A to Z."

"Was there anything that impressed you about him from the start?" I said.

"All heart, that'sall," Jimmy said. "A big gangling kid, about 140, like what you call, an ostrich, but all fighter."

"I'd like to meet him," I said.

I met him a few days later. It was the middle of the afternoon and raining, and we walked up from Stillman's to The Neutral Corner and sat across from each other in one of the booths in the back room.

The Neutral Corner is a bar and grill on the southwest corner

of Eighth Avenue and Fifty-Fifth Street, in New York City, half
a block north of Stillman's. It is owned and operated by Frankie
Jay, Chickie Bogad and Nick Masuras. Frankie used to manage
fighters, including Tony Janiro, a good-looking welterweight of a
half-dozen years ago who almost broke Frankie's heart; Chickie
grew up with the good Jewish fighters who came out of the lower
East Side about thirty-five years ago, and once, for a few months,
he was matchmaker for Madison Square Garden; Nick used to
be a fighter himself, a middleweight.

"That scar under your right eye," I said to McNeece, after we
had talked a few minutes. "Where did you get it?"

McNeece is twenty-three years old and stands six feet and
weighs about 165. He has pale, freckled skin, red-blond wavy hair
and pale blue eyes.

"Scar?" he said, feeling with the fingers of his right hand across
the scar and then around it. "I haven't got any scar."

"It looks like a scar," I said, and reached across the table and
placed my fingers on the little crescent of tightened skin on his right
cheekbone. "It's an old one, but it's there."

"I don't think so," he said, puzzled. "I was never cut there."

In the bar and in the back room at the Neutral Corner the walls
are hung with black-framed photographs of prize fights and prize
fighters, managers and handlers. In each of the half-dozen booths,
centered on the wall between the pictures, there is a small, narrow
mirror.

"Take a look in that mirror," I said. "You'll see it."

The fighter turned to the mirror, and then he moved his head to
get the light right. Then, with his fingers, he went over the small
scar twice and turned back with a half-smile on his face.

"You're right," he said. "I didn't even remember it. I got it in a
kid fight so long ago I forgot it."

"What about the fight?"

"I don't remember it. I just vaguely remember that I got cut
there once in a kid fight. I don't remember anything about the
fight, and I didn't even remember that I had the cut."

"The bridge of your nose," I said. "It's starting to broaden. Was
it ever broken in a fight?"

"No," he said, feeling his nose. "It's just from my amateur fights
and my fights as a pro."

"Does it bother you that your face is getting marked?"

"No."

"When Billy Graham was a kid in school," I said, speaking of the fighter and not the preacher, "he used to box in the boys' clubs. After a fight he'd wear a patch over his eye to school. There wasn't any cut under the patch; he wanted to look like a fighter. Did you ever do that?"

"No," McNeece said. "I never did that, but I was never ashamed of anything for sure. When I get banged, I get banged."

I would say that tells a lot about what makes a fighter right there. I go along with the poet who said my body is the mansion of my soul. I can tell you exactly how I got the scar on my lower lip and the one on the index finger of my left hand and the one on my right knee. That's one of the reasons why I was never a fighter, and why McNeece is.

McNeece grew up in Central Islip, Long Island. There were three kids in the family—his sister Mary, who is a year older than the fighter, and his brother Jimmy, who is a year younger.

"Have you had hard time around your home?" I said.

"Sure," McNeece said. "My father's a laborer, a construction worker."

"Was he ever out of work?"

"Sure. When the weather is bad or you're sick, you can't work. Ever since we were little kids my mother worked in the state hospital, too. We never had much money."

I will admit that not all fighters are impelled by financial poverty. I have known a few who attended college, but they were less as fighters because of it. There was always the knowledge within them that they could make a living in another way, and so it has always been that most fighters, and the best fighters, are those who know that fighting will give them their only chance to make a real pile.

"I never wanted to be anything else but a fighter," McNeece said. "Me and my brother—he's in the Navy now—I guess the first thing we ever got was boxing bloves. They threatened to burn the gloves a million times, the fights we used to have."

He was sitting there, friendly and alert to my questions. He had on a pair of grey slacks and a soft yellow sports shirt, open at the neck, and a light-tan wind jacket. He is big-boned and, although considered to be a middleweight, he will probably build up with proper training and with proteins to add about ten pounds of good weight and become a light-heavyweight.

"From a little kid on," he said, "I got all the record books and

I know every fighter from away back. My mother used to wake me up at ten o'clock so I could listen to the fights."

I think that's important in this, too. Some fighters have to go against their families to do it, but in the majority of cases the resistance is what the Army used to call sporadic, at best. That is why I decided to drive out to Central Islip to try to find out what forces, outside of himself, impelled this fighter toward the ring, and why, at home, the climate, as they say, was right.

Central Islip is a crossroads town about fifty miles from New York City and in about the geographical center of Long Island. Robert Ripley once ascertained, after what could have been some very pleasant research, that there were more bars per capita in Central Islip than in any other town or city in the United States. Its population has been about ninety per cent Irish Catholic, and most of its residents work in the three nearby state mental hospitals and in the Grumman and Republic aircraft plants.

"This is a fighting town," Joe Barlin, the physical-education instructor and coach of Central Islip High School, told me. "Kids around here fight more than in any other town I've ever known."

Barlin, McNeece and I were in the small faculty room off the stage in the gymnasium. Barlin, still a young man, was smoking a pipe.

"I was quite aghast when I first came here," he said, "But I've come to let the kids throw a few punches. You see, it's a hospital town. The parents work around the clock, and the kids are left to shift for themselves more than in most places."

I suppose McNeece was amused by the efforts I was making to reconstruct the background that propelled him into professional fighting. In his own mind it is all very simple. He always wanted to be a fighter.

"If you ask me why he became a fighter," Barlin said, "I'll give you three reasons. One, he's Irish. Two, he's got a younger brother. Three, he was always a fierce competitor."

"My brother and I, we'd be mad at one another about almost everything," McNeece said, smiling. "We fought all the time. When we played on the same teams here they would never put us both into the game at the same time."

While in high school, he had played varsity basketball, soccer and baseball. He had never failed a subject, but after his third year and at the age of seventeen he quit to enlist in the paratroops.

"What ever he played here," Barlin said, "he fought like hell all the way. I wish we had more like him. He'd just as soon tell you to go to hell as not, but he'd always tell the truth. He has what I'd call an open personality."

A slim, neatly dressed man in his thirties came in carrying a book and some papers. Barlin introduced him as Ted Jamison, the assistant principal, and after he had shaken hands with me and greeted McNeece warmly, he sat down and I explained my interest in McNeece.

"Would you," I asked him, "say that there is something in the general environment here that Billy has been trying to escape?"

That is, really, the way we regard fighting in our time. We examine the exponents of it, and their origins, as if they were confirmed criminals.

"Definitely," Jamison said. "We have that problem here constantly, and I've even held up Billy, here, as an example of what one individual can do about it. A lot of kids here have a defeatist complex. They say: 'What have I got to look forward to? To work in the hospital or the aircraft plant all my life?' "

"I always said I wouldn't be working in the hospital," McNeece said.

"Exactly," Jamison said. "I just couldn't see Billy doing that. I think he'd go crazy in a factory, too. I think he'd walk out and tell the boss what to do."

"I think I would," McNeece said, smiling.

While the McNeece children were small, the family lived in an aging grey frame house behind a lumberyard near the center of town. Six years ago they moved into a home of their own, a new ranch-type bungalow in a development of small houses on the northeast edge of the town.

When we arrived at the house the fighter's older sister, Mary, was there with her two-year-old son. As I talked with her it was apparent that she sees nothing surprising about the fact that her brother has become a fighter and, as a result, has never attempted to analyze the reasons for his choice of this profession.

"But when you and your brother were small," I said, "I'm sure there were occasions when your parents punished you. Do you recall how your brother reacted to punishment?"

"Oh, yes," she said. "I remember that when my mother would smack him, he'd just stand there. I remember he'd never cry or anything."

The fighter's mother is a small, auburn-haired woman, now forty-four years old, who came to this country alone from Ireland when she was sixteen to live with relatives. On this particular day she got home early from the hospital.

"He wasn't difficult as a child," she said. "I would say he was just adventurous. They used to have the Tarzan movies then, and I'd come home and find rope strung from tree to tree. I did worry a little, but he always seemed to come out all right, and I got over that."

Mrs. McNeice—the fighter changed the spelling of the name when he began to box—said it was much the same when her son started fighting. At first she was nervous, but when she saw that he was not being hurt she ceased to worry deeply, and she has attended each of his fights in and around New York.

"I went to his first one here, at the Eastern Parkway," she said. "He won, and then I felt that I never wanted to change anything, so I still go."

"The chance to make a lot of money draws all fighters to the ring," I said. "Would you say that your son has always been conscious of how difficult it is for many people to make a good living?"

"Often," she said, "he would say to me: Someday I want to make a lot of money."

"When I was in the Army," the fighter said, "I used to read about guys I boxed in the amateurs moving ahead. I'd tell my mother: 'Wait till I get out of the Army, and then we'll have some of the nice things.' "

"Billy worked after school, too," Mrs. McNeice said.

"Once I worked in the ravioli factory here," the fighter said. "I labeled jars from five in the afternoon to ten. I was about twelve years old, and one day the inspector came in and found me."

When the fighter was thirteen he piled lumber for the Central Islip Lumber Company. When he was fifteen he worked at Camp Upton, Long Island, on a construction job with his father.

"He always brought home the money," Mrs. McNeice said, "and waited for his cut."

Shortly after four o'clock, William McNeice, Sr., came home. He is a thin, ruddy-faced, sandy-haired, blue-eyed man, now fifty years old.

He was born in the Williamsburg section of Brooklyn and left school in the eighth grade at the age of fourteen to work as a truck helper. Then he became a brick handler and finally a construction laborer.

"Coming from the Williamsburg section," he said, when I began to question him about fighting, "I followed fighters since I was a kid. I thought there was nobody like Mike O'Dowd."

This reminded me of the one question I had saved. I wanted to ask it of the mother and father together.

"All of the motion pictures and all of the fiction that are written about boxing," I said, "depict the rosy side. They're concerned with death in the ring or dishonest fights or dishonest managers or gangsters. Were either of you worried about your son getting into a business that is always portrayed in that manner?"

"I never believed that stuff about the cheating managers or the fixed fights," the father said. "I never worry about the boy getting hurt, either. I've seen many fights in my line of work, and I saw many a fight in the Ridgewood or the armories or Ebbets Field. I saw the boy in all his Golden Gloves bouts, and from the way he handled himself I figured he wasn't being hurt."

"But didn't what you had seen in the movies or read about boxing concern you?" I asked the mother.

"Billy used to talk so much about boxing that it never bothered me," Mrs. McNeice said. "I never believed the other things, and I met Jimmy August and Billy's manager and they're nice men."

When McNeece finished his four years in the Army early last year and resumed professional fighting, August turned over the management of him to Irving Cohen. Cohen, a short, semi-stout, round-faced, blue-eyed, soft-spoken man, manages Billy Graham and managed Rocky Graziano to the middleweight championship. He is completely honest in his dealings with his fighters, and is so cautious that seldom does he put one of them into a ring unless he is reasonably certain that the fighter has better than an even chance to beat the other man.

"Out here," the fighter said now, "I guess the guys that follow boxing were surprised that I got Irving Cohen for a manager."

I did not see the fighter again until the evening of the fight. He had been at Greenwood Lake, New York, for twelve days training to fight Jackie La Bua, another young middleweight, at the Eastern Parkway, and he and August had taken a room at a hotel just off Times Square for the night before the fight.

La Bua had had twenty-five fights and had won twenty-two—

McNeece had won ten of twelve—and was working on a winning streak of eleven. Although the New York newspapers had not given much space to the fight, they had been unanimous in the opinion that La Bua was the logical favorite to lick McNeece.

"How is he?" I said to August when I met him in the hotel lobby.

"He's resting," August said. "He'll be down in a few minutes."

"How will he do?"

"Who knows?" August said. "He can lick this guy, but it depends on him. The trouble with him is that he fears nothing."

"I know," I said.

"It's a tough job for a conscientious trainer and manager to put fear and respect in a guy like this," August said. "He takes chances he shouldn't take. He can box like hell, but he gets hit on the chin and then he's a sensational fighter for no reason at all.

"A guy with too much guts is hard to teach. A guy with a little geezer in him is the greatest fighter in the world. You teach him a trick and he'll learn it. This guy, he says, 'Aw, I'll run him out of the ring.' "

"So the other trainers," August said, "they say to me, 'Why must he go wild. Why can't you cool him down?' How am I going to cool him down? In one fight he went wild altogether, and he came to me and he said, 'Why can't you control me?'

"He's asking me? I've tried everything. I've conned him and I've abused him, because let's face it. You know what an Irishman or a Jew who can fight can mean at the gate."

"I know," I said.

"Even managers get excited when they think about it," August said. "If I can cool him off and let him use the ability God gave him, good. If I can't, he'll have a short career, and that's what it'll be tonight. If he loses his head, he's gone. If he fights his fight, he'll lick the guy without too much trouble."

The fighter came down and went out and got into his second-hand Dodge convertible. With Jimmy Moulton, a young lightweight who was to box a four-rounder on the card, driving, and with McNeece sitting up front with him, we started for the Arena.

"How are your folks?" I said to McNeece after a while.

"They're fine, thanks," he said. "That is, my mother's fine, but my father's sick. He can't move."

"He can't move?" I said.

"They brought him home from work," McNeece said, "and he couldn't move. He's lying there in the house and he can just move one hand."

"Did he have a stroke?" I said to August who was riding next to me in the back.

"It must be," August said, shrugging. "They didn't want Billy to know before the fight."

"They tried to keep it from me," the fighter said. "I heard about it and I went out there yesterday."

"The dough you'll get for tonight," August said, "will come in handy."

In the preceding twelve months McNeece had earned $900 in purses in five fights. For this one, however, he would clear about $1000 after expenses for his end.

"I'll say," he said. "I'll go out there tomorrow, and we'll take him to the hospital. I'll have the money to put right down."

The Arena's dressing rooms are to the left of the lobby; half of the preliminary fighters are in one room and the men they are going to fight in another, and because McNeece was boxing the ten-round main event, he had a private cubicle, about ten feet by eight, with the shower curtain separating him from the preliminary boys.

In the two-and-a-half hours that we waited there he was more quiet than he had been on the other occasions when I had been with him. If he heard the talk of the preliminary boys he paid no attention to it, resting on his back on the rubbing table and then later he sat up while August bandaged and taped first one hand and then the other, and I thought of what he had told me about his feelings before a fight.

"When you enlisted in the Army," I had asked that afternoon in The Neutral Corner, "why did you pick the paratroops?"

"For the extra pay," he said.

"Had you ever been up in a plane before?"

"Not until I jumped."

"Were you scared?"

"I was as nervous as anybody else, but I think you do it because it's just follow the leader. I always had pride, and if anybody said I couldn't do something I'd do it."

"Did you know any men who wouldn't jump?"

"Sure. They have a heck of a lot of quitters. Maybe almost half the class were quitters, but I never thought about them one way or the other. Some of the guys laughed at them, but at times even I myself felt like saying, 'The hell with this stuff.' That's the reason I wouldn't quit. If the other guy could do it, so could I."

"Did you pray before your jumps?" I said, remembering that he had told me that he and his brother had been altar boys and had attended parochial school.

"I went to church the night before my first jump. I always make a visit to church just before a fight, too."

"For what do you pray?"

"I ask for a real good fight, and that I don't get my eyes busted up."

"Do you pray to win?"

"No. If I ask to win, I still might get beat, and I don't want to be disappointed."

There were about 500 spectators in the Arena, which will hold four times as many, when McNeece, with August and Cohen and Whitey Bimstein behind him, came down the aisle. When he was introduced from the ring, about half of them set up a noise, and when La Bua, who lives in East Meadow, Long Island, took his bow the effect was about the same.

As the bell rang, McNeece came out fast and he was three quarters of the way across the ring when he and La Bua joined. Immediately it was apparent that La Bua was the calmer of the two, and he met McNeece's rush with two jabs that brought the color to McNeece's face.

"Easy, Irish," Bimstein hollered up. "Hold it, Irish."

It was that way through the first minute of the first round, with McNeece's anxiety showing in the punches he was missing and with La Bua pacing himself nicely. Then, suddenly, halfway through the round, McNeece landed a right hand to the body that hurt La Bua and backed him up. The moment he felt La Bua give under the punch, McNeece moved in after it, forcing, and it was apparent now that this, unless La Bua could do something to change it or McNeece lost his head, would be the pattern of the fight.

It was the same in the second round, with McNeece pressing, keeping La Bua from getting set. La Bua's corner must have noticed this, because in the third round La Bua came out and tried to take the lead. He was putting more authority into his jabs, snapping McNeece's head back. For a moment he backed McNeece up, but then McNeece started to drop inside the arcs of La Bua's follow-up punches and hook to La Bua's body, and when he did that it was the same as it had been in the first two rounds.

It would in all probability have been the same for ten rounds except that, in the fifth, a cut opened over La Bua's left eye from one of McNeece's overhand rights. It opened again the sixth, and at the end of the round Doctor Samuel Swetnick, of the New York State Athletic Commission, climbed into the ring. He looked at the eye and then spoke to the referee, and the referee threw his hands out flat to signal the end.

All the way from the ring to the dressing room McNeece, grinning now, his face and hair wet, was accepting the congratulations of his friends. A few minutes later, his green robe over him, he was sitting on the dressing table, holding an ice pack to his left eye, which had purplish welts above and below it.

"You see?" August was saying, bending over McNeece. "When you jabbed and moved under, his right went over your head."

"I know," McNeece said. "It was good."

"You looked very good tonight," Joe Lee, a sports writer, was saying. He was standing by the table with pencil and paper in hand.

"He was a very tough guy, a very tough guy," McNeece said, and I could see he was starting to unwind now. "He takes a good rap. I'd just wait for him to start, and then I'd shoot inside to the belly."

"Who'd you like to fight now?" Lee said.

"Anybody my manager says," McNeece said.

"You see?" Bimstein said.

"I know," McNeece said.

"You got a little Jew sense in your head tonight," Bimstein said. "Let the Irish out later."

"He means be more deliberate," McNeece said, smiling and explaining the reference to Lee.

"Let me tell you something," Izzy Grove, who had just come in, said. "You got a lot of ability. You can make a lot of money."

"Thank you," McNeece said, smiling and removing the ice pack.

During the middle and late Twenties, Izzy Grove was a good middleweight who fought most of the best in and around New York, several champions among them. Now he books dance bands for a living.

"Don't thank me," he said. "Thank yourself. I don't want to tell you how to fight. You got a manager and a trainer to tell you that. Just behave yourself. Don't abuse this body. You got only one."

"I know," McNeece said.

"Have a good time, sure," Grove said, "but not tonight. Wait a couple of days. Don't get drunk."

"Sure," McNeece said.

"Let these words become imbedded in your brain," Grove said, tapping his own forehead. "I know. I been through it. There's no business in the world where you can make more money if you take care of yourself."

"I know," McNeece said.

"Remember this," Grove said. "The whole world loves a winner and the losers are on Strike It Rich."

"Thanks, Mr. Grove," McNeece said.

In the lobby, fifteen minutes later, there were still several dozen men and women waiting near the door to the dressing rooms. They were talking loudly and kidding one another and laughing, and every now and then one of the men would slap another on the back. They were waiting for a young man who, for many reasons, all of them interwoven, always wanted to be a fighter. They were waiting for Billy McNeece.

FORGET THE "WAS"

By Bill Leiser

From The San Francisco Chronicle, December 10, 1955

You can write Sugar Ray Robinson back into the present tense. Forget the "was." He must still be the greatest fighting man, pound for pound, in the world.

At least he is once again middleweight champion of the world, having just knocked out San Francisco's Carl (Bobo) Olson nine seconds before the end of the second round of their title bout here tonight.

It happened quick and it was difficult to tell who was the more surprised, the Hawaiian born Bobo rolling over and taking the ten count on the floor, or "Old Man" Robinson who was having his hand raised as the first battler ever to win back this crown the second time.

He won the title way back in 1951. He later lost it to Randy Turpin, and he won it back from Randy Turpin again, which was accomplishment enough, but he next gave up the crown to become a dancing man, and then decided he wanted it for his own once more, and he came back to qualify to meet the new champ and blame me if he didn't knock that champ flinging tonight.

Our boy Bobo seemed to be in shape and seemed willing enough, and he was moving forward or boring in through the first round, but he still lost that round by a 10-9 or 10-8 score to the man who was "too old" to be in the ring.

Over a 15-round span that opening score wouldn't have mattered much, for Sugar Ray was surely due to tire down before his 27-year-old foe as the evening wore on, but it didn't wear.

Over by the ropes on our left in round two, Bobo seemed to be getting in a couple of fair punches when suddenly he straightened up for no reason except this Sugar Ray man had connected with a left hook to the face.

But Bobo didn't stay straightened up very long. Something of a right uppercut delivered by the "old man" hit him in the jaw and down he went, sprawling, and looking wide-eyed and dreamy as he looked when another old man, Archie Moore, flattened him in New York in June.

This time he didn't seem so much dazed as surprised. He had enough strength to roll over, and we thought he was going to push himself up but he stayed there listening to the referee.

And Robinson's friends rushed into the ring, lifting the "new" champ to their shoulders as though they were carrying the college touchdown hero off the Big Game field.

If there was one element in common in their combined expressions it was surprise, as if they were all celebrating something they had dreamed of but never believed actually could happen. Most surprised of all seemed to be Robinson. He cried and he laughed and he beamed for everyone who looked his way.

Olson still acted as a surprised man, wondering "How could this happen to me?" as manager Sid Flaherty ushered him out the pavilion aisle.

It was quite a short-short story. Leo Leavitt, former Hawaii promoter, who came all the way from Bangkok to see the boy he started as a fighter in Honolulu, didn't think he got enough action to reward him for his 15,000-mile trip. "How could he lose so quick, like that?" Leavitt then left to pack up for the return home.

They said it would be the end of the trail for Robinson if he couldn't win. We don't know what it is for Olson. Left hooks have "killed" him twice, now. Moore's lefty followed a right; tonight Sugar Ray reversed the combination.

Robinson's slight lead in the first round did not begin to suggest the dramatic end to come 2 minutes 51 seconds later. Both Judges, Ed Hintz and John Bray, voted Robinson the winner, 10 to 9. Referee Frank Sikora called the round even.

Sugar Ray reached Bobo with an early left hook to the body. He was jabbing sharply, but he didn't hurt the champion. Midway in the round Olson smashed a solid right to the ribs, and that was about all.

Olson seemed to be trying to bore his way in, but Robinson's snake-whip left jabs seemed full of sting. Robbie stayed outside. The second round was not exciting—at the outset. They clinched twice after short exchanges. No damage. They met again on the south side of the ring, with Olson's back to the television cameras.

Bobo flashed a hard right to the body, and he tried to rip forward with a higher right, but this time Sugar Ray backed off quickly. Almost as quickly as he had slipped away, he was back again. Left hook. Right. The champion sagged, and a new champion who has twice before been champion, was reborn.

Surprisingly enough, Olson who was supposed to be having a battle with weight came in at 159¼ while Ray scaled 159¾, the heaviest ever for any of his title bouts.

Attendance was 12,441. Gross receipts were $139,725. Net receipts were $114,929. Television paid $75,000. Olson got 35 per cent and Robinson 25 per cent.

One fan is happy. Dr. Joyce Brothers, the $64,000 question winner told us on the way over from the Parkway Hotel, "I don't think Robinson has a chance, but he's been such a fine fighter I hope he wins."

Olson has been a pretty fair fighter in his day, too, but now perhaps it's Bobo we'll have to write back to the past tense.

Some of his friends have hinted he wants to retire. It's either that or the long, hard road back for the youngster who started fighting in bare feet in Hawaii, and has won 65 while losing eight, including only three knockouts—one by Moore and two by Robinson.

Yet this same Sugar Ray Robinson can tell him that "impossible" comebacks are not impossible at all.

THEY NEVER HURT ME

By Tex Maule

From The Dallas Morning News, July 25, 1955

(THE LINES *of old scars crawl through the heavy eyebrows like white worms. Scars make faint tracings around the mouth and the nose is battered and shapeless and the voice is hoarse and whispery from a hundred blows on the throat.*)

"I guess I had—lemme see, now, musta been—I don' know, maybe two, t'ree hunnerd fights, see? Seem like I don't remember like I useta. One t'ing I'm sure, I never got knocked out for the ten count, see? Sometimes I get a loss but it's a TKO, see? One thing 'bout me. I never took no eight count like they do now. You know. I get knocked down, I never stay there, always made myself get up before they could start countin' an I never got knocked out for the ten count, see?"

(Your brain is about the consistency of a cantaloupe. A ripe cantaloupe. It's protected by a tough skin called the dura and by the skull. You can live a whole lifetime and most people do without any injury to the brain because it is so well protected. It has to be because the brain itself isn't tough. No tougher than the meat of a ripe cantaloupe.)

"I'm kinda wai'n 'round now to make a comeback. Seem like nobody wants to gi' me any fights, an' take these punk kids they got now, I can lick 'em. Lick 'em, easy. I been ever' where fightin'. Main events, too. Couldn' none of 'em ever knock me out, see? TKO, once ina w'ile. Man can't help gettin' cut up, see? But not no knockouts with a ten count, see? Useta fight alla time. One time I fight fi' times ina week an' some people might say the man was pushin' me too fas' but I'da been fightin' anyway, see?"

(The skull is a wall to keep hurt from the brain, but it can bruise and tear, too. A hard blow to the head will slap the soft, heavy brain against the inside of the skull and cause tiny tears in the thread-like capillary blood vessels that feed the brain. The tears heal, but they leave little scars across the surface of the brain. A few of them won't make any difference in the way you feel or

177

act or talk. If the scar tissue keeps on piling up from repeated injury, lots of things can happen to you.)

"Kids fightin' now ain' tough anymore, see? People don' git what they come for with them kids. Say I'm a fighter an' you're a fighter. Right? So we're fightin'. Right? People out there, they payin' for us wearin' nice clean clothes, got money in the pockets. They payin' the money to see us fight. You got to have it here if you gonna fight. I 'member one fight, I got cuts over both eyes an' blood ina mouth so I can't hardly breathe an' my manager say, 'Baby, don' go out there no more' but I go on out. An' I ain' never been hurt, see?"

(If you keep getting hit in the head and the soft, heavy brain jostles against the inside walls of the skull, the little tears multiply and heal and the scars spread out over the surface of the brain. The first thing affected, usually, is the motor reflexes. You don't react quite as quickly as you did and you don't co-ordinate as well. But you can get along all right that way and so far your mentality has escaped, anyway.)

"I dunno. Seems like theys worse things than fightin' in the ring. Where else am I gonna make the money to wear nice clean clothes? Laborin'? I'm a fighter an' I guess I'd rather die in there in 'at four-square ring. You kin git killed out there ina street brawl an' ain' no one payin' any money to see it, see? That makes neither here nor there, though. Big thing, you gotta have heart, gotta think you kin be champion, gotta be tough an' take it. Right? I useta fight alla good ones, see? I can't remember alla good boys I been in there with. Right? You know what I'm talkin' about?"

(When the motor reflexes go, the hard, jarring blows to the head that rattle the soft, heavy brain like jelly in a coconut come more often and the tears are bigger and still they heal and leave more of the little white scar lines on the surface of the brain. Then the memory begins to fail and the tongue thickens. Sometimes, a personality will be completely reversed and, if you were a happy, kindly person, you'll be mean. Or if you were mean, you'll be easy to get along with. Lots of the time a state of euphoria sets in and, no matter what kind of life you have to live, you'll feel good and happy. You won't be good for much, but you'll feel good.)

"Thin' about me, soo, I never got hurt. An' 'ats why I think maybe I kin come back an' w'ip some a' these punk kids. Right? I been in the ring I think 'bout 15 years, or 14, or sumpin' like 'at, I don' remember, but I never been hurt. Right?"

(There's no cure for the little scars. They don't often kill, either. Maybe, if you get a very severe blow, the dura will tear and the brain rip and you'll die. But the little tears won't kill. Maybe you're lucky if the tear is big enough.)

12 MINUTES SHORT OF 70 DAYS

By Jerry Nason

From The Boston Globe, June 11, 1955

GREYHOUND LEAN and wolfpack mean, Carmen Basilio, 28-year-old onion farmer, tonight wrested the world welterweight championship from Tony DeMarco of Boston with a 12-round technical knockout.

Harry Kessler, millionaire, whose hobby is arbitrating boxing bouts, pulled the snarling Basilio off the weary, battered, dully-eyed Bostonian at 1:52 of the round.

It was a merciful gesture. The youngster from the North End had fought on instinct alone from the middle of the 10th round. Basilio's vicious hooking attack had dropped him twice for eight counts in the 10th.

DeMarco, younger at 23 and bulldog-strong in the early rounds, when he bossed the ring, suddenly ran out of gas.

The end came to him in lingering style. Early in the ninth round he seemed to be sure-footed on the road to victory. He was hacking at Basilio and driving him off with hard, accurate punches.

Suddenly Basilio, himself split over the right eye and dribbling from the nose, lodged a terrific left hook on DeMarco's cheekbone. The fight suddenly turned over on its back.

Stung, DeMarco stormed angrily at the gimlet-eyed challenger who was soon to end his reign just 12 minutes short of 70 days. DeMarco missed three, four, five, six wild punches. Each time he missed, Basilio stabbed out with a left jab that painted young Tony's face from chin to brow.

To now DeMarco had pulsed with power. Several times he had buckled Basilio's knees with the velocity of his hitting. Now, starting the 10th round, he combined a right-left combination. Both punches landed. But they no longer carried the authority of those which had made Basilio an anxious, cautious man back down there in the early rounds.

Now Charmin' Carmen started to take chances. He laughed out of the side of his mouth and when DeMarco charged him he met

180

head-on. They both were hooking and uppercutting without a letup—two young bull buffalos in unyielding combat.

Now it was Basilio who carried the firepower. They exchanged nine punches, then suddenly DeMarco's head came shooting up as if a giant hand had snarled itself in his hair and yanked him.

It was a Basilio left hook, and it sent Tony over backward along the ropes. Kessler bustled over, picked up the count as he peered exploratively into Tony's bloodied face, both eyes gashed and the nose spurting.

DeMarco was obviously hurt. A veil was drawn over his eyes. His arm hooked across the rope. But he got up. He was around when they passed out guts, this boy.

He got up and faced the wild-eyed Basilio across the ring. He was going to catch pure hell, and in his heart he knew it. He had nothing left, really. For nine rounds he had gone head hunting, draining his energy with his ponderous swings and misses, and now he was drained to the dregs.

All but his store of courage. He got up and Basilio came after him, with a minute to go before the bell. He got up, and almost instantly he was down again. A long Basilio right, thrown with abandon since Carmen needed to fear no countering blow that might derail him so close to the title, smacked off DeMarco's head.

As his black shock of hair bounced with the punch, Basilio hurled his dreaded left hook—his meal-ticket punch. It caught the unprotected, weary Bostonian flush. Down he went for another count of eight.

This time he seemed to have somehow absorbed the blows with less damage, and he got up, fairly strong, and just before the bell rang to end the 10th it was DeMarco who was boring in and sledging at the title hungry onion farmer from nearby Chitteango.

They got him out for the 11th, although Dr. Charles E. Heck, ring physician, trundled his bulk up the stairs and into DeMarco's corner to inspect the sabred face of the battered boy from the North End.

The bell got them up for the 11th. Sammy Fuller pushed De-Marco toward the center of the ring. Dr. Heck was still trying to get his 200-pound bulk through the ropes. Basilio moved across but he looked tired. He was blood spattered and arm weary, and he fell back on his long left jab for the entire round, pot shotting like the canny, sharpshooting veteran he is.

Toward the round's end Carmen walked in on the staggering champion and potted him with six punches, with no return.

And so it came to the 12th. You knew nothing kept DeMarco on his feet except his huge heart. He had left his strength down there in the rounds from one to seven, when he had barreled into Basilio with sometimes wild, occasionally accurate efforts to take his man out with one punch.

Now on the threshold of defeat, his 70-day-old title slipping from his hands, DeMarco sought to throw that one salvaging punch from the haze that held him.

He walked out for the 12th and threw it—and missed. Now Basilio stabbed his face apart with that long left jab. He backed off and let Tony come seeking him as he jabbed relentlessly.

He backed off toward the ropes to the left of DeMarco's corner, luring his wavering opponent with him, then suddenly turned like a tiger and churned up a 12-punch flurry that snapped the champion's head around like a lobster buoy in a stormy sea.

It was getting pretty brutal. DeMarco refused to go down. Basilio apparently didn't have the strength to put him there. But he was strong enough to tear this stubborn target to ribbons.

So Kessler, therefore, who had been carefully surveying the situation for two rounds, walked between them. He shouldered Basilio to one side, guided him toward his corner with a gesture.

Then he took DeMarco by the arm, as Tony leaned, half conscious, against the ropes, and said, "That's all, Tony."

That is how the end came, with the Fleet street boy who'd come from obscurity to the world welterweight title overnight, out on his feet but refusing to go down again.

The 9170 patrons, naturally partisans, filled the beautiful war memorial auditorium with a tumult of sound. As DeMarco trudged unsteadily toward his corner, Basilio leaped wildly in the air, then fell on his knees in a prayerful attitude. Then his mother and his wife and aunts in profusion poured in there with him.

In his corner Tony DeMarco cried as they wiped the blood from his tortured face. But for Basilio, bypassed by two former champions, this was the night of his life.

But in his hour of triumph Basilio, who fights mean and viciously, did not forget the man who fought him toe to toe all the way.

He turned and sped across the ring, and patted DeMarco on the head and raised his arm as much as saying to his wildly exuberant followers, "Here's a man."

Basilio had escaped a bear trap early in the fight, and well knew it. In the first round he had taken a smash on the face which drove his rubber mouthpiece almost down his throat.

In the third he was almost on the way out from two hard right hooks DeMarco landed almost as the round started, and a following left hook which snapped Basilio's head back and sent him bowlegged in retreat.

In the seventh DeMarco left-hooked him and hurt him terribly. Basilio started to come, nourished himself back to health behind that spanking left jab.

He is a cutey. A year from now he won't go the distance with young Tony, but tonight he fell back on all he had learned over the years and saved himself three or four times.

And, finally, it was DeMarco, five years younger, who reached the bottom of the gastank and went dry.

Thus DeMarco's sensational streak, 17 bouts long, came to a violent and bitter end—but Syracuse will never forget the stand he made tonight against the 2-1 favorite fighting in his home town for the world title.

A man, you suspect it was Tom Lea, once wrote a remarkable story called the Brave Bulls, and Tom Lea—who obviously appreciated unflinching courage—would have adored young Tony DeMarco here tonight.

His tactical plot, his violent and rash and energy-robbing head hunt of the early rounds, is suspect . . . but never his tremendous courage.

He was so well beaten, on the official score cards, that only by a KO could he have retained his newly fitted title. Referee Harry Kessler scored it 8-2-1. Judges Bert Grant and Frank Forbes scored it 7-4 and 8-3, respectively. The Globe card was 7-3-1.

This is the beginning of an old, old dream for Basilio but let us state, with no reservations, that it was not the end of a dream for Tony DeMarco of Fleet st., North End, Boston.

He is merely 23. He is two years away from reaching the pulsating peak that will know him as the champion again. There will come the day when no man of his weight will be able to stand up to him in the ring and survive.

He was the noblest Roman of them all tonight. He refused to be carried off on his shield.

THE GAY GOB

By Gene Ward

From The New York Daily News, March 14, 1955

THERE WAS a short piece of copy out of Waltham, Mass., the other day concerning Bob Murphy, the battling gob, and it brought back a flock of memories. Perhaps you saw the item. Murphy pulled three kids out of a burning building and lost his job. It seems the building contained a bar which the old redhead was tending.

This is not designed as a hero-worshipping stint. Murphy had more faults than most fighters, and a supply of foibles to last half a dozen ordinary humans a lifetime. But he was the most personable, colorful, dead game and generally intriguing fightin' guy I've ever met, and a few more like him would go a long way toward curing boxing of what ails it.

His training methods consisted of story-telling and elbow-bending, and he was an accomplished artist at both. If the report is true that he's been on the wagon since marrying Ann Moore of Boston, and starting to raise a family, I suppose it's all for the best. But I just can't help remembering Murphy when he came out of the West, a rip-snortin' guy in and out of the ring who, for a little while, battered down the old adage that you can't have your cake and eat it, too.

He was a continual source of amazement to his stablemate, Billy Graham. To this day, Billy never has been able to understand how a man of Murphy's appetites could find the physical resources to ply his trade. Murphy played as hard as he fought. He lived life to the hilt, and rightly belonged in an era far more swashbuckling than this one. He might have been most anything he chose to be, but a war, in which he served aboard battlewagons in some of the toughest Pacific action, left him unfit and restless. And so the redhead turned to fighting as the quickest method of making up for lost time. Edwin Lee O'Connerty became Irish Bob Murphy, fist fighter.

There was a night in Milwaukee he took on the brewing community's local hero, Cecil Hudson, and knocked him out in the fifth round. It wasn't a particularly good fight, and the crowd had been sitting on its hands throughout the evening. The ring announcer was ready to intone the time of the kayo and thus wrap up a dull card. At this point, Murphy turned to his manager, Irving Cohen, and said: "Get me the mike!"

The redhead talked for what must have been 10 minutes. He thanked the fans for coming out to see the fight. "I want to thank every one of ye," he said, "and to tell you that your boy, Cecil Hudson, is a very fine fighter. I learned more from him tonight than in all the other fights in my career. From now on I want to be billed as coming from Milwaukee, and before you leave, I want every one of you to come to my dressing room. I want to shake hands with all of you and give each and every one of you an autograph."

And he did, too. The fans loved it, and they loved Murphy. For three hours, he stayed in his dressing room shaking hands and signing autographs, and then went out on the town with the enraptured citizens.

A week later, Murphy was in Chicago knocking out Danny Nardico and playing the night spots on the loop with his pals. Next came kayoes of Jake LaMotta in New York, and Joe Rindone in Boston, with Murphy ever the hail-fellow-well-met, the convivial companion for whatever fun could be found on the bright light beat. When he met Joey Maxim for the light-heavyweight crown in August of that year, the terrific pace had begun to tell, the marvelous physical machine to run down.

He always was the answer to a promoter's prayer. His match with Harry (Kid) Matthews in the Garden was drawing little advance notice mainly because Harry's pilot, the usually voluble Jack Hurley, refused to work up any enthusiasm for his fighter. New York sportswriters didn't know much either. "Matthews may prove himself," Hurley said, "but he hasn't so far."

Murphy thought this was a helluva way to promote a fight. He called a press conference at his Greenwood Lake training quarters and told the writers: "I've seen this fellow Matthews fight and he's terrific. It will be my toughest fight, and I'll be lucky to win."

Well, he didn't win it. He might have, for his rugged, Pier 6 crowding had the superior boxer on the run in the fourth and fifth frames. Then, suddenly, Murphy stopped crowding and began to box Matthews just when Hurley's golden boy appeared ready to fold. When the sixth round was over, Murphy returned to his corner with a smile on his face. "I told you I could outbox that guy," he said to his perplexed handlers.

The gay gob ran out of juice completely one night in Syracuse when Joey DeJohn belted him out in three rounds—and it was the beginning of the end for Murphy as a fighter. He went to bat four more times on the small club circuit, but, by now, he was merely dragging his body through the motions. After being beaten twice, knocked out again, and then held to a draw, all by nonentities, he hung up the gloves.

He went a long way on very little ability—almost to the top. He gave everybody he met, inside ring and out, a run for their money, and I hope he never comes back. Because, if he does, it won't be the same. And I'd rather remember Irish Bob Murphy the way he was—a guy with a lust for life and a knack for day-to-day living that is an all but lost art in a neurotic world which has forgotten how to laugh.

Golf

JACK THE GIANT KILLER

By Herbert Warren Wind

From Sports Illustrated, June 27, 1955

Copyright, Time, Inc.

WHO IS JACK FLECK? If you had been able to answer that question a week ago on a television quiz and had been able to answer it correctly, there is no knowning how many refrigerators and home freezers it would have won for you. Today it is different. Everybody knows who Jack Fleck is. He is the angular 32-year-old Iowan who accomplished two miracles two days hand running. On Saturday at the Olympic Club course in San Francisco, he tied Ben Hogan for first place in the 55th National Open Championship with a 67 on his last round. On Sunday, playing crisp, precise shots from tee to green and putting like a man in a trance, he stopped Ben's tremendous bid to become the first five-time winner of the Open by outscoring him 69 to 72 in the play-off. In short, Jack Fleck is the new National Open champion.

Late on Saturday afternoon, just about an hour after Hogan had finished his fourth and final round with a 70 and had trudged up the hill to the locker-room to sweat out Fleck, the only man on the course with a chance to tie his four-round total of 287 strokes, a tall, spare, somber-faced young man, his dark eyebrows edging from beneath his large gray cap, walked calmly and easily down the fairway of the 18th hole. This rather Lincolnesque figure was Fleck, a pro with just the suspicion of a reputation who operates two municipal courses in Davenport, Iowa when he is not competing in tournaments, who plays with Hogan clubs, who never before had finished as high as fifth place in any circuit competition and who had had an 87 in a warm-up round.

On the 337-yard 18th, Fleck walked to the edge of the rough where his drive had ended a scant four inches off the left edge of the fairway, about 110 yards from the small plateaued green which lies in the U at the base of a steep-banked natural amphithetater.

As some 10,000 spectators peered down from the hillside, Fleck undramatically prepared to play his pitch—a very big shot indeed. On it rode, to a very large extent, the success or failure of the magnificent attempt to catch Hogan this highly unregarded young man had been making all afternoon after Hogan's pace (and their own errors) had killed off all of his experienced competition.

At the time Hogan had holed out on the 72nd green, Fleck, who had started the final round three shots behind him, had been playing the 12th hole, the 66th of the tournament. He had then stood two under par for the round. He had gotten his par nicely on the twelfth and had rescued his par on the 13th with an excellent trap shot, but when he had gone one over par with a five on the 14th, Fleck's chances of catching Hogan had seemed absolutely forlorn. To do so, he had had to finish with two pars and two birdies on the last four holes, and on the Olympic Club course this is a considerable feat on a lazy non-tournament afternoon let alone on the last round of the world's most important championship.

Fleck had immediately picked up one of the birdies he needed on the 15th, a short par three, where he dumped his iron about nine feet from the cup and holed his putt. On the 603-yard 16th, after he had pulled his third in the rough behind the apron, he had all but holed his delicate chip. Par. Playing now like a man who has been "touched," as golfers say, hitting every shot superbly, he had laced two woods to the back of the green on the 17th, a par four 461 yards long which swings uphill all the way.

His try for his birdie from 40 feet had just slid by the cup. Par. So now it all depended on whether or not he could birdie the home hole.

From his lie in the rough—not too difficult a lie since the rough was not too heavy at that spot—Fleck played a three-quarter seven-iron and hit a simply wonderful shot. Flying in a low trajectory, the ball just cleared the bunker that guards the front entrance to the green and sat down hole-high, seven feet to the right of the cup. This home green tilts severely from back to front and its surface is slippery. All the tournament long, the players, and with reason, had been babying their putts here, hoping to catch just a corner of the cup. There was nothing tentative about Fleck's putt, downhill with a faint right-to-left borrow, as he read it correctly. He struck the ball firmly and it rolled right in, right in the center. He had gotten that birdie, he had tied Hogan, but for minutes and minutes after they had seen him do it, no one in the gallery could actually believe what they had witnessed.

Jack Fleck's fantastic finish and his equally incredible golf in the play-off were the ultimate chunks of drama in a championship which, even before Fleck came ghosting down the stretch, had made its progress one of the most exciting additions of the National Open. It had just about everything. To begin with, after only one man had broken par (70) on the opening round—Tommy Bolt with a 67—there had been the annual controversy as to whether or not the USGA and the host club had made the course unfairly tough in their efforts to provide a formidable test for the present brigade of precision golfers.

Along the narrow fairways—narrower in "feel" than their actual measurements since they are lined with dark green cedars, eucalyptus and pine—lurked rough that was really rough. Mainly made up of a rye grass imported from Italy 33 years ago, grass whose single stalks measure about three-eights of an inch in width, this rough, whether cut to two inches adjacent to the fairways or allowed to grow first to five inches and then to a foot in height farther from the fairway, was extremely thick, matty and resistant. To play more than a six-iron from the deeper strips was quite impossible. Moreover, the clumpy rough around the perimeter of the greens was terribly potent. To get out of it, a golfer had to strike the ball a pretty decisive blow, and it was quite impossible to do this without the ball's picking up a terrific overspin that sent it racing, sometimes, over the opposite edge of the green. To cope with this rough, a sharp-edged wedge was required equipment, and as Bob Drum of the *Pittsburgh Press* remarked, this Open, among its other distinctions, could boast of "the sharpest wedges ever honed."

In any event, since scrambling was out of the question, the major problem for anyone who hoped to score well was to sacrifice distance and keep straight and meet this examination in tight target golf on its own terms. On his opening round, Sam Snead did just the reverse. After missing three putts of under five feet which had taken the edge off his concentration, Sam had begun spraying his tee shots, had been unable to get home from the rough and had ended his sad safari with 79 blows.

Although it later turned out not to be the case, it seemed at the time that Sam had shot himself completely out of the tournament

and, in his understandable chagrin, had stomped from the clubhouse to his auto still wearing his spikes. On this opening round,
82 of the 162 starters took 80 or more to get around. At the half-
way mark, a total of 155 strokes was low enough to qualify for the
final 36 on Saturday, the highest figure for the "cut" in a good
many seasons.

By Saturday, the big day, when a mild San Francisco fog rolled
in (on little caddies' feet) and obscured most of the white city in
the distance, "the cream" had come to the top, as it invariably does
on a demanding course. Leading at 144 were Bolt and Harvie
Ward. With a chance to run away from the field if he added a
fairly low second round, Bolt had taken a 77, fading his irons
chronically and stroking his putts anything but like the golfer who
had taken only 24 putts in the process of his opening 67. A stroke
behind at 145 stood Ben Hogan (73-72) and Julius Boros (76-69)
along with Fleck (76-69) and another unknown, Walker Inman, a
youngster from Augusta who had been Fleck's playing partner the
first two days and who is his present traveling partner on the
tournament circuit. Snead, relaxed again and playing superlatively
from tee to green, had leapt back with a 69, and he stood at 148
along with Jack Burke, only four strokes off the pace.

It was an amazing dramatis personae for the final day, a story-
book lineup if there ever was one. Here was Harvie Ward, the
local boy who lives across the street from the club, with as good a
chance as any amateur has had in a long, long time to take the
Open. Here was Snead once again in a position, if he could muster
all his talent, to finally take the Open, the only major championship
he has never won though, heaven knows, he has had his chances.
And here, to be sure, was Hogan. On his first two rounds, Ben's
play had not been too impressive, not for anyone who remembered
the complete authority that had been his in 1951 and in 1953, his
peak year. The old sense of attack was missing in his putting. His
swing seemed somewhat flatter and shorter than usual. He seldom
opened up with his full cut, and when he did, he had trouble getting
through on the shot. He was swinging faster too, sort of punching
into the short shots with his forearms forcing the blow. But Ben
was controlling the ball, hitting the fairways, hitting the greens,
retaining his composure and his keenness since the tiredness that
came into his legs as he climbed up and down the hills was largely
burned away by the inner drive that stayed with him every second

of the way as he strove to achieve his appointed goal of becoming the first player ever to win the Open five times.

By midafternoon it looked as if Ben had that fifth championship, and with strokes to spare. One by one the other contenders had faded away. Young Inman went out with a 76 in the morning, and Harvie had shot his wad on the third round also, with a 76. Bob Rosburg, who had rushed into the contention with a 67 in the morning, played himself out of it early in the fourth round. Boros' chances were finished after he took a double bogey on the short 3rd (or 57th). For all intents and purposes, the tournament had resolved itself into another duel between those two ancient rivals, Hogan and Snead.

Playing about three holes in front of Ben, Sam started the final round one shot behind him. He quickly fell three behind when he led off with 5-5 against Ben's 4-4. He remained three behind when he turned in 37 and Ben in 35. At this stage of the tournament, both of these great golfers were playing great golf. You just can't hit a golf ball any better than Sam was hitting it. On the 12th, 13th and 14th, for example, he played, in succession, an 8-iron approach nine feet past the pin, a 4-iron five feet past and a 5-iron approach about seven feet to the left. He made none of the putts and, in truth, never looked for a moment as if he would. The definitive comment on Snead's pathetic failures on the greens came on the 13th (or 67th) hole, a 187-yarder, where he all but holed his 4-iron. As the ball barely missed the cup and slid five feet by, Sam's rooters almost conceded on the spot that, having missed his one, he would now have to settle for a three.

Some 40 minutes later, Hogan, pelting the short 13th, went one over par, to cut his lead over Snead to two strokes. Immediately on top of this, he faded his drive on the 14th, a long par four, into the five-inch rough. The decisive action in the Hogan-Snead duel then took place. After chilling his rooters by taking a four-wood from his bag, Ben played his finest shot of the round. Hitting the ball with a slight cut, he swatted it out of the grass and on a dead line for the center of the green some 210 yards away. The ball hit on the upslope to this hilltop green, bounded up between the two flanking bunkers and expired some 20 feet from the hole.

Almost simultaneously, the report came through that Snead had bogeyed both the 16th and the 17th. Hitting the ball with a freer action and more juice as the adrenalin released by the prospect of winning raced through his system, Ben finished with a birdie and three stalwart pars for a 70. He walked off the 72nd green, the apparent victor, to one of the greatest and most honestly earned acclamations in the history of a game which will go a long time indeed before it knows another champion of his stature.

And then along came Fleck.

The story of the play-off really began on the 6th hole. One stroke ahead at this point, Fleck had not played a bad shot. It is not unfair to the new champion to say that everyone in the gallery wondered when he would make his first error and what effect this would have on him. Well, he pulled his approach on the 6th, a par four measuring 437 yards, into the trap to the left of the green. He followed this with a rather loose recovery 25 feet past the pin. He then proceeded to knock the putt into the hole, and his errors had hurt him not at all. On the short eighth, after Hogan had rolled in a 50 footer for a deuce, the amazing Mr. Fleck coolly rolled in his eight footer for his deuce. The gallery had hardly digested this when he holed another long one for a birdie on the 9th, this one from about 25 feet. By this time everyone was almost conditioned to the fact that Fleck might hole anything, and on the very next green he holed still another. This one, however, was a mere 18 footer.

After this, Fleck holed no long ones, but this staggering putting spree had put him three under par and three strokes up on Hogan. It proved to be a sufficient cushion. Summoning all his heart and skill, Hogan fought back to chop one stroke off Fleck's lead with a birdie on the 14th, to chop off another with a fine four on the 17th. Now, with the positions of the previous day reversed, as it was, with Hogan needing to pick up one stroke on Fleck on the 18th, Ben just couldn't make it. He had no chance, in fact, after his drive. He hooked it into the foot-high rough, into an exceptionally healthy patch that all but obscured the ball. It took Ben three strokes to reach the fairway, one to uncover the ball, another to budge it three feet, a third to punch it laterally to the fairway. Both men finished like champions. Hogan holed a 25-foot downhiller. Fleck played a perfect four.

Perhaps all of us who saw this play-off can appreciate a bit better now how it felt to be at Brookline in 1913 when another complete unknown—the name was something like Ouimet—defeated the peerless Harry Vardon and that other contemporary giant, Ted Ray, in that historic Open play-off. This too, some 42 years later, was quite an afternoon, and the new champion, Jack Fleck, revealed himself to be quite a golfer.

THE BIGGEST VICTORY

By Whitney Martin

From The Associated Press, February 1, 1955

AT FIRST the vagrant idea seemed a little morbid, and you tried to brush it aside as unworthy of contemplation.

Then, suddenly, you saw something glorious in the picture of Bob Jones, Ben Hogan, Babe Didrikson Zaharias and Ed Furgol seated near each other on the dais at the Metropolitan Golf Writers dinner.

Glorious, because each is a glittering example of courage, and determination, and stoicism in the face of physical misfortune, and you realized there was something ironic in that such misfortune should descend upon the two greatest male golfers in the sport's history, the greatest woman performer, and the current National Open champion.

Jones, whose niche is secure for all time, whose historic grand slam probably never will be repeated, and for whom the word "gentleman" might have been coined, maintaining the gracious manner when every movement of his lower limbs is an ordeal because of a spinal injury.

Hogan, whose name can be coupled with that of Jones with credit to both, now trim and sound, but who had to battle his way back to health after suffering injuries so grave his golf future, and even his life, were periled.

The incomparable Babe, No. 1 in anybody's book, winning tournaments again after winning something infinitely greater—a conquest of cancer—in a grim struggle which won the admiration of the nation, and brought hope to untold thousands similarly afflicted.

Furgol, victim of a boyhood playground accident which left his left arm maimed and withered, but failed to quell a spirit which has carried him to the top and which refuses to concede an inch to a handicap which would have prompted less resolute athletes to give up without a struggle.

Strange, and cruel, have been the tricks fate has played on these

193

headliners, and the manner in which they have met the challenges is a fine chapter in a fine old sport.

So there they sat, these four, and only they know the physical pain and mental anguish they have, as individuals, suffered. And you marveled at their serene outlook on life, and thought how each has grown in stature in the eyes of the public because of a refusal to bow to misfortune.

Bob Jones would have ample cause to curse the fate that has left him hobbling about on canes, his once-sturdy legs encased in braces.

He has known the joy of the sport, the competition, success unmatched. Now he is sidelined, and to watch others pass to receive the plaudits of the crowd would create a situation which in a lesser man would bring only self-pity, and resentment.

Yet he retains the avid interest of his glory days, helping promote the game, lauding the young fellows, with no speck of jealousy or effort to bring up the past to the discredit of the present.

He had his day in the sun—and what a day it was! He may dream of his triumphs. He would be less than human if he didn't. But he is living in the present, and future, and in an active sport he is as much a participant as if he still were swinging a club.

Jones . . . Hogan . . . Didrikson . . . Furgol. Their biggest victories weren't on a golf course.

BROOKLYN'S MAD GOLF COURSE

By Jane Perry

From Sports Illustrated, August 22, 1955

IN ALL OF Brooklyn, from Coney Island to the Gowanus Canal, there is only one 18-hole golf course. And as might be expected, the game played there, although outwardly resembling golf, is quite different from the gentlemanly sport performed under normal, country club conditions.

A hundred thousand players use the Dyker Beach Golf Course each 12-month season. In addition to being the course with the world's most well-trodden fairways, Dyker is also the one where the incumbent pro, Tommy Strafaci, was brought up on the course (his father had a house on what is now the first tee and raised goats, hogs and vegetables on the second fairway); where the undershirt is a classic costume for hot summer days (topped by a bright plaid cap); and where the insult is the common and formal method of communication ("Hey, drop that ball, ya crumb!").

The Dyker course is municipally owned and commands a rather fine view of Lower New York Bay past the Narrows, although it is doubtful if any golfer has ever lifted his head long enough to admire it.

Duker players, all graduates of Ebbets Field and stormy days with the Dodgers, have been tossing pop bottles at umpires since infancy and enjoying nothing quite so much as a loud, vigorous hassle. Their game is rowdy, democratic and argumentative; and Dyker fairways resound with threats and the noise of Brooklyn voices raised in altercation. At the shriek of "fore!" players automatically drop their arguments and their clubs and assume a crouching position with arms wrapped over their heads—a defense similar to that recommended for an atom bomb. There is no way of telling from what direction the ball might come, since at Dyker so many fairways are cozily adjacent and so many players have spectacular hooks and slices.

It takes stamina and a rare sense of dedication to become an authentic Dykerite. It is helpful to have been born in Brooklyn, or at least to have moved there early in life. Out-of-town golfers who wander onto the course, either ignorant of its reputation or fascinated by the stories they've heard, have been known to quit after a few holes, thoroughly baffled and unhappy. In many cases the uninitiated may register but become so frustrated during the long wait that they never get to tee off at all.

Waiting time on a fine Sunday ranges from three to five hours. The alltime waiting record—about six hours—was set on a purely local holiday, Brooklyn Anniversary Day of 1940, when 860 players signed up.

As at all New York City municipal courses, each player is given a number on registration, and these numbers are posted by the starter on a blackboard directly behind the first tee. If anybody is waiting, golfers are required to play in foursomes—and on a Dyker weekend there is always somebody waiting. The first players arrive before 3:30 a.m., deposit their golf bags in front of the clubhouse and curl up in their cars for a nap. By 5 there are dozens of people milling around in the chill gray light, breakfastless, belligerent and talkative.

"So I get up at 4 o'clock with all the other nuts, and there's still this bunch a jerks ahead of me!" ... "You laughin' at my swing? What's so funny?" "Nuttin's funny. I'm just laughin' to be social." ... "That guy over there, I ain't seen him for 25 years, not since he beaned me with a 2-iron shot when I was 11." ... "So this bum got sore when I sneezed on his drive. After that I don't talk no more. Even when I step on his foot, I don't say 'excuse me.' "

The members of a pickup foursome introduce themselves informally, by first names only. A Dyker golfer may find himself teamed up with a municipal court judge (Joe), a Flatbush housewife (Mabel) and a city bus driver (Hoibert)—a state of affairs which has led to the breakdown of the few remaining social distinctions in Brooklyn. Women, who make up one-fourth of the players, are shown no mercy and little respect; in fact there is no look as openly horrified as that on the face of a male Dykerite who finds himself inextricably involved with three lady duffers. Occasionally a quick-thinking man in such a predicament will invent an urgent phone call and allow his number to be pushed back on the board, but most trudge along, audibly lamenting their fate. They will permit their lady partners to remove and replace the flag on each green, to locate their lost balls and will even condescend to give a few well-chosen pointers on the game ("When ya hit through, honey, ya gotta be square with the hole—get the pernt?")—but they are not happy.

Once a foursome starts on its way, it is at the mercy of eight people, the foursome immediately in front and the foursome behind.

The four in front will hold up the game by searching for balls, by mysteriously acquiring friends and becoming a sixsome; they will accuse the four behind of cutting in and trying to play past them. Sometimes they will charge at offenders with raised clubs—especially the females, who are, in this respect, the more deadly of the species *Golfer Dykeriens*.

The four behind will snap and snarl at the heels of the foursome ahead. If a player so much as stops to tie a shoelace, they will drive a warning ball whistling past his head. They are masters of the impatient stance, the sneering look, the "Hurry up, willya!" cries of outrage.

There are some players who have spent years trying to figure out various strategies of advancing their numbers on the blackboard. The powerful custodian of the numbers is the starter, a city employee of modest salary but heroic caliber, a man armed with only a piece of chalk, an eraser and a whistle, but capable of withstanding the deadliest bribes, insults and threats, often delivered simultaneously by the same golfer. The starter is able to handle minor emergencies himself—such as five players suddenly teeing off when only four have been called—but all requests for playing ahead of turn are referred to the supervisor of park operations who maintains a day-long vigil in the clubhouse.

Appeals to the director fall into several popular categories: *The Professional Engagement*—"I'm Dr. Smith, and I wouldn't ordinarily bother you, but I have several patients coming to the office . . . or (variation) a serious appendectomy scheduled for one o'clock"; *The Social Engagement*—"Have a heart, pal, and let me tee off. I can just get in nine holes before my mother-in-law's funeral"; and *The Train (Boat, Plane) Schedule*—"You gotta let me play now. I'm sailing for Tasmania in two hours, and there ain't a golf course in the whole damn country." Not one request has been urgent or unusual enough to melt the supervisor, who after nearly 2 years at Dyker has observed human nature at its most mendacious.

Before the 1930s, Dyker was a private golf club, first called Dyker Fields and then the Marine and Field Course, but from the beginning it possessed a unique Brooklyn personality. In the earliest days of the motion picture industry, according to one old hand, when the Vitagraph Studio was located in Brooklyn, Lillian Russell enacted a notable golfing sequence at the old Dyker. The story called for Miss Russell to sink her putt, and this she was able to do adequately enough in the rehearsal. When the cameras went into action, however, Miss Russell's meager golfing skill failed. The crisis was solved by an ingenious Dyker caddy who tied a string around the ball, and as Miss Russell went through the motions, the caddy gently pulled the ball into the cup. This sort of maneuver became a specialty with some Dyker caddies, one of whom figured later in a tempestuous scandal when he was accused of picking up a client's ball, racing 20 yards to the green, and dropping it in for a hole-in-one.

Some old-timers recall that the old course was a popular dumping ground for hot goods during the days of Prohibition, and even for victims of gang rides. Bodies were promptly removed, but other inanimate objects often were not. A Ford that had been driven onto the 5th fairway remained there for years, unclaimed and gently rusting away, viewed by players after a while as simply another natural hazard.

The present enlarged city course was designed in 1934 by John R. Van Kleeck, who, with a great deal of foresight, retired to South America, thus removing himself from the range of the always-articulate Dykerites. During succeeding years Dyker became more and more streamlined, with most roughs minimized in the interest of speeding up play. Ten minutes wasted by one golfer searching for a lost ball can set off a chain reaction involving a hundred lost tempers, up to and including actual physical conflict.

One of Dyker's first pros was Brooklyn's Wiffy Cox, winner of the 1931 North and South Open. The five Strafaci brothers, including Frank, an amateur holder of many titles, and Tommy, the family's only professional, grew up in and on the course, starting their careers as Dyker caddies. Tommy, with his dark, John Garfield-type of good looks and impeccably tailored clothes, has raised the sartorial standard of Dyker an appreciable degree during the last few years. He and the assistant pro, Harry Dunn, give about 2,200 lessons a season, possibly a world-wide record.

Dyker has many low-handicap golfers but is famous for its beginners, especially those whose sole previous experience has consisted of hitting one pailful of balls at a driving range. Duffers have been known to take 55 strokes on Dyker's first hole. One beginner attempted to play with the covers still on his clubs; another lady duffer inquired at the pro shop for a box of divots. Then there was the caddy who came back to the clubhouse sobbing indignantly: "Dat guy tell me I gotta keep my eye on his ball, and then he hooks it into the swamp. He yells, 'Put down the clubs where ya seen the ball go in,' and I done it and found the ball. But now I can't find the clubs."

Golf ball snatching, a problem at all busy courses, has achieved the status of a science at Dyker. Among the most skilled snatchers are the small boys who operate on several fairways adjacent to the city streets. When directly accused, the boy might be standing on the ball or has just slipped it to an accomplice, but he is all snub-nosed, freckled and dirty-faced innocence. "I ain't got ya ball, mister. Wanna soich me?"

The most successful ball snatcher in Dyker's history was a harmless-looking old party who had a habit of slipping in and wandering over the course, always leaning heavily on a bamboo stick—one end of which was later found to be hollowed out. Although balls began to disappear at an alarming rate and Dyker tempers began to soar proportionately, nobody suspected the old gentleman, who had never been seen to stoop, look at a ball, or even be aware that the game was played with little round objects. Finally the snatcher became so brazen that he stole a ball on the fairway right from under the nose of a golfer who had turned during his upswing to observe the position of the club head. The golfer completed his swing but hit only air—the ball had vanished. Completely unnerved, this Dykerite ran off yelling, "Let me outta here. Trained snakes!" Shortly afterwards a special policeman caught the old man with his capacious pockets full of balls and a Spalding Dot still concealed in the hollowed-out cane.

Not only golf balls but larger objects, even rain shelters, when they had them several years ago, were pilfered at Dyker. The wooden shelters, standard on almost every course, lasted here only until winter, when ice skaters using the swampy pond chopped them up for fuel. Plans at one time were made to erect cement block shelters, stark and monolithic, but incapable of being burned, knocked down, or carted off by Brooklyn burghers or burglars.

It is inevitable that regular Dyker players should tend to seek the solace of one another's company during non-golfing hours too. After a five-hour wait and five hours of playing, the Dykerite is apt to feel strange and lost in the outside world and in need of the companionship of his own kind. Three social clubs—the Shore View, the Brooklyn Golf club and Brookridge (for women only) —have arisen. The second was dedicated to the improvement of golf etiquette on the course—no fighting, replace divots, no throwing clubs. The organizations all take official notice of wives and children of members, who are encouraged to emerge at intervals from wherever golfers customarily stow their families and mingle with the Dyker world. It is a common sight on Sunday to see a golfer in the Dyker cafeteria, sweaty, dirty and rumpled, being visited by his wife and little ones dressed in their pretty, starched, church-going clothes.

One weekend a wife who had decided she'd had just about enough, arrived not with the children but with a policeman to arrest her golfer husband on a charge of neglect. However, during the week they came to an understanding, and by golf time the following Sunday, they were *both* at the course, honeymooners again, ready for a round of play.

There was the other golfer who had waited four lenthy hours to tee off, when a phone message arrived, informing him that his wife was being rushed to the maternity hospital. He picked up his clubs and started to run; then stopped, looked back, and yelled in anguish, "Hey, don't take my number off the board!"

Dyker was even host to a fugitive from justice, the operator of a stolen-car racket. This sportsman, after dutifully paying his greens fee, was not extracted from his hideout near the pond for several days.

And then there was the man, fast becoming a legend, who appeared at the clubhouse on a stormy day with a bag of what looked like golf clubs slung over his shoulder. Stepping out to the first tee in a cloud-burst, he drew a bow from the bag and shot an arrow toward the green. He then walked up to the arrow, imbedded in the grass of the fairway, and shot it again, reaching the green in two. The archer finished the 18 holes slightly over par, walked back through the clubhouse in his soaking clothes, and disappeared into the Brooklyn streets, never to be seen again. The spectacle had a curious unreal quality to the few who had observed it, but they were unsurprised. This was Dyker.

Some stalwart golfers profess to have read a newspaper article telling of the proposed building of a new course in Brooklyn— undoubtedly the fantasy of a sports reporter of the late Brooklyn

Eagle on a dull day when the Dodgers weren't playing. A few Dykerites, credulous and hopeful, even claim to have seen bulldozers at work on this new course. They are vague about the location, however, and no two accounts are exactly alike. It is very possible that the whole story can be explained as a unique combination of daydream and mirage, compounded out of the pungent Gowanus air and the fertile Brooklyn imagination.

Basketball

ROOMMATE: BOB COUSY

By Al Hirshberg

From Sport, March, 1955

FOR THE swing around the western half of the league, the Boston Celtics had chartered a Northeast Airlines DC-3 which, complete with crew and flight agent, would carry us on the whole trip, from Boston to Rochester to Minneapolis to Milwaukee to St. Louis to Fort Wayne and back to Boston. I arrived at Logan Airport in East Boston with a few minutes to spare and hurried aboard the plane. There was a single row of seats on the right and a double row on the left, and everyone seemed pretty well settled when I arrived. Bob Cousy was in the front single seat, busily shuffling a deck of cards. Bill Sharman was directly across the aisle from him, and Johnny Most, who broadcasts the Celtics' games on radio, was on the window seat next to Sharman. Fred Scolari sat right behind Cousy, with Ed Crowley, the radio engineer, and sportswriter Larry Claflin of the Boston *American* opposite him. The six of them were deep in a card game before the engines had begun warming up.

I was curious to know what they were playing but I couldn't see; another card game was blocking my view. This one numbered Ed Macauley, Red Auerback, the coach, Bob Brannum and Dwight (Red) Morrison. Sitting on aisle seats opposite each other, they had constructed a card table out of a blanket spread across the aisle and hooked on the arm rests of each of the four seats. They were playing bridge.

Further back in the plane, I sat down next to Jack Barry of the Boston *Globe* and said, conversationally, "I'd like to sit and talk to Cousy for a while."

"You might as well forget about talking to him until we get to Rochester," he said.

"Why?"

"Because he won't get up off that seat and neither will those guys playing bridge."

"What's Cousy playing?"

"Oh, hell," Barry said.

"What's the matter?" I asked him.

"Not a thing," he said cheerfully. "Why?"

"Why'd you say 'Oh, hell'?"

"Because that's the name of the game."

"Oh," I said, relieved. "How do you play it?"

"Hanged if I know," Barry said. "You'll have to ask Cousy."

We took off at 10:45 and Cousy lit a cigar the moment the "No Smoking" sign went off. I passed the time talking to Barry and to the non-card-playing Celtics, Togo Palazzi, Frank Ramsey, Don Barksdale and Jack Nichols. Joan Barrett, the pretty, blue-eyed stewardess, came by from time to time with cookies and coffee. Once in a while she handed cartons of milk to Cousy and Sharman, who would surely drink up all the profits if they were dairy farmers. The trip to Rochester took about two hours and 15 minutes and they must have guzzled a quart and a half apiece.

It was bitter cold at the Rochester airport, but the boys in the "Oh, hell" game were in no hurry to get into the terminal. Instead, they crowded around Cousy as he stood beside the plane, working with a pencil over a complicated chart of figures on a sheet of paper. Finally, Cousy announced the results. With nothing at stake, I was already retiring to the warmth of the airport building.

"How did you come out?" I asked Cousy, as he came in.

"Lost a half a buck."

"Anybody lose more?"

"Not much. Nobody ever loses more than a buck or so at this game."

"And you guys stood around and froze to settle fifty-cent accounts?"

Cousy shrugged. "I'd rather die from freezing than from worrying," he said.

Since we weren't staying overnight in Rochester, those of us who were supernumeraries left our luggage on the plane. Only the players carried their grips into town. In the lobby of the Hotel Seneca, Auerbach said, "Mind if your career as Cousy's roommate doesn't start until we get to Minneapolis? The boys will only be here for the afternoon."

Cousy's regular roommate is Sharman. The two were standing in the lobby, staring at a 1955 model automobile on display.

"Reminds me of a Christmas tree," Cousy said.

"I'll bite," I said. "Why does an automobile remind you of a Christmas tree?"

"Because I can't figure out how they got the car in here and how they'll get it out again."

"What's that got to do with a Christmas tree?"

"Because I can't figure out how they'd get a Christmas tree in and out of here either," he said.

"What are you going to do this afternoon?"

"I'm undecided whether to sack out or go to the movies. I might even eat."

He ended up eating—about a side of beef, two glasses of milk and a huge plate of ice cream. By the time he got through, it was after three o'clock. Then, with Sharman and Palazzi, he went to the movies. After that, he had a quick sandwich and some more milk, then headed for the Arena.

The Rochester Arena is a big, barn-like building, with tiers of seats rising from the floor on both sides of the basketball court. There is a reverberating echo in the place, and the name that bounced around it most was Cousy. Everyone was either cheering or jeering him, but, apparently impervious to the crowd reactions, he played a solid, steady game. The Royals won, 107-101. Cousy, with five field goals and 14 successful foul conversions, had 24 points, a good night's total.

"Those noises bother you?" I asked him later.

"I'd be out of business if they did," he said.

"Some of the riding was pretty rough."

"They paid their money. They had a right to say anything they felt like."

"Some guys resent it," I remarked.

"Any professional athlete who resents anything a paying customer says ought to have his head examined," Cousy said.

We ate at a diner near the airport, with Cousy packing away two sandwiches, a huge piece of pie and two glasses of milk. As we walked to the plane for a midnight takeoff, he asked, "You going to play 'Oh, hell'?"

"Don't know how," I told him.

"Want to learn?"

"Sure," I said.

We got back into the plane, and I took the front window seat. Cousy was beside me and Sharman sat in the single seat across the aisle. Crowley sat in one of the seats behind us, with Houbregs, who had met us at the airport, in the other. When the game began, I figured we'd play for an hour or so and then call it a night, but I was living in a fool's paradise. Hour after hour, the boys kept dealing, and by 3 a.m. I was ready to throw in the towel.

"Look," I asked, "how long are you guys going to play?"

"Until we get to Minneapolis," Cousy said blandly.

"Until *when?*"

"No sense breaking up the game right in the middle, as long as we've got players."

"Don't you intend to get any sleep?"

"You one of these guys who sleeps his life away?" he needled me. "Come on, now, don't be a spoilsport."

So I played "Oh, hell" all night.

Well, not exactly all night. We stopped in Milwaukee at 4:30 in the morning to fuel up, and had sandwiches and coffee (milk for Cousy and Sharman) while we were waiting. On the way back to the plane, we bought chocolate-covered ice cream sticks out of a slot machine and ate them as we walked toward our DC-3. When we got aboard, we found Crowley and Houbregs asleep, and the game had to be rearranged. Scolari sat in the seat behind Sharman, and he played for an hour or so. When he wilted, Brannum moved in. By the time we reached Minneapolis at 6 a.m., Cousy, Sharman, Brannum and I were staggering through the last hand. I lost $2.70.

"I thought you said nobody ever loses more than a buck at this game," I remarked.

"Never in my entire career," Cousy said earnestly, "have I run into as lousy an 'Oh, hell' player as you."

"I'll learn."

"You'd better. There are only eight people in the whole world who know how to play it and they're all on this trip."

"Oh, hell" is not a difficult game to learn, as I found out later when, refreshed from a whole three hours of sleep, I could think fairly straight. Depending upon the number of players in the game, eight or ten cards are dealt on the first hand, and a card is turned up as trump. Each player announces how many tricks he expects to take, and the cards are then played out as in bridge. Players who take exactly as many tricks as they predicted get a 15-point bonus; otherwise, only as many points as they take tricks. In each succeeding hand, one less card is dealt, and the game ends on the one-card deal.

I played the game practically every single minute we were airborne and I never did learn how to keep score. Furthermore, Cousy, Sharman and Scolari weren't too sure of themselves. Even Cousy and Sharman who, for all I know, might have invented "Oh, hell," were half-way into the next game before they had figured out the results of the last one.

Minneapolis was cold, colder than Rochester. Between a long delay waiting for luggage and a long ride in from the airport, we couldn't check into the Hotel Nicollet until about 7:30—an hour and a half after we landed. Just before we got into the elevator to go to our room, Auerbach said, "Leave a call in time to meet at 12:30." Cousy just looked at him and nodded. I shuddered.

We rode up without a word, then headed for our room. The only sound that came from either of us was Cousy's grunted "Long halls —I hate 'em" as we struggled with grips which suddenly had become as heavy as lead. Once in the room, Cousy left a call for noon. The two of us took off our clothes and flopped into bed without even opening our suitcases. It was was nearly eight o'clock.

The next thing I knew, Cousy was wheezing, from the depths of his blankets, "What time is it?"

I looked at my watch and wheezed back, "11:30."

He got up, jumped out of bed, took his toilet kit from his suitcase, rushed into the bathroom and started shaving. Ten minutes later, he poked his head out and barked, "What time did you say it was?"

"11:30."

"What did you wake me up for?"

"I didn't wake you up. You woke me up," I said.

"The hell I did! I messed myself out of half an hour's sleep. Well, I'll get it now." And he flopped back into bed again.

Fifteen minutes later, the operator rang with our noon call, which we had both forgotten. With murder in my heart but sugar on my tongue, I thanked her, then got up. At 12:15, I woke Cousy, and a quarter of an hour later, we were on our way downstairs to meet the rest for the ride to the game.

"Do you do this sort of thing often?" I asked him.

"This," he said, "is practically routine."

"How do you feel?"

"Terrible."

"Then how can you play?"

By this time, we were getting off the elevator in the lobby. Cousy turned to me and said, "I can play all right. What worries me is how I can eat. It's too soon before the game to have a big meal."

"But the game doesn't worry you?"

"Oh, I'll have trouble trying to score. I always do in this town."

"Why?" I asked him.

"On account of Slater Martin. That little guy is the greatest guard in the league. He sticks to me like court plaster. Whenever I play him, I'm glad to settle for ten points."

"And the way you feel now—?"

"I'll settle for five," Cousy said.

He had a light breakfast—orange juice, toast and milk—and we headed for the Armory at about 1:15 for a 2:30 game. Everyone looked tired, although some of the boys had slept fairly well on the plane. Neither Cousy nor Sharman, who had sat up all night, appeared to be ready to play a basketball game, and, with the Lakers in their own hometown, this one figured to be a slaughter.

But Minneapolis was lucky to win. Once the game got under way, the Celtics got their second wind, and they put up a real battle before losing, 115-108. The Lakers didn't clinch the issue until the last two minutes of play. It was the second time in a row that the Celtics had scored over 100 points in a losing cause.

Cousy, a hard loser, was grim and silent for an hour or so after the game. He had hit for 21 points, with five baskets from the floor and 11 foul shots, in spite of the fact that he had neither eaten nor slept well. Yet he was very unhappy.

Later, I said to him, "You didn't really expect to win, did you?"

"Well, I never go into a game expecting to lose."

"I know, but look what you guys had been through. And you certainly scored more than five points off Martin."

He smiled, then said, "Y'know something? That's the best day I've ever had against him."

We had dinner a couple of hours later, and Cousy, as usual, demolished a tremendous slab of roast beef. Sharman and Palazzi, who were rooming together, joined us, along with Ed Crowley. At about 6:30, we went to the movies. When we came out, it was nine o'clock.

I yawned and said, "Well, guess it's time to go to bed."

"Bed—at nine o'clock? You crazy?" Cousy said.

"Have you got any better ideas?"

"Sure. There's another movie across the street."

That was too much. I watched the boys buy their tickets and go into the show, then I picked up some newspapers and went back to the hotel. Playing cards all night on an airplane was all right. So was going to one movie. But two movies in one night was more than I could take.

"You must be daffy about the movies," I said to Bob when we got up Monday morning.

"Once in a while, you see a real good one. Mostly, I just go to pass away the time."

"Do you ever see the same show twice?"

"That I won't do," Cousy said. "But I can always find a show somewhere I haven't seen before."

"What time did you get in?"

"About 1:30. We had something to eat after the show."

"Aren't you tired?"

"Sort of," he said. "But there's no sense in my going to bed early. I just toss around half the night and then get up exhausted."

The phone rang, and Cousy, after talking for a few minutes, hung up and said, "That was one of my campers. He apologized for not coming to the game."

Bob is part owner of Camp Graylag in Pittsfield, New Hampshire. He has 100 boys, ranging in age from eight to 16, and they come from all over the East and Midwest. Last year, he ran a post-season basketball clinic and it was so successful that he plans to make it a permanent fixture. The clinic lasted ten days and drew 100 boys, some from as far away as the West Coast.

"Basketball is the greatest game in the world," he said, "and I'll do anything I can to sell the game. Now, take our league. We've still got a few kinks to iron out, but we're getting there. I'd like to see teams in cities like Chicago and Detroit and I think we'll have them some day. The new rules have worked great. They've made for a faster, better, more exciting game than ever."

He was referring to the 24-second rule, which makes it necessary for a team to take a shot at the basket within 24 seconds after getting possession of the ball, and the six-foul rule, which gives an extra penalty shot for every foul over six in a given period.

"Before the new rule, the last quarter could be deadly in a pressure game," he said. "The team in front would hold the ball indefinitely, and the only way you could get it was by fouling somebody. In the meantime, nobody dared take a shot and the whole game was slowed up. Of course, the new game is tougher on the ballplayers, and I'm trying to work something out to protect them."

Cousy has spent considerable time in the last two years forming a players' association, similar to the group operating among professional baseball players.

"The players have as much at stake as the owners," he said. "If the league weakens or folds, it will cost a lot of guys their living. I think we should have more to say about how the league is run."

"What would you want done?" I asked.

"Well, we've kidded around a lot about this trip, for example, but it's really a killer. Just imagine—playing in Rochester one night and in Minneapolis the next afternoon! Today's our only day off this trip—Milwaukee tomorrow night, St. Louis Wednesday night, Fort Wayne Thursday night! And we're not the only ones. That sort of thing happens to everyone in the league. We've got to work something out that makes more sense.

"And there should be some kind of a minimum salary, and better incentives. We don't even have a Most Valuable Player award, or an award for the highest scorer or anything like that. The boys should be given more to shoot for than just those post-season bonuses.

"I'd like to see a good minor league developed," he said. "The way it is now, there's no place for a boy to go if he's dropped from an NBA squad. There are only a few independent teams and no real league. Some of the younger fellows need nothing more than experience, but where can they get it? Instead of taking a chance on struggling back into the NBA some day, most of the promising kids quit the game altogether if they don't make the big league on their first try.

"I don't know what the solutions are, but I want to do something to help find them. We're all college men and we've got normal intelligence. There's no reason why we can't be consulted for ideas. That's one of the big reasons why we're forming this association."

On the way to the airport—we were scheduled for a 1:30 p.m. takeoff for Milwaukee—I said, "How come you didn't drop dead during the game yesterday afternoon?"

"It really wasn't so bad."

"But didn't you *ever* feel so tired you thought you'd have to call it a day?"

"Well," he said, "there are always times when I feel that way. I can run up and down the floor twice at constant top speed without getting tired, but when I have to do it a third time, it really gets me."

"That's right," said Sharman, who was in the taxi with us. "You run the ball down, lose it at the other end and then run back, all without stopping, and you're all right. But if you steal it at your end and have to move back down again without breaking your stride, it's murder. As a matter of fact, it's easier on the Cooz than on any of us."

Cousy is not a robust-looking athlete. On the contrary, with his long, thin face and his sloping shoulders, he looks actually frail. And at six feet two inches, he is a great deal shorter than the average professional basketball player.

"Where does all the stamina come from?" I asked.

"My legs," Cousy answered. "They're my strongest asset. The bulk of my weight is below my waist. I look about 160, but I weigh around 185. Nobody ever believes that until they see me standing on the scales."

"This guy can run forever," Sharman said.

"I grew up playing basketball on concrete outdoor courts on Long Island," Cousy pointed out. "I never played indoors as a kid. I built up my legs on those hard courts, and when it came time to play on wooden floors, it was that much easier for me."

We took off from Minneapolis at 1:45 p.m. and landed in Milwaukee an hour and three-quarters later. During that brief time, Cousy, Sharman, Scolari and Houbregs officiated while I dropped six dollars at "Oh, hell."

"If I hadn't seen it with my own eyes, I wouldn't have believed it possible," said Scolari.

"Don't let him get away, boys," Cousy added. "This is his only trip."

At the desk of the Hotel Wisconsin, Auerbach said, "You've got two roommates instead of one this time. Sharman's going in with you."

As soon as we had checked in, Cousy and Sharman went to the Milwaukee Auditorium, where the Hawks were working out, to visit Chuck Cooper, who had roomed with Cousy when he was with the Celtics. The two are close friends. Cousy had once refused to stay in a Raleigh, North Carolina, hotel because it wouldn't accept Cooper, a Negro.

I didn't see Cousy until four or five hours later when he and Sharman walked into a movie palace around the corner from the hotel. The theater was advertising a triple bill, so I knew it would be a long evening. It was. The boys got out at one o'clock in the morning, and by the time they had eaten and gone to bed, it was after two.

When we got up the next morning—Tuesday—I asked them why, on the one day off, they didn't take advantage of the chance to get to bed early.

"Because it throws our schedule all out of kilter," Cousy said. "We play most of our games at night, so we gear our lives accordingly. We eat a big meal at around three in the afternoon, then take in a movie or loaf around the room and go to the arena an hour or so before the game. Then we eat again after it's over and get to be at 1:30 or 2:00 in the morning. On our days off, we do the same thing, because we don't have enough days off to shift to a more normal routine."

"You know how baseball players hate to go from day games to night games and back again," Sharman pointed out. "Well, we're the same way, except we play more nights than ballplayers do. The worst thing for us is a day game, because that messes everything up."

Sharman is an authority on the subject of baseball players. He is still an outfielder in the Brooklyn Dodgers' chain. He didn't play in 1954, but he's toying with the idea of returning to baseball this year.

The boys had a big breakfast at about 10:30 Tuesday morning, and then went to the movies. They ate again in the middle of the afternoon, then rested for an hour or so. That ended their longest free period of the trip.

The game Tuesday night was played in the Milwaukee Auditorium, and it marked the Hawks' debut of Frank Selvy who, like Houbregs, was a refugee from the Baltimore Bullets. The rookie star from Furman got a big buildup locally, and a good crowd showed up for a well-publicized Cousy-Selvy duel.

The fans were on Cousy all night, but, as usual, he showed no signs of being annoyed. One leather-lunged observer kept yelling, "Cousy, you're a bum! Cousy, you're a bum!"

But Cousy was no bum that night. On the contrary, both he and Selvy built up impressive point totals. When Cousy scored his 34th point late in the game to set a new Milwaukee record, his heckler yelled, "Don't that bum ever miss?" A minute later Selvy, who had 33 points himself, racked up two more, and Cousy's tormentor was back in business. As the game ended, the walls were jumping again with the raucous, "Cousy, you're a bum!" But Cousy was all smiles as he ran off the floor. The Celtics, hitting the hundred mark for the third straight game, won a 118-99 victory.

Cousy was bubbling and grinning and swapping wisecracks when I walked into the locker room ten minutes later.

"Now everything's fine," he said. "We finally won one."

"Did you hear that guy yelling at you?" I asked.

"You mean the fog-horn? There's one like that in every town. 'Long as they pay their way in, they don't bother me any."

Later about ten of us sat down for a "snack." Cousy's consisted of a full-course dinner, complete from soup to nuts and featuring a thick, juicy steak. It was exactly midnight when he started cutting into it.

"Hey, Red, what time do we meet tomorrow morning?" he asked.

"Nine o'clock, in the lobby," Auerback replied. "It's two and a half hours to St. Louis and I don't want to get there too late."

Cousy turned to me. "How about a card game back in the room?"

"You mean tonight?" I said.

"Sure."

"But we won't get started until about half past one."

"That'll be all right."

"How long do you want to play?"

"Well," Cousy said, we have to be out of here by nine. We can't play any longer than that."

So we played cards—but not until nine in the morning. That would have been all right with Cousy and Sharman, but the rest of the boys broke it up at four. Grateful for small mercies, I was happy to settle for four hours' sleep in the pungent atmosphere of drying uniforms. Both Cousy's and Sharman's were draped along the radiators.

"How come I never noticed this fragrance before?" I asked, as I struggled out of bed Wednesday morning.

"Very simple," Cousy explained. "I didn't have time to hang my suit up after the Rochester game, and by the time we got into the room Sunday night at Minneapolis, it was all dry. We had an afternoon game there—remember?"

"I wish they were all afternoon games," I muttered.

It was snowing hard when we took off from Milwaukee, and we found out later that we ran away from a blizzard. We got off the ground at about 10:30 a.m., and landed in St. Louis two and a half hours later. On this trip, Johnny Most, the radio announcer, helped Cousy, Sharman, Scolari and Houbregs relieve me of $3.75.

"A game of pennies, and the guy loses in dollars," said Most. "Where have I been? You been keeping him to yourself?"

"Don't worry," Cousy told him. "We've got time for a couple more sessions. Don't worry, you'll get your share."

Scolari, the elder statesman of the ball club, rode with Cousy, Sharman and me into St. Louis from the airport.

"How old are you really, Freddie?" Cousy asked him.

"I'm 32. I'll be 33 in March."

"You've been 32 for years. You were playing in this league before I was in high school."

"This is my ninth year. I started when I was 23," said Scolari, haughtily.

"That's your story. Hey, Willie," Cousy said, turning to Sharman, "how many ages have you got?"

"Three," said Sharman. "One for baseball, one for basketball and one for when I first got into Southern California."

"Which is the right one?" Cousy asked him.

"I don't remember which is which. Anyhow, I'm 26."

"Twenty-six?" roared Scolari. "Why, you've got a daughter in high school!"

"That's my kid sister," said Sharman.

"How old do you claim you are, Cousy?" Scolari demanded.

"I'm 26."

"And I'm Childe Harold. Why don't you guys be like me and tell the truth?"

The game at the spacious new St. Louis Arena was scheduled for 9:30 Wednesday night. Sharman roomed with us again, and after we checked into the Hotel Melbourne, he and Cousy had their big dinner and then went off to the inevitable movie.

The Hawks, who came in from Milwaukee by train, arrived early in the evening. A fair-sized but hardly neutral crowd was on hand for what turned out to be an easy game for the Celts. St. Louis is Ed Macauley's hometown, and as far as the Celtics were concerned, the game might just as well have been played in Boston.

Cousy had another great night. Besides piling up 31 points to lead both clubs, he put on a bewildering show of dribbling behind his back, scoring from odd angles and looking in one direction while passing the ball in another. He banged in 12 baskets from the floor and, as usual, played practically the whole game.

The Celtics won their second in a row, and, for the fourth straight time, scored over 100 points. The score was 101-90, thanks not only to Cousy's hit streak but also to Macauley's 28 points and a magnificent job of defending against Selvy on the part of Sharman. The Hawks' rookie, who had finished up with 44 points the night before in Milwaukee, was held to 15 points.

It was Cousy's game all the way, but he was particularly brilliant in the last period. The Celtics had a seven-point lead going into it, and Cousy made some unbelievable shots as he racked up five field goals. When the lead had increased to 16, he dug into his bag of tricks and delighted the crowd with his passing, shooting and dribbling.

"The guy's the greatest," said Auerbach, after the game. "There isn't anyone in the business who can come close to him. He's had 65 points in two nights. And when he gets a chance to put on a show the way he did tonight, he's in a class by himself."

"Why don't you do that sort of thing more often?" I asked Cousy, later.

"The only time I can do it is when we've got a safe lead," he said, "and in this league, that doesn't happen very often. I can't fiddle around out there just for the sake of fiddling around. My job is to help win ball games. When a stunt will help me out of a jam, I'll use one. Otherwise, I have to play it straight.

"That behind-the-back dribble which seems to attract a lot of attention was originally a desperation measure. I picked that one up while I was at Holy Cross. We played Loyola one night, and the only way I could get around a guy was by shifting the ball from one hand to the other. He had me so well guarded that I couldn't do it in front, so I did it behind my back.

"As a matter of fact," Cousy added, "I'm not the only guy who can do that. I've seen others work it, and I imagine everyone on a club like the Harlem Globetrotters can do it as a gag. I guess maybe I'm the only one who does it consistently, and as a strategic measure during a regular game."

"Do you mind being called a basketball magician?"

"Hell, no. It suits me fine. If people want to think of me as a magician, that's wonderful, just so long as they don't think of me *only* as a magician. I'm a professional basketball player, and I have to be a lot more than a so-called magacian in order to be a successful one."

Cousy, as a matter of fact, is almost as proud of his defensive ability as of his passing, shooting and legerdemain. When he first joined the Celtics five years ago, he had some defensive weaknesses. They since have been ironed out, and he is now a comparatively stingy opponent.

"Of course, I'm not the best in the business," he said. "Nobody on our club is a defensive genius. If we were as good on defense as on offense, we'd be unbeatable. We're the highest scoring team in the NBA, but we lose a lot of ball games because opponents score heavily on us. But the game we play is wide open, and I'm sure the customers like it better that way."

The usual midnight "bite" was another steak. At about 12:30, I went back to the room for what I hoped would be a night's sleep. We had to meet in the lobby at nine o'clock the next morning for the flight to Fort Wayne, where the Celtics were winding up the trip Thursday night. I left a call for 8:30, read the papers for a while and put out the light at one o'clock.

It didn't stay out long. Just as I was dropping off to sleep, the door burst open and in trooped Cousy, Sharman, Houbregs and Ramsey.

"Come on, come on, get up!" yelled Cousy. "This is no time to be sleeping."

"Ga-a-a-" I grunted.

"Half-past one and you're in bed? Where do you think you are—in a hospital?"

"I will be by the time you guys get through with me."

I struggled up to a sitting position, while the boys dragged a table and some chairs over by my bed. Cousy took a deck of cards out of his pocket and started shuffling. Before he began dealing, he said, "We're going to play buck-up."

"Buck-up?"

"You know the game?" asked Cousy.

"Never heard of it."

"Well, Ramsey never heard of 'Oh, hell,' and he's too young to teach."

Buck-up is a fast, three-card game which we played for a fast two hours. At 3:30, when Ramsey and Houbregs finally left the room, I collapsed.

"Look at that crumb, Willie," I heard Cousy say. "He died on us."

"Better it should happen to you," I snarled from under the pillow.

"You going to bed, Willie?" he asked Sharman.

"I guess so," was the reply. "There doesn't seem to be anything else to do."

"Well, I'm not tired," said Cousy. "I'm going to read a while."

Cousy and I were the last ones out of the hotel the next morning. Sharman was up and dressed before either of us had set our feet on the floor.

"What time did you get to sleep?" I asked.

"About 4:30, I guess," Cousy yawned.

"Did you read all that time?"

"Sure."

"What did you do that for?"

"Good book," he said.

Palazzi was waiting for us on the sidewalk. The youngster started to get into the back seat, but Cousy said, "Why don't you sit in front, Toge? It's more comfortable."

Cousy and I climbed in back and, when the taxi started rolling towards the airport, Cousy said, casually, "Say, Toge, did you notice that sign on the dashboard?"

When Palazzi shook his head, Cousy told him to read it aloud.

"The right front is the most dangerous seat in the car," Palazzi read, slowly. "Please do not sit here unless all other seats are taken."

Cousy killed himself laughing. He was still chuckling when we arrived at the airport. Palazzi climbed out of the cab looking like a man who had just sat in an electric chair with the power off.

It was exactly 10:30 when we took off from St. Louis, and, with a one-hour change back to Eastern Standard Time, we got into Fort Wayne at 1:45 p.m. During the two and a quarter hours, I lost only $1.25.

"You're getting there," said Cousy.

"In another week you'll be playing us even," Sharman added.

I lost my roommates at the Van Orman Hotel. Since we were leaving right after the game to fly back to Boston, there was no purpose in my checking in. Besides, I couldn't be with Cousy anyhow, since several of his campers live in Fort Wayne and he would be busy until it was time to go to the Coliseum, which, incidentally, is the most beautiful arena on the NBA circuit. We arrived there during the early stages of a game between Milwaukee and Minneapolis, since the Celtics-Pistons contest was the windup of a doubleheader.

With no Sharman to guard him, Selvy had a field day against the Lakers. He scored 42 points, setting a new Coliseum record, and the first to congratulate him after he left the floor was Cousy.

"That boy's great," Cousy said, later. "He'll be good for a long time, too. He's only a kid, fresh out of college."

The game at Fort Wayne started as if it would be a cinch for the Celtics. At the end of the first quarter, they had a 28-21 lead, but they slipped in the second and held only a one-point advantage at half-time. It was 71-71 at the three-quarter mark and then the roof fell in on the Celtics. The Pistons scored 45 points in the last session and piled up a 116-98 decision. It was the only game on the whole trip in which the Celtics failed to score 100 points.

After the first period, when he scored four times from the floor, Cousy was held to one basket. He was glum and uncommunicative when the game ended, but hamburgers and milk at the airport helped bring back his normal good humor. He didn't even get mad when I asked, "What makes a bad night?"

"Maybe you—maybe the other team—it all depends," he answered.

"Well—like tonight."

"I guess it was a combination of the two. We were hot at first, and then we cooled off. And the Pistons are in a terrific streak. A good club going well is the hardest combination in the world to beat."

"You started out as if you were going to have another big night."

"It looked that way, didn't it?" he nodded. "But I went cold. Those shots that rolled in when we played at Milwaukee and St. Louis just dropped out here."

"Do you keep track of your baskets during a game?"

He shook his head. "I don't even try," he said. "If I only get a few, I don't want to know the total and if I get a lot, I can't add them up."

We were sitting at the airport, waiting for the writers, who were still filing their stories from the Coliseum. Someone griped about the delay, and Cousy quickly turned on him.

"Never squawk when writers are working," he said. "If you're lucky, they might be writing about you."

"They might be beating my brains out, too," the other man remarked.

"I'd rather have them beat my brains out than not mention me at all," Cousy said.

"There are athletes who don't have much use for writers," I commented.

"I feel sorry for them. They don't realize how much help writers can give them. I don't know where we'd be without the writers. Basketball is over 50 years old, but the game never really caught on until the writers began telling the world about it."

He leaned forward. "Y'know," he said, slowly, "there are some people who think they're more important than anyone else just because they have some God-given talent—maybe they're atheletes, maybe artists, maybe stage or screen people, maybe even writers. But I'll tell you this, no matter how big a person is, there's never an excuse for his having a big head."

We got off the ground at 1:15 in the morning, with two stops before Boston ahead of us. We were hitting Washington to refuel and landing in Worcester to drop Cousy off.

"They always do that for you?" I asked him, as we sat down for the last "Oh, hell" game.

"What do you want 'em to do—drop me off by parachute?"

"That wouldn't be so bad?" Scolari commented.

"Deal the cards, Gramps," Cousy said, "and try not to look at them while you're doing it."

The game lasted all night. At about 3:30 a.m. the plane began pitching and tossing. Joanie, the stewardess, walked by and Cousy asked, "Is this Washington or bad weather?"

"Washington," she told him.

We were there nearly an hour. Back in the plane, we picked up the game again, and kept going until we started coming down in Worcester. Just as the wheels touched, Sharman, who was keeping score, was ready with the results.

"How did I do this time?" I asked.

"You won a quarter," he said.

We were on the field now, rolling toward the main building.

Cousy stood up, bowed deeply and said, "Congratulations. I never thought you'd do it."

He walked up the aisle toward the door. When he got there, he turned and yelled something that sounded like, "Don't think it hasn't been swell, buddy, because it hasn't!" I can't be sure. I was practically asleep.

I slept all the way to Boston—the whole 30 minutes. It's lucky Cousy wasn't there to see me. He'd have thought I was an awful sissy.

THE KID THEY CALL 'THE HOT ROD'

By Andy McCutcheon

From The Richmond (Va.) News Leader

HIGH IN THE mountains of Morgantown, W. Va., where the beauty of white snow is marred only by the thick layer of coal dust that covers it, basketball is more than just a game to keep thinly clad college boys busy during the winter.

It is a live-and-die business with the natives, who, to be sure, have had few West Virginia University victories—by comparison with earlier years—to warm the hearth the past few seasons. But it is still like the hostess in the dining room of the city's only hotel said:

"When it comes to basketball this town doesn't have any sense at all."

Poised to drive the city—and this entire area, perhaps—to further distraction is a mature (?) 6-4 sophomore named Rodney Hundley, who, in one freshman season and four varsity games, already has added his share of zany performances to a sport known for its craziness.

Already he has restored box-office vigor to the Mountaineer basketball scene. Already he is the campus hero of the fans and townspeople who have had to pour all their adulation the past few years on Coach Art (Pappy) Lewis' beefy football players.

And to look at the slope-shouldered, skinny 19-year-old you might never believe it. He's a show-off from the word go, with enough tricks of his own to make the Harlem Globetrotters stop and watch. He appears to be a college misfit academically, with a record that had to be bolstered by 12 hours of school work this past summer.

But he's a basketball player—and an all-business one when the occasion demands, as it did last Monday night when he quarterbacked the Mountaineers from a nine-point deficit to a 62-66 victory over the previously unbeaten University of Richmond Spiders.

Against the Spiders, Hundley's shooting percentage was poor (only six for 26 from the floor) but it can hardly be taken as a mark against him. He didn't get an easy chance against a UR defense that forced him to use a fadeaway hook and a jump shot from the outside.

And his past records show no sign of a shooting deficiency. Hundley averaged better than 34 points a game as a freshman and hit on better than 50 per cent of his shots in West Virginia's first three games.

In every other department against UR he was something better than all right for a sophomore in his fourth varsity game. He had six rebounds and one extra-special assist. On defense he played tenaciously in a surprising man-for-man alignment that well may be the making of this year's Mountaineer team.

Offensively, he directed the West Virginia operations—with a bit of show that the 6,000-plus fans paid to see. He passed the ball behind his back, he offered the Spiders the ball only to flip it into his other hand when they tried to accept and he faked long overhead passes with his right hand only to wind up with the ball behind his back in his left hand.

But it didn't suffice for one disgruntled fan.

"You ought to see him," he said, "when he doesn't have to tend to business."

Above all, however, Hundley's principal asset seems to be his basketball maturity—his wiseness in the ways of the game.

West Virginia Athletic Director Robert (Red) Brown illustrates it by tapping a finger to his own temple ("smart"). Hundley illustrates it with his work on the floor, performance he has not yet matched in the classroom.

His followers say his slow classroom progress is due to disinterest and not to lack of intelligence. They point to his intelligence in basketball, a game that seems to occupy his every thought.

In one brief display against the Spiders he made at least one believer who went North through the snow and ice to scoff. Freezing the ball with time running out, Hundley dribbled—forwards, backwards and behind his back—untill hemmed in by the Spiders.

Then, without a dribble left, he controlled the ball from his pressing adversaries by rolling it over his shoulders and around his back while trying to distract the enemy by pointing with his free hand in every direction.

With the crowd showing the proper amazement, he heaved the ball some 50 feet in the air and laughed aloud as the gun went off, ending the game, while the ball was still coming down.

In the excitement only Hundley, it seemed, had the presence of mind to know that the game was that near its finish. Even a teammate, Big (6-6) Willie Bergines, had a question after the game.

"What if the clock had said 11 seconds left instead of only one?" he asked.

The kid they call the "Hot Rod" just laughed again.

A likeable boy, despite a "showboat" approach to his sport, Hundley has to be admired, if only for his complete devotion to the one thing—basketball—that has helped him make something of a somewhat confused start on the road of life.

Less than two months ago he was in the hospital, being operated on for a knee injury. He has played in every West Virginia game and went the full 40 minutes against the Spiders.

Unbelievable? Not when you consider that Hundley spent every free moment after his operation conscientiously lifting heavy weights with his injured leg.

He likes the spotlight, certainly, and will never pass up a chance to make the opposition look bad, even silly. Yet when the time comes for seriousness he's prepared.

Hundley followed Richmond Guard Ed Harrison, who had fouled out, to the bench Monday night as the first Mountaineer to congratulate him.

After the game Hundley was asked what he thought of the Spiders.

"Rough, man," said Rod. "Real rough."

COACHING THE PROS IS A CINCH, HE SAYS

By Stanley Frank

From The Saturday Evening Post, February 19, 1955

"I DO ALL RIGHT with the pros, but I couldn't coach a college team," Charley Eckman says. "I don't know enough basketball. Working with a pro line-up full of All-Americans is a cinch, though. What do you have to teach them? How to comb their hair?"

Eckman, the new coach of the Fort Wayne Pistons, will wind up with a blunt instrument etched on his brow if he continues to imply—and prove—that almost anyone can be a mastermind in the National Basketball Association. Such measures seem to be the only recourse left to rivals for cooling off a subversive who has made the racket look too easy. Although Eckman's previous coaching experience was limited to amateur softball, he turned the league upside down the first half of this season with the same personnel that languished in the lower depths last year. For a long time the opposition needed radar to keep within sight of the Pistons. They roared into the back stretch at close to a .700 pace, leading the Minneapolis Lakers, defending champions, by five and a half games in the Western Division.

Eckman has been the most intriguing feature of one of the pleasantest sports surprises of the year. Nobody thought that the team from Fort Wayne, which is by far the smallest town in the N.B.A., would run wild for any part of this season. The league's seven other cities are all, in baseball parlance, either major-league, or Triple-A. Fort Wayne, with a population of less than 140,000, is the only surviving carry-over from the recent past, when pro basketball was largely the game of small Midwestern cities. Its team was a powerhouse in those days as the Fort Wayne Zollner Pistons—bearing the full trade name of the club owner. Since joining the modern big-city league in 1948, however, the Pistons have never made much of a splash until this year.

The fact that Fort Wayne's upsurge coincided with Eckman's installation as coach has been irritating enough to the league's established coaches, but that is not the most unkindest cut. Before he went to Fort Wayne, Eckman was a referee in the N.B.A.—and the hostility of basketball coaches for referees is duplicated only by the antipathy between the mongoose and the cobra. Eckman never lost an argument while he was tooting a whistle, and as a coach, he went right on showing old sparring partners that he still was the boss.

It is a tossup whether Eckman's methods or the results he has achieved are the more striking aspect of the story. There is general agreement that Eckman's predecessor, Paul Birch, operated with the grim intensity of a cop looking for his stolen patrol car, and seemed to go out of his way to antagonize the players and fans. Eckman, a blithe extrovert, acts more like a cheer-leader than a coach.

"Winning is fun," he told the team at the opening practice. "Let's have a lot of fun this year." His light touch is such a refreshing switch from Birch's browbeating that the Pistons are giving him the full measure of their effort and capabilities. That, in essence, appears to be the explanation for the team's early transformation.

"Birch tied the players into knots and tore down their confidence with incessant criticism," says Hilliard Gates, sports announcer for WKJG, in Fort Wayne. "Eckman lets them cut loose and do what comes naturally. They're like a swing band getting a chance to improvise after grinding out dull, long-hair stuff they hated."

Thirty-three-year-old Eckman, the youngest and smallest coach in the league, barely made his high-school basketball team in Baltimore. "I had two handicaps," he says. "No height or talent." Like many frustrated athletes, he is awed by the astonishing skills the pros take for granted.

He roots so strenuously for the team that he loses his voice in every game. At New York he leaped to his feet after a spectacular play against the Knickerbockers and missed the bench on the descent. He landed on the floor and went on screaming ecstatically, "Go! Go! Get more!"

Eckman always got a terrific kick out of basketball as an official, and he sees no reason to change his attitude now that he has a personal stake in the outcome of games. If a player was having a rough night, Referee Eckman would try to relieve the tension in him by saying, "Come on, live a little. Take two foul shots. Be my guest." He swapped gags and amiable insults with fans and newspapermen along the side lines. He gave the customers an extra

fillip by pantomiming the fouls he called, and sometimes, in his
exuberance, he inflicted more punishment on himself than the
offended player had suffered. Eckman was a clown, but he had
fewer hassles with players than any of his colleagues—a reflection
of the confidence in his decisions—and he usually was the coaches'
first choice in their annual rating of officials.

It is characteristic of Eckman that he prefers to talk of his
amusing experiences as a referee rather than discuss his coaching
exploits. Last year, Philadelphia's Joe Fulks, a good-natured giant
who was finishing a glamorous career, stunned one and all by
squawking violently when Eckman called a foul against him in the
final seconds of a nationally televised game. From the stands it
looked as though the six-five Fulks had blown his top and had
every intention of dismembering the five-eight Eckman.

"Stand right here with me, you little squirt," Fulks was saying. "This is the last time my mother down in Kentucky is gonna
see old Joe on TV, and I want to give her a good, long look. Turn
around so the camera can get me on my good side. Now hold still
while I jaw at you. O.K. Now throw me out of the game so I can
act real indignant."

On another occasion Eckman was in the middle of a sticky
situation at Moline, Illinois, cosponsor of the since-disbanded Tri-
Cities Blackhawks. An appeal was made for the Heart Fund before the game, and the fans responded so generously that Eckman
and Max Tabacchi, the other official, helped a crew of pretty girls
collect the coins showered on the court. It was one of those nights
when every close decision went against the home team, and the
crowd began to cast coarse doubts on the integrity and ancestry
of the referees. During a time-out, Tabacchi drew a handkerchief
from his pocket to mop his brown—and to Eckman's horror, a
dollar in small change clattered noisily to the floor.

"Max thought his money might be stolen if he left it in the
locker room, so he took it with him," Eckman explains. "He tied
the change in his handkerchief. The knot must've slipped and the
coins shook loose. The fans thought we had pocketed some of the
money donated to the Heart Fund. Now they were sure we were
robbers—from charity, yet. A hotel could've been furnished with
the chairs and cushions that were thrown at us. We needed a police
escort to get out of town."

There there was a delicate contretemps at El Centro, California,
after the war, when ex-Corporal Eckman needed ready money to

support his wife and three children—he now has four. He went on tour as a referee with the All-American Redheads, a girls' team that played any bunch of men foolish enough to venture into the arena with them. The Redhead center was a six-foot, six-inch misanthrope who committed frightful indignities on male opponents, taking outrageous advantage of the maxim that a gent never slugs a lady in public regardless of the provocation.

"That dame had a build that would make a skinny boy look like Marilyn Monroe," Eckman says reflectively, "but her bony elbows and knees cut guys to ribbons. What a beast!"

After watching the hatchet women in a couple of games, Eckman felt he would lose his union card in humanity if he did not curb her atrocities. He finally called a foul on her when she ran into a man so violently that he was struck in the face with a pass and suffered a broken nose.

"What's the foul for?" she screeched.

"You can't bump into a player and use your—your chest that way," Eckman retorted.

The Redhead was a real pro. Her competitive drive was stronger than her vanity. "Where do you see a chest?" she demanded.

"I'm giving you the benefit of the doubt," Eckman snapped.

The young lady patted Eckman on the head when the fans within earshot stopped whooping hysterically. "That's a great gag, kid," she said. "We'll have to use it tomorrow night."

Referee Eckman always had a penchant for pulling wisecracks. Last season he submitted a report to Maurice Podoloff, president of the NBA, on the progress made by a new referee assigned to work with him. "I believe he will prove satisfactory to you, since I have told him the most important rule to observe in the league," he wrote. "I always instruct a new man to hold the ball so that the people in the stands can read your name on it."

Eckman does not exempt his own sudden prestige as a target for the needle. He shrugs off the hullabaloo over his switch from officiating to coaching, which is so rare that there are few precedents for it in big-time sports. Bill Stewart, former National League baseball umpire, was a hockey referee before he won the Stanley Cup with the Chicago Black Hawks in 1938. Hank O'Day and Georgie Moriarty, also big-league umpires, took fliers at managing, then fled back to their original occupation, where no one ever is second-guessed successfully.

"What's such a big deal about a referee doing a good job on the

other side of the street?" Eckman demanded recently. "Every pro
player can shoot, pass and dribble like he invented the game. If he
wasn't great he wouldn't be up here in the first place. You don't
have to show him anything. It's a breeze compared to coaching in
college. I'd be a stiff there because I was a lousy player myself, and
I don't know enough to teach techniques.

"You hear a lot of talk about strategy. Who's kidding who? In
sixteen years of refereeing, I saw all the hot-shot coaches operate,
and they never showed me a new trick. How could they? Basketball
is a game of spontaneous situations. There are only three or four
basic set plays, because it's impossible to anticipate rebounds or
how the players will be scattered over the court. It's different in
baseball and football, where there's a break in the action before
every play and you can plan your next move. You can't pull a
surprise in pro basketball. You meet every team in the league about
ten times a season, and after watching a player for a couple of years,
you know what he's going to do before he thinks of it himself.

"All the teams are loaded with so many All-Americans it's a
wonder every game doesn't end in a tie. To win consistently, you've
got to make the most of each player's extra talents. That's where
I have an edge on other coaches. As a referee, the outcome meant
nothing to me and I got a more objective look at the players."

A provocative statement. Would Eckman elaborate, please?

"Sure, I'll give you for-instances. I refereed a game at Milwaukee a few years ago when Max Zaslofsky scored a bushel of
points on the pivot play. Zaslofsky is six-two, short as pros go, and
most coaches think only big goons are effective in the pivot, so he
wasn't used there again. I remembered how great he looked in the
pivot that one time, and I told him to try to play whenever the
defensive man was his size. He won three games for us in the first
month of the season.

"Take Frank Brian. Everyone had him tabbed strictly as a
backcourt feeder because that was his function in Birch's deliberate offense. When Brian broke in at Anderson six years ago,
though, he was a helluva man leading a fast break. Knowing that,
I was able to mix up our attack instead of sticking to one style.
George Yardley always had a swell one-handed jump shot, but
Birch had an old-timer's prejudice against it. I gave him the green
light to let 'er go whenever he thought he saw an opening, and
he's doubled his scoring average. Mel Hutchins is driving more
under the basket, the way he used to when I got my first impres-

sion of him as a rookie at Milwaukee. Nobody knows better than
a referee what a beating a center takes, so I'm giving Larry Foust
more rest for a Garrison finish.

"Don't get the idea I'm building myself up as a big brain. I'm
just trying to show that a referee isn't a blind bum who doesn't
know what's going on. Anyone can win with good material. All you
have to do is match up personnel on defense and make substitu-
tions; then sit back and take the bows."

Eckman is oversimplifying the case, of course, for the sake of
getting back at agitators who blasted him when he was a referee,
but there is something in what he says. He admits that every
coach in the league can give him cards and spades in technical
basketball, yet it may be that he sees the game in broader scope
than men who get wrapped up in abstruse maneuvers.

The Pistons' early jump on the field could be traced in large
measure to Eckman's liberal use of substitutes. He was the first
coach to realize that the new N.B.A. rule requiring a team to
shoot within twenty-four seconds after getting possession of the
ball would be a severe drain on the players' endurance. Eckman,
constantly shuttling all ten men on his squad in and out of the
game, ran ragged opponents who were trying to stagger through
forty-eight minutes of almost continues action with six or seven
key operatives.

A typical example of Eckman's tactics was given on December
twenty-third against the Philadelphia Warriors, in a game that
meant a good deal more than just another schedule commitment.
The Warriors had licked the Pistons in three previous meetings,
and Eckman was anxious to scotch notions of a hex that might
undermine his team's confidence. With the score tied at 59-all
going into the final quarter, Eckman took out Foust, his center,
who had outscored Philadelphia's Neil Johnston by 21-14, and
put in Bob Houbregs, a recent acquisition from the disbanded
Baltimore team. Pitting the inexperienced Houbregs against
Johnston, the league's leading scorer for the last two years, had
all the earmarks of a first-class boner. Eckman figured, however,
that a fresh man would pull the cork on Johnston's dwindling
stamina, and that's the way it worked out. Houbregs threw in
eleven points while holding Johnston scoreless, and the Pistons
won, 92-82.

A revealing tip-off on Eckman's effective use of his players is
found in the unusually equal distribution of points among the

Pistons. The same two or three men generally can be expected to lead an amateur or pro team in scoring in any given game. With the Pistons, every man on the squad has had a turn at being high gun except Paul Walther, a defensive specialist.

Eckman has been getting more drive and team spirit from his men than they ever gave another pro coach, a development that began long before the first field goal of the season was registered.

It started last May, when Eckman went on a unique transcontinental sales trip immediately after his appointment. He was selling himself and morale to the players. The team's resistance to him as a rank outsider was intensified by the fact that Andy Phillip, the oldest player, had applied to Fred Zollner, the owner, for the job. Morale was a word the Pistons associated only with payday.

Although Zollner was paying the best salaries in the league after the Boston Celtics—the scale for top-flight Pistons ranged from $9000 to $13,000 for Foust—he was getting less for his money than any other owner. Now we are not intimating that athletes should be kept hungry to make them hustle. We merely are suggesting that spirit is as important a motivating factor as money, even among professionals who play games for a living. The purpose of Eckman's trip was to rehabilitate the spirit that had gone to pot under Birch.

Eckman shrewdly observed protocol on his strange mission. From Baltimore, the first stop on his itinerary was Santa Monica, California, the home of Phillip, dean of the team. "I'd be disappointed, too, in your place," he told Phillip, "but I want you to know I didn't go after the job. Zollner came to me. I need you on my side because you know a helluva lot more basketball than I do, and the other guys look to you as a leader. We've always been friends. I'd like to keep it that way."

In Santa Monica, Eckman also saw Yardley, and he made a phone call to San Francisco to Fred Scolari, a veteran since traded to Boston. He next visited Brian, the second-oldest Piston, in Coushatta, Louisiana. Brian had been nominated by the newspapers as a coaching candidate, and Eckman made a similar appeal for his cooperation. Then he doubled back to New York to see Zaslofsky, a member of the league since its founding in 1946.

The last stop was Fort Wayne, where Foust lives. Eckman traveled some 6000 miles to speak briefly with six players, a tour that paid handsome dividends in the increased mileage he has got from the team.

The key personnel is essentially the same as that which, although playing better than .500 ball, still finished next to last in the Western Division in 1954. The only noteworthy addition to the squad is Dick Rosenthal, a good rookie, but hardly in the class of Frank Selvy, Bob Pettit and Frank Ramsey. There are at least three men in the league who are rated higher at every position than the Piston incumbents, the team's height is below the league average and it plays orthodox basketball. By the players' own testimony, Eckman is the difference in the team.

"The tension is gone," Phillip says. "Charley treats us like mature men who want to win instead of dumb jerks with no pride or ambition. He's as sharp as anyone correcting mistakes, but he doesn't set himself apart from the team. If somebody has an idea that can win a game, he'll adopt it."

Former teammates and employers thought an interview with Max Zaslofsky in a Philadelphia newspaper was a typographical error, when he was quoted as saying, "We don't care who gets the points or who plays a lot. We just want to win and make Charley look good." Zaslofsky, long labeled a self-centered bloke concerned only with the points he scored himself, was traded in successive seasons by New York, Baltimore and Milwaukee before he landed with Fort Wayne.

"I'd heard all the stories that Zaslofsky was just for Max," Eckman confides. "Maybe he isn't a rah-rah boy. How could he be, after nine years in this rat race? I put myself in his place. Max isn't the big star he was a few years ago. He thinks his job is in danger if he doesn't play regularly. If you pat him on the back and tell him you're saving him for a crucial spot, he won't give you any trouble. Show Max a little consideration and he's no headache. Handling a pro basketball team is like any other job. You'll do fine if you know how to get along with people."

That is Eckman's chief asset and he has been exploiting it ever since he began to scramble for a living at the age of fourteen. After the death of his father, who had been gassed in World War I, Charley worked at night on a laundry truck to help support his mother. During the day he attended Baltimore City College, a high school, and played on the baseball and basketball teams, but his ingratiating personality was a springboard to easier money when he was seventeen. He started to referee basketball games in the CYO and Municipal leagues, and his work was so satisfactory that presently he was getting nineteen assignments a week at two dollars apiece.

"I'll never forget my mother's bewildered look when I dumped thirty-eight dollar bills in her lap," he recalls.

" 'Why,' she said, 'this is more than your father ever made in the grocery store.' It was a long time since she'd seen so much money in one lump. My father was an invalid for six years before he died, and we had to get along on his Government pension of ninety-five dollars a month. My mother's remark gave me a new slant on refereeing as a career. I dreamed up stunts to make games dramatic and entertaining for the fans. Let's face it. I hammed it up calling fouls, but the fans seemed to like it and I got a lot of work."

Charley also fancied himself a baseball player, and following graduation from high school in 1940, he signed with Mooresville, North Carolina, as an infielder. A .200 batting average against Class D pitching in the North Carolina State League disabused him of that foolish notion, but he was offered a contract for the next season. In those early days of the military draft, ball clubs had use for all youths who bore a vague resemblance to professionals and were willing to work for $125 a month. Charley was a great one for laughing it up and keeping the team's morale higher than its standing in the league, but the management thought his enthusiasm was an excessive expense when he was side-lined by a leg injury.

He returned to Baltimore with another Mrs. Eckman to support on the twenty-nine dollars a week he earned as a stock clerk. He had married Wilma Howard, a Mooresville girl. The outbreak of war eased the financial strain temporarily. He was put in charge of the Westinghouse Company's local storerooms at eighty-five dollars a week, and inflation jacked up his basketball fees to a giddy $7.50 a game.

In 1942, Eckman enlisted in the Signal Corps and was sent to a civilian code school at night, an arrangement that permitted him to stay on at Westinghouse and referee on weekends. When he was called up for active Army duty eight months later, he transferred to the Air Force for pilot training, but he washed out of the course and finished the war as a physical instructor at Yuma, Arizona. There, after his discharge in 1945, Eckman had brief preparation for his present eminence. He organized an amateur softball league and was the playing manager of the stalwarts representing La Mesa

Stables. "Remember to mention we won the championship," he says. "I don't want people to think I'm a green pea in the masterminding department."

Basketball officiating was Eckman's meal ticket as he drifted from dispatching buses to managing a poolroom in Yuma. The steady jobs he was qualified to hold were no more attractive when he moved back to Baltimore with his expanding family. He was an umpire in the Tri-State League, but the working conditions were so grubby that he quit after three weeks. Forced to return to Westinghouse in a subordinate position, Eckman would have been in severe straits without the money he picked up refereeing high-school and college games. His competency brought a staff appointment in the pro league in 1947, and two years later his worries further were relieved when he was hired as a sales-tax investigator for the state of Maryland.

The recent improbable turn of events dates back to a certain night in Milwaukee in the winter of 1951. A heavy snowstorm had stalled transportation after a double-header in Milwaukee, and a group of basketball people, including the Fort Wayne owner, Fred Zollner, met around a convivial watering hole in the Schroeder Hotel. George Mikan, who had just scored twenty-seven points, was in a benign mood. "That wasn't a bad game you worked to-night," he said condescendingly to Eckman.

"I called a better game than you big oafs played," Eckman snapped. "Some day I'd like to coach you monkeys and teach you new tricks."

"It was one of those flip answers Eckman always pops," Fred Zollner relates now, "but something in his voice convinced me he was serious. I wasn't in the market for a coach. Birch had just signed a three-year contract, and there were no complaints against him yet. I filed Eckman's crack for future reference. The more I thought of it the more sense it made. If I ever needed a new coach I would choose someone thoroughly familiar with the league, and a referee knew the players and the styles of the teams as well as anyone.

"During the next two years I made a point of bumping into Eckman and chatting with him. He didn't suspect I was scouting him. I discussed everything except basketball to get an idea of his philosophy and attitude toward people. I listened to players talk in the locker room and found they all respected him."

Meanwhile, relations between Birch and the Pistons deteriorated so badly last year that Zollner, the head of a manufacturing business that grosses $14,000,000 a year, had to fly to Minneapolis to avert an open rebellion. The situation improved after Birch heard the players air their grievances. The team won five straight, but then Birch alienated the men all over again. Fort Wayne fans staged a testimonial game for Dike Eddleman, but Birch did not use him until the last four minutes. Zaslofsky twice was yanked from a game in Miami after playing thirty seconds before a large delegation of tourists from New York, his home town. "What am I, a Yo-yo?" the incensed Zaslofsky yelled at Birch.

"I decided by midseason to get rid of Birch," Zollner says, "but I didn't want to make the change then because anyone else would have been a stand-in for Eckman. I couldn't approach him. It would have been unethical while he still was refereeing games involving my team."

When the two finally did get together, the news that Eckman had signed a three-year contract to coach the Pistons can be described conservatively as a bombshell in Fort Wayne. Zollner previously had announced that Birch's replacement would be a man who had been associated with the N.B.A. for many years, and everyone assumed he was negotiating with an established coach or a veteran player. The reaction to Eckman's appointment was decidedly cool, but he broke the ice with a disarming quip at a boosters' dinner. "I've been booed by the best fans in the world," he said. "I hope you were among them."

The Pistons' spectacular opening surge under Eckman has posed a curious dilemma that is touching off tremors throughout the still-struggling N.B.A., which has yet to get on as stable a footing as the baseball and football big leagues. Indiana is the traditional hotbed of basketball, and Fort Wayne has been drawing more than 4000 admissions at home games. A special "Appreciation Day" in January brought out 6653. This is good attendance in relation to population—better than the turnouts in some of the much larger cities. But, still, league owners are beginning to wonder whether such a small city ever can do right by a big-league franchise. There are several straws in the wind indicating that Zollner doubts it too.

Wealthy sports nuts absorb losses in the hope of being identified with a winner, but Zollner is beyond that stage. He was the industrial sports tycoon of America ten years ago, when basketball and softball teams representing his company captured world championships.

The basketball team topped the old National League from 1943 to 1945, and the softball outfit had the remarkable record of 1253 victories in 1442 games, an average of .869 against all comers in the United States and Canada. The team was disbanded last September, a victim of major-league baseball broadcasts that killed interest. The $150,000 softball stadium that Zollner built will be used in the future by the Knothole Gang, now his favorite community project, with a membership of 31,000 children.

Zolner has trimmed his basketball budget so sharply that it is clear he no longer is lavishing money on the Pistons as a civic enterprise. He willingly accepted inevitable deficits when the team played in the North Side High School gym, which accommodated only 3800 spectators. Since 1952 the Pistons have been playing in the new Memorial Coliseum, with a capacity of 9500, and Zollner is miffed that a winning team is not drawing consistently the 4700 admissions a game he needs to break even.

"I've dropped more than three hundred thousand dollars in pro basketball during the last fifteen years," he said a few weeks ago. "It never bothered me until this season. I'll be honest and admit the team does not cost me a nickel personally. I write off the loss as a tax deduction for consumer advertising. I'll also concede the team is priceless publicity for my company. It offends me as a businessman, though, to lose money with a good product offered in fine facilities."

We asked Zollner point-blank if he was thinking of abandoning the franchise. He pondered the question and corrected a scribbled statement before he answered. "I expect to continue basketball during my reasonably active life. Fort Wayne is my home town, and I intend to play as many home games as the community wants. It may be, however, that a community of this size cannot support more than one home game a week. In that event, it may be necessary to review the situation."

Charley Eckman was too far up in the clouds last month to be disturbed by rumblings of an upheaval at Fort Wayne. The crowded Eckman household was jumping with the master's ebullience. "We're having the time of our lives," Mrs. Eckman said. "I love being able to root my head off for the Pistons. I always had to watch games like a bump on a log because people would get funny ideas if a referee's wife was partial to one side. Charley's like a kid with a new toy. I know coaching must be more of a strain than refereeing, but he never shows it."

"This is a swell setup," twelve-year-old Barry agreed. "When pop wins we collect a little." Handing out quarters regularly to four kids runs into money, but Eckman feels like a millionaire on a salary of $7500.

"We're really living it up," he chortled as his Pistons rode high. "We've got meat on the table every night, and my tigers are tearing the opposition to pieces. I'm too young to get an ulcer worrying how long it will keep up. If I fall on my kisser, I can always go back to blowing the whistle. One way or another, I'll be around stirring up excitement."

kids runs into money, but Eckman feels like a million on his

Racing

THE COMET FROM CALIFORNIA

By Earl Ruby

From The Louisville (Ky.) Courier-Journal, May 8, 1955

Copyright, 1955, The Courier-Journal

THUNDER ROLLED and exploded. Lightning flashed in vivid streaks
across a gray sky. Rain whipped down from the north. And a comet
from California came whirling down the stretch.

It was Swaps by a length and a half ahead of Nashua, the favorite
in the richest and perhaps the truest-run Kentucky Derby of them
all.

The gates housing the 10 starters at the head of the stretch flew
open less than a minute after the racers entered their stalls.

Nashua came charging out in short, choppy strides. Trim Destiny and Honey's Alibi were right with him. They seemed to be
volunteering to set the early pace and that suited Willie Shoemaker, astride Swaps.

Eddie Arcaro on Nashua quickly got his horse in hand. Honey's
Alibi wasn't serious. But Trim Destiny was making a run for it.

Willie started in eighth post position and had to find a route to
the rail without losing any ground.

Hunched like a bug on the broad shoulders of the first California-
bred colt to win since Morvich in 1922, Shoemaker barreled
straight down the stretch past the grandstand, trailing the game
upstart by a length.

He rounded the clubhouse turn still trailing. Then he looked up
and saw daylight ahead—nothing between him and the rail at the
head of the back stretch.

Trim Destiny still was on the inside, but fast losing leg. Arcaro
was holding Nashua to a hard, steady pace, but not pushing for an
opening to move up from third.

Shoemaker sped straight for the rail. Trim Destiny fell back and
Nashua assumed second position. They raced down the back
stretch and into the far turn.

236

Shoemaker hugged the rail so tight you'll probably find white-wash on his left boot this morning. He rounded the last turn. He heard the roar of the crowd ahead—and the pounding of Nashua coming up behind.

Out of the corner of his eye he saw the favorite and Arcaro edging up almost even.

It was now or never. It was time to find out what he was riding —a champion or a—.

At that moment Swaps caught sight of the white starting gate, which had been pulled just off the track to the left.

Being, as his trainer Meshach Tenney said, a horse that "spooks" easy, Swaps shied out to the right. He might have shied right out of the race, but for quick, firm handling by Shoemaker.

Arcaro saw the leader swerve and thought this was it. This was the opening he had sat back and waited for. He clucked to Nashua and swung his whip hard.

The fleet winner of the Wood Memorial, sweat streaming down his flanks, responded quickly. In a mighty effort he drew even with the swerving Swaps.

"They are head and head coming into the stretch!" cried the announcer.

"Nashua's making his move," rippled along the rows of writers in the press box.

Every binocular held shakily on the thudding pair.

"I believe he's going to make it," cried an Eastern writer.

Shoemaker barked a sharp command to the iron son of Khaled and swung his whip.

Swaps took off like a comet and streaked down the stretch and across the finish line. He won pulling away—pulling away from the greatest money winning horse ever to come to the Derby.

Nashua and Arcaro, who caused winter books to close early because of their nation-wide popularity, were beaten a full length and a half. Summer Tan was third, more than six lengths behind Nashua, and Racing Fool fourth. Then followed Jean's Joe, Flying Fury, Honey's Alibi, Blue Lem, Nabesna and Trim Destiny.

The dark day, threatening cloudburst, popularity of the trainer and a record of solid racing and training, made Swaps second favorite. The mutuel return of $7.60, $3.40 and $2.60 was less than early backers anticipated.

Before the race trainer Tenney let Swaps smell a faded rose from Morvich's blanket of roses—a good luck charm from an admirer.

But Tenney and Owner Rex Ellsworth don't believe in charms. . . . Devout members of the Mormon Church, both believe the Lord looks after those who look after themselves.

Ellsworth volunteered for three years of missionary work for his church in South Africa some years back.

While there he sought out and met H. H. Aga Khan, a fabulous horse breeder.

From Aga Khan he bought Khaled. . . From Khaled came Swaps. From two years of earnest, honest training and racing has come one of the fourth fastest Derbies ever run—and a brilliant new champion.

THE COOK WAS FROM RICHMOND, KY.

By Red Smith

From The New York Herald Tribune, December 18, 1955

NASHUA WEIGHS 1,200 pounds, give or take an exercise boy, and stands second to Citation in the Dun & Bradstreet ratings of four-legged capitalists. At $1,251,200, he sold for $1,042.67 a pound, which puts him ahead of marinated larks' wings and right behind Jackie Gleason in the international meat market. He also ran second to Swaps in the Kentucky Derby. Just a hard-luck horse.

Ever since the bid of Leslie Combs and his friends was opened and read with bugging eyes down at the Hanover Bank, people have been asking one question: "Can any horse be worth a million and a quarter dollars?" (They always ignore the addition $1,200, which is $1 a pound.)

The answer is that Les Combs' Spendthrift Farm was named for a horse, not an idiosyncracy. Spendthrift is a gracious domicile outside Lexington, celebrated for the best mint juleps in Kentucky and fodder so succulent that on one memorable occasion a guest, finishing his third wedge of pecan pie, offered 5 to 2 that the cook had to be a Northerner.

Les Combs did not acquire these creature comforts by pouring silver into gopher holes. He can estimate the potential value of a horse, and it is not unlikely that his figuring went something like this:

Sound as he is, big and muscular and presumably able to carry the weight he will get in handicaps, Nashua might win another half-million on the track, leaving $751,200 to be picked up in more leisurely style. Bred to twenty-five mares a year at a fee of $10,000, he would earn $750,000 in three years, before his get had a chance to demonstrate whether he was good at getting winners.

That would pay off all save $1,200 of the original investment, which could be picked up at Sunshine Park in a claiming race for eight-year-olds and up. Meanwhile, there'd always be the chance for a member of the syndicate to get a horse by Nashua that would win a million on his own.

So much for finance. Published discussion of Nashua's fertility

—nobody knows whether he has any, since no test has been made— has led laymen to inquire about the love life of thoroughbreds. If a single answer could be made to all their questions, it would be as follows: It varies.

After the triple-crown winner, Assault, was retired to stud and proved sterile—it was not for want of trying, for he was well named—Max Hirsch, his trainer, remarked casually that this was a trait which ran in Assault's family. A man who heard him say this in a front box at Jamaica got all the way up to the press box before he was struck by the biological import of this case of inherited sterility.

When Tom Fool was retired to stud at the age of four, he displayed alarming symptoms of misogyny. They'd introduce him to a comely mare, and he'd shrug his sleek bay shoulders and go down to play pool with the boys. He, too, was aptly named.

Tom Fool was getting a reputation on the banks of Elkhorn Creek as "the celebrated celibate," but after a while he got over his boyish diffidence. Some of his progeny ought to be showing up on the track in 1957.

On the subject of testing a horse for fertility, there is a classic tale that has been told here before, but not lately. It concerns Calumet Farm's light-headed, swift-footed Whirlaway, which was retired from racing in midsummer of 1943. Spring is the breeding season for race horses, so it was not planned to open Whirlaway's court until 1944.

However, it was deemed advisable to test him for fertility. Ordinarily a cold-blooded mare is drafted for this purpose, but it happened that a farmer down the Versailles Pike had a thoroughbred mare named Mary V., possessed of a roving eye. Ostensibly to make a fertility test, she was introduced to Whirlaway in the autumn of 1943, apparently without the knowledge or consent of his owner, Warren Wright.

A child was born of this clandestine union the following fall, and Mr. Wright was fit to be tied. Under the rule establishing Jan. 1 as the universal birthday for thoroughbreds, the foal was due to become a year old in a matter of weeks after his birth, so, of course, if he ever got to the races he'd always be in with horses almost a year more mature than he. Wright didn't want that to happen to Whirlaway's first son.

The laird of Calumet fired farm help right and left, cut off diplomatic relations with the owner of Mary V. and, it was said, vowed that he wouldn't permit the foal to be registered, though actually he had no authority there. The commotion roused the attention of Charles Fisher, the automobile tycoon of Dixiana Farm, who had given Mary V. to the farmer in the first place. Mr. Fisher had as much money as Mr. Wright, so Whirlaway's love child was registered under the name, First Whirl.

It was taken for granted that First Whirl would be withheld from the races as a two-year-old and given a chance to grow up. He must have matured rapidly, however, for during the autumn meeting at Keeneland, the name of First Whirl appeared in the chart on a two-year-old race.

He trailed into the stretch, then poured on coal and won going away, just like his old man. That was the last ever heard of him here.

COWBOY RACE KINGS

By Marshall Smith

Courtesy LIFE Magazine, August 9, 1955

Copyright, 1955, Time, Inc.

THE EXCITEMENT which precedes those rare occasions when two superb horses meet by special appointment has already set in. It will reach a peak, barring an accident or an act of God, on the afternoon of Aug. 31 when the two contestants, Swaps and Nashua, have it out on a winner-take-all basis for $100,000 at Washington Park race track near Chicago.

Of the two horses Nashua is in the familiar tradition of a plush eastern stable and a plush eastern owner, the wealthy New York financier William Woodward Jr. But Swaps is a strictly unorthodox horse, raised without fanfare on a far from splendid ranch by a man who breaks all the most cherished traditions of bigtime racing, and who even goes out on a limb before a big race. When the Swaps-Nashua match was announced, Swaps' owner said candidly, "I just hope it doesn't come up to a big rainstorm. Then people would say we didn't win fair and square and we'd have to do it all over again."

This man is Rex Ellsworth, a tall, lean, taciturn and extremely shrewd ex-cowboy from Arizona. He is listed as the owner of Swaps and 230 other Thoroughbred horses which, together with two ranches near Chino, Calif. totaling 380 acres, are worth close to $5 million. But in the approved manner of the old West, Ellsworth has a side-kick, an equally lean but shorter Arizona cowboy named Meshach Tenney, who has been with Ellsworth even since the days when they roped calves and broke wild horses together in the Gila Valley. Tenney has a share in the ranches and race horses and the two are actually partners, even though they have never bothered with a written agreement. Tenney is the trainer for Swaps and all the other racers, and the two men think almost identically—especially on the subject of how to win races.

They outrage all the romantic notions that kings and milkmen and people from Kentucky have about horses. After riding hundreds of them for thousands of hours across lonely wastes and trying to figure out what makes them tick, they are convinced that

242

horses are not only unaffectionate but unintelligent. "I just know for sure that they are stupid," says Ellsworth.

"They are dumber than a dog or even a mule," he said. "A dog will dig to water where a horse will stand there and choke to death, and if a mule gets hung up in a wire fence he will wait for help where a horse will tear its leg off trying to get loose. Horses do things only because they are too dumb to figure out a way not to do them. When they nicker it is because that lump of sugar is there. They cannot recognize people by sight. A mare cannot even recognize her own foal without smelling it. The most you can say for them is that they like the company of humans and other horses. They get lonesome—but they will slash and kick and bite each other over a handful of feed or a drink of water."

Ellsworth and Tenney handle their high-priced stock in an efficient impersonal way with no frills or folderol. Unlike other race-horse people they personally break their own yearlings, maneuvering their trained cow ponies with one hand while teaching the young Thoroughbred galloping alongside to respond to the reins with the other. All the while, as they stop, start, wheel and turn, kicking up a suffocating cloud of dust, a whip flicks back and forth, sharply emphasizing the lesson.

When they finish, the horse is thoroughly and completely disciplined. As a result Ellsworth and Tenney have only well-behaved, tractable Thoroughbreds in their barn. This enables them to do strange and unusual things. Instead of walking their horses for half an hour after a workout as other stables do, they put a boy on them bareback and jog them five times around a figure 8 ring. They think the traditional cooling-off method is just plain unnecessary. Their method saves time and money, both of which Ellsworth and Tenney respect. If a horse should step out of line, he gets the equivalent of a quick trip to the woodshed and promptly snaps back into line.

The two men discipline themselves as well as their horses. Being Mormons, they do not drink coffee, tea or alcoholic beverages. They do not touch tobacco or take the name of the Lord in vain. Although they have been rubbing elbows with pari-mutuel machines for years, they have never placed a bet on a horse. Ellsworth laughs this off by saying, "I can't afford to bet on horses. I've got to feed them."

Their one vice is an irresistible desire to be photographed in the winner's circle along with one of their horses. It is a weakness which they have been exposed to constantly this year, having won 55 races and more than half a million dollars. But up until the moment that the camera clicks they show admirable restraint. During a race they sit like stone figures with binoculars glued to their eyes, the two most composed people in the entire grandstand.

After one of his horses, El Drag, set a new world record for seven furlongs at Hollywood Park this spring, Tenney showed no undue emotion. "People can't understand why I don't come back grinning if I win and cussing if I lose," he said. "If the horse runs his best, that's all that matters."

The day before the $100,000 California stakes, with Swaps' regular jockey unavailable and a decision to be made on whether to run him or not, Meshach Tenney finished his morning chores at the barn with a relaxed shrug.

"It's peaceful here," he said. "I sleep here sometimes. I hate hotels. Don't like the smell of them." He wore spurs, a string tie of bright blue, a fringed buckskin jacket and cowhide leggings. "Rex Ellsworth made these for me," he said, pointing to the leggings. "He learned leather work back in Arizona, and he makes them better than anybody else. Made this jacket too. I found me a jacket that fit 20 years ago and he's been cutting from the pattern ever since. He made that saddle over there. It's his own design. Keeps me from getting bowlegged."

Tenney excused himself and sauntered toward the tack room on unbowed legs. "I've got to tack on a shoe," he explained. He tied on a blacksmith's apron which he said Rex made and, jamming a stalljack into the dirt, began hammering on a horseshoe. He explained that Rex did most of the shoeing until he got too busy running the ranch. Tenney fitted the shoe carefully to a hoof, drove the nails and rasped them smooth.

Shoeing horses is a task that other race horse people leave to blacksmiths. The insistence of Ellsworth and Tenney on doing it themselves has kept alive a smoldering war with the powerful race track blacksmith union. In Chicago one year, when the smithy threatened to go on strike because of them, the Washington Park management pleaded with them to desist. They refused to stop shoeing but offered to withdraw their horses from the races. They had reasons other than saving the $15 blacksmith fee: "We take pains with a shoe where the others are hurrying to get on to the next horse."

But basically the two men just like doing with their two hands everything there is to do with a horse. "I enjoy every nail I drive, every lick I hit. I can't get on my pony enough or manipulate him enough, no matter how tired I get," says Tenney. Ellsworth feels the same way.

The bond between Rex Ellsworth and Meshach Tenney amounts to more than a deep-set obsession with horses. In trying to explain it Ellsworth fumbled for words and then said simply, "If Meshach needed my right arm, I would give it to him." They were born in the same year, in 1907, Ellsworth being one day older. They share a common heritage in that their fathers, both devout Mormons, migrated south from Utah.

At the age of 8 Tenney came to live with the Ellsworths on their ranch near Safford, Ariz. He and Rex went to school together and sat in the same classroom. They inhabited a tract of mesquite and cactus which began six miles south of the Ellsworth home and extended for another 20 down the long, dry San Simon wash.

The horses on the Ellsworth ranch were about as wild as horses ever get. Range-bred, they were allowed to run free in the hills for six or seven years before being touched by human hands. In the dusty corral by the bunkhouse, battles raged periodically between wild horses and men in leggings and spurs who looked limber in the saddle and stuck there despite all the pitching and squealing and fishtailing. By the time Rex Ellsworth was 16 he had won a hundred such battles. "I was thrown a time or two," he admits, "but the horse had to work at it."

No matter how tractable a horse seemed, Ellsworth and Tenney learned never to grow careless around one. "Horses have no sentiment, no reasoning power whatever, just instinct," says Ellsworth, "and their instinct is unpredictable."

At 17 Rex Ellsworth took charge of his father's cow outfit with Tenney as his first assistant. His father had land and cattle but never had much actual cash. They were running about 1,000 head on the open range where cattle can roam at will. At roundup time Rex's younger brothers, Reed and Heber, came out to help. They killed and cooked their own beef, hanging it outside at night and putting it in a bedroll by day to keep it from spoiling. They rode up to 30 or 40 miles a day, a chore hard on men and brutal on horses.

A horse rested four days for every day it worked, and with a rider using a different horse each day it was easy to spot the advantage of a fast pony over a slow one. A fast one ran and caught cattle more easily and consequently did not wear out so fast. While Meshach and the others joked and argued about which horses were faster, Rex, who had bigger dreams, envisioned a range full of horses that could fly. He became hipped on the subject of breeding faster horses. He subscribed to *The Blood-Horse,* a publication devoted to the breeding of Thoroughbreds, not with any idea of raising race horses but of crossing Thoroughbreds with range stock to get faster cow ponies.

On his long rides he sketched a mental picture of what a horse should look like. It had to be long, high and wide—long and high for a big, ground-eating stride, wide in the hindquarters for power. It had to have long, straight, driving hind legs and low hocks and knees. From experience on the range he wanted no calf-kneed horses; they went limber after two or three hours' work and began stumbling. "I've seen many a man hang his saddle on a tree and walk home because his horse fell," he said. "I did it once myself. There's no hitch-hiking out there."

Rex Ellsworth had no chance to put his theories into practice before getting a call that comes to all able and willing young Mormon men. At 19, a few months after marrying Nola Ferrin, he was told by the bishop that he was to go on a mission teaching the gospel and making converts. "I like to fainted," he said when he heard that South Africa was his destination. In the summer of 1927, paying his own expenses, he set out for Cape Town.

In South Africa he made his calls on a bicycle, which to a cowboy was almost as humiliating as walking. As an elder of the Mormon Church he blessed babies, baptized adults, presided at wakes and weddings and moved from house to house hopefully trying to interest people in God.

When he wasn't worrying about saving people's souls he was crystallizing plans for the improvement of cow horses. When he returned to Arizona after three years, his mission completed, he was ready to put the plans to work. Meshach Tenney, who had served his two-year mission in Colorado, came back to fall into step beside Ellsworth. They borrowed a Thoroughbred stallion from the U. S. Army Remount Branch and crossed him with wild range stock.

The results were exciting. They got trimmer, obviously faster foals which turned out to be ideal cow horses. This helped them financially at a time when Ellsworth was making only $50 a month and board as foreman and Tenney was earning only $40 and board as cowhand. Because of their skill with a rope and the excellence of their mounts, they picked up prize money in rodeos at places like Pima and Thatcher.

They shunned the bucking events simply because they had no faith in official red tape. "I never compete in anything left to the opinion of judges, where there is no line to run to, no clock to go by," said Ellsworth. But when they paid $2 to enter the calf-roping contest one of them invariably took home the $60 first prize. When they joined forces in the team tying event—Ellsworth going for the head with his rope and Tenney for the heels—they were unbeatable.

The final turning point in Ellsworth's dream of fast horses came in 1933. He and his brother Heber had been talking about going into racing, and that spring Heber, returning from his honeymoon trip to Kentucky, brought back a Thoroughbred brood mare. That fall Ellsworth and Heber pooled all their ready cash, about $625, and headed for Lexington, Ky. in a dilapidated Ford truck.

At the fall sales in Lexington they could not afford to buy brood mares on their racing record because performance was too expensive a standard. The pedigree standard was less expensive but still beyond their meager bankroll. So they bought by the only standard they could afford, conformation, using the length-side-height-and-straight-legs rule that Rex had devised back on the range. They paid $50 for this mare, $75 for that one, buying eight in all. They put them in the truck and headed for Arizona, stopping at every lumber yard along the way to rebuild the rickety partitions the mares kept kicking out.

When they got home there was trouble. Their father, a man of strict conscience and Puritan principles, was aghast at the thought of his sons getting mixed up with race horses. A storm stirred in the Ellsworth household with Will Ellsworth losing his temper and his sons standing their ground. The argument rumbled on for years with Rex maintaining that if a carpenter built a saloon he was not responsible for the whisky sold in it.

"It isn't my fault," he said, "if people bet on race horses I raise."

But he was not going to raise any race horses without being able to breed his mares, and there was no suitable stud in all of Arizona. He circled back to Kentucky to shop for a bargain in stallions. He found one for $1,250, a ridiculous price for good horseflesh even during the Depression, only he did not have even that much money. He told the man he would be back. Meshach Tenney mortgaged everything he had, a herd of heifers, to help raise $600. His brothers kicked in what they had and Rex went back to claim his stud, a well-put-together gray named Silver Cord.

"I've been on borrowed money ever since," he confesses. Since the day he bred his first Thoroughbred horse he has been on a financial tightrope that would have scared anybody but a seasoned speculator. As the operator of an expanding cattle business, he carried bank loans up to $350,000 on his herds. Sometimes the cattle carried the race horses and once, when the bottom fell out of the beef market, the horses picked up the slack and carried the cattle. But his cash on hand never caught up with what he owed, mostly because Ellsworth never stopped buying more brood mares.

His first stud, Silver Cord, was also the first that ever raced for him. He ran at the fairgrounds in Phoenix the day Meshach Tenney was married and won by four lengths. Spring Flower, one of the mares that Ellsworth had brought back from his first trip to Kentucky, turned out to be a superior dam whose foals won some 25 races. "Every foal she threw was a flying machine," her owner says respectfully.

Ellsworth Sr.'s protests were beginning to die down by 1946 when U-Time swept everything before her and won almost $100,-000. It was a bad year for cattle and what she and the rest of the stable won hardly made up the deficit at the ranch. But when Movie Magnate Louis B. Mayer offered Ellsworth $100,000 for her, it was his father who stepped into the breach and said, "No, son, you can't sell her." Rex's father might not approve of racing, but he could not bear to sell a great horse.

Ellsworth's theories on breeding fast horses, put into operation on a shoestring, took a costly turn nine years ago. He felt that he had to have a super stallion, one with perfect conformation, a royal pedigree and a fine racing record. No such animal was for sale in the U. S. His first stop was a bank in Denver where he explained that he wanted to borrow $100,000. When they asked him why, he said truthfully, "I want to buy a horse." He got the money, with his ranch as collateral, and headed for Europe with his brother Heber. They inspected and turned down eight stallions in France and even more in England.

In Paris they met Prince Aly Khan, proprietor along with his father, the Aga Khan, of the finest blooded horses on earth. "They showed up to look at horses," said Prince Aly. "They looked so funny in their big cowboy hats. Well, I thought they had nice faces.

I was going to Ireland and I said to myself here are these two nice chaps wandering around in big hats like a couple of cowboys, so I asked them to come with me. They spent a few days with me and looked at my horses."

Ellsworth looked at one of them, a fine hunk of horse known as Khaled, for only two minutes and asked, "How much?" The prince said $160,000 and Ellsworth looked again just to make sure. The horse was without a fault. He bought Khaled but told the prince that he had to go home "and rustle up another $60,000." He went home and pried the additional money out of the banks.

Khaled was shipped to the ranch near Chino, Calif., which Ellsworth had just bought, also on borrowed money. It was a startling change from the Aga Khan's sumptuous show place in Ireland. The country was dull brown rather than green and no money was spent on luxuries, such as paint to keep the place looking presentable. All Ellsworth's time and money went into making it look like the Chicago stockyards with its efficient but unlovely system of pens and runways.

There was one expensive innovation which Ellsworth dreamed up himself and which he believes brings his horses to early maturity so that by the time they are 3-year-olds they are as strong as 4- or 5-year-olds. This is a machine, a monstrous 90-foot-high maze of cogs and conveyors known as the "feed mill." Ellsworth figured out by trial and error what a horse should eat, built a smaller test machine and then had the monster designed by an engineer and put together by a contractor. Worked by push-button, it measures ingredients, chops hay, mashes grain, removes dust, extricates bits of baling wire and dishes out a scientific mixture of corn, barley, bran, alfalfa, oats, linseed meal, de-worming powder, molasses and even kelp, which Ellsworth says is full of valuable minerals. Ellsworth now feeds his formulas into the machine as though it were an electric brain.

There are economies which make up for big expenses like the feed mill. At the track Tenney uses only half as much straw as other stables, believing that lush straw bedding a foot deep keeps the air from circulating around a horse's feet. The big saving is in stable help. Where other stables have one man for every three horses Tenney has one for every 10. "People think that horses are people," says Tenney. "They aren't people, they're horses. Horses are 10 times as tough as people."

When Khaled had produced four crops of foals he had paid for himself. In 1952 he was the country's leading sire of 2-year-olds and among his fifth crop was a chestnut colt which looked fine physically but seemed in danger of never racing for lack of a name. Three times Ellsworth sent in names for him only to have them rejected because they were already taken. Ellsworth and Tenney and their families were sitting around swapping ideas for the nameless waif when somebody suggested calling him Swaps—and it stuck.

Swaps, the horse that lifted the mortgage, started out modestly winning three of his first six races. He got a case of influenza last year and then an infected foot. Blacksmith Tenney put a special pad between the shoe and the hoof, packing it with disinfectant. The horse seemed to be more tolerant of human beings than other horses and equipped with more intelligence. He seemed to grow up suddenly as he turned 3, filling out his long, high, wide frame. He has won all his races as a 3-year-old, including the Kentucky and Santa Anita derbies, but this has not caused Ellsworth or Tenney to show any sentiment toward him.

"Swaps wouldn't wink his eye for me if he didn't have to," says Tenney, but he could not help noticing with pride how readily Swaps oriented himself on his first train ride en route from California to the Kentucky Derby. He sniffed around the railroad car, investigating the noise and vibration, then lay down and went to sleep, leaving the cow pony that was brought along as company to squeal and thrash around.

For two weeks before the Derby, Tenney cat-napped in Swaps' stall at night—not for sentiment's sake but just to make sure nobody tampered with him. On the big day at Churchill Downs he ran away from Nashua, the pride of the east, while Ellsworth and Tenney sat stoically behind their field glasses. After making note of the fact they were $108,400 richer, a help toward paying off some of the mortgage, they had their pictures taken with Swaps and then Meshach Tenney said with a casual grin, "Well, that's the Kentucky Derby."

One of the few times that Ellsworth or Tenney has shown anything but a poker face during a race was one month later at Hollywood Park. Swaps, a young 3-year-old, was stepping far out of his division to face the classiest old pros on the West Coast in another $100,000 race. His regular rider, Willie Shoemaker, had been suspended and his substitute, Dave Erb, had been given explicit instructions to hold Swaps back. When Erb followed orders too literally and Swaps came by the stands the first time throwing his head and fighting to run, the blood drained from Ellsworth's face and he became deathly pale. He began pounding the rail with his fists and finally shouted, "Let him go! Let him go!"

As if some hidden transmitter had got the message through, the jockey eased his hold and the horse settled into a smooth, powerful stride. He caught the leader at exactly the right time and, taking the lead in the stretch, won under wraps. Without ever being touched by the whip, Swaps had not only humbled older, more experienced horses but had set a new world's record of 1:40 2/5 for 1 1/16th mile.

All things considered, it was one of the greatest races ever run by a horse on the North American continent. As a result Ellsworth is relatively calm about the match race with Nashua this month. "We feel kind of confident that we have quite a bit the best horse," he says. "I guess Nashua will try to push us a bit early. We've been pushed before. Any horse that's ever pushed us has wilted."

But Ellsworth has other things to interest him besides the match race. One is Swaps' full brother, a 2-year-old named Like Magic, who is better right now than Swaps was a year ago. Next year, if all goes well, Ellsworth doesn't see how Like Magic can miss winning the Kentucky Derby.

But the only foal ever born that turns Ellsworth to jelly inside is Swaps' 3-month-old youngest brother. Every time Ellsworth sees him he gets excited and starts jabbering like a doting parent. He points to the bulging quarters and the slope of the pastern, the straight legs and beautiful balance. He insists that anybody could study this colt forever without finding a blemish, and he finishes by saying, "If anybody else owned this horse it would kill me."

WEEP FOR THE WINNER

By Si Burick

From The Dayton (Ohio) News, September 2, 1955

Copyright, 1955, The Dayton Daily News

EXULT WITH NASHUA, but also shed a tear for the handsome champion 3-year-old colt of this year, who is about to be rated with the great running-horses of all the ages.

Weep for the son of Nasrullah and Segula, though, only yesterday, he erased the lone blot on his 1955 escutcheon by soundly whipping Swaps, his California conqueror in the Kentucky Derby last May.

Cry a little for the victor by six and a half lengths in the two-horse joust that will be recorded in history as the Washington Park Match Race for $100,000, winner-take-all, over a mile-and-a-quarter route.

There were, to be sure, cheers and admiring glances for Nashua from 35,262 spectators and perhaps millions of televiewers. There were endearing caresses from those whose business it was to be in the winner's circle and from interlopers who did not belong.

There was Nashua's bank account, going for a million, built up in less than two years of racing, to $882,565, minus the customary fees to his trainer, bent-over old Sunny Jim Fitzsimmons, and to his regular jockey, Eddie Arcaro.

There was a good feed for Nashua last night and a rubdown and special water and a bed that would suit any king, human as well as equine.

But there must have been pain in the champion's sides and perhaps welts on his withers, for Arcaro had whacked away at him with his whip at the start of the run, at stages through the middle, and through most of the 1531 feet of what is known as the world's longest stretch. The long-nosed genius who pilots Nashua did not swing his bat idly. He belabored him like a prisoner taking his lashes at a medieval whipping post.

This reporter, an interloper on the happy scene in the winner's circle, asked: "Eddie, why did you whip Nashua so hard when you had it won so early?"

252

"Oh, Mr. Fitz will rest him up now and get all those whip marks off him," he retorted.

Arcaro couldn't have been happier if he had just won a million himself instead of a mere $10,000 for his afternoon's work.

The jockey usually collects 10 per cent. So homely that he is almost handsome, the 39-year-old jockey seemed to gurgle with delight. Everything about him shone in the very reflection of his happiness. Even the scarlet tassel on his cap seemed to be beaming.

"Did you have to whip him like that?"

"He's a strange one, you know," Eddie said. "He doesn't run easily on his own. He doesn't like to get far in front. I couldn't afford to let him relax. If I hadn't batted him, chances are he'd have slowed right up. I knew Swaps was a dead-beat horse coming into the stretch, but if I'd let up on Nashua, he'd have eased right back to Swaps. That's why I had to go to the whip so early and so hard.

"You might say," he laughed, "I tried to put some fire in his rear."

And William Woodward Jr., Nashua's owner, excusing the whipping, said, "This horse takes a lot of encouragement."

There were no doubts about this one. Nashua had shot to the front from his inside position in the starting gate, placed an eighth-of-a-mile from the finish on this narrow mile-and-an-eighth oval. Swaps, who had taken the lead early the day he beat Nashua and the Derby field last May 7, ran slightly behind, but nobody thought anything of it at the time. There was a long way to go on this "off" track that had started out "slow" but had dried out to a "good" condition by match-race time.

On at least three occasions tiny and taciturn Willie Shoemaker, who had piloted Swaps to six of his nine consecutive triumphs since Dec. 30 of last year, called upon his horse to take the leader. Each time, Swaps would make his move, then Arcaro would talk to his horse in the only language he understands—with a club— and Nashua would pull away.

This was a little different from what had happened in the Derby. Then, it will be recalled, Nashua had challenged Swaps in the stretch, had moved right up even with him, but the California horse would take none of that nonsense and pulled away. He was a "go-ing-away" length and a half to the good on the occasion.

But that was Churchill Downs in May and this was Washington Park on the last day of August.

It was actually pathetic in the stretch. Nearing the last turn,

Shoemaker made one last urgent request of Swaps and punctuated it with his whip. But Arcaro wasn't buying. Nashua ran away so far he could have hidden. And on this "off" track, the mile and a quarter was run in dreadfully ordinary time, Nashua crossing the finish line in two minutes, four and one-fifth seconds.

Rex Ellsworth, disappointed owner of Swaps, and his cowboy-partner-trainer, Mashach Tenney, were unwilling to make excuses. But first Shoemaker was saying, "Gosh, I don't want to sound like I'm trying to alibi, but I don't think Swaps ran his race on this kind of track.

"On the backstretch," Willie said, "I was running alongside Nashua with a good hold on Swaps—but not real tight like I usually do, because the horse wasn't acting right. Suddenly, it came to me that he wasn't going to be able to do it. I guess the best way I can explain it is that it felt empty underneath. You feel when a horse has something in reserve. Swaps didn't have it.

"No, Nashua's fast pace at the start didn't surprise me. All I wanted to do was go along with him. But Swaps didn't respond when I put the whip to him. He was bearing out on the turns and in the stretches, too."

And later, Ellsworth was saying, "Swaps is a placid horse, real peaceful. When he was being saddled, maybe you noticed that he was wiggling around—just a little fractious—and that's unlike him." (Both horses were saddled in front of the crowd at the finish-line of the grass course inside the rail.)

"Willie," Ellsworth continued, "said he had quite a time keeping Swaps on the course. The horse wanted to bear out and that wasn't like him either and I have to figure he's got some little thing aching him. When a horse doesn't run his race, you've got to feel something's wrong. I hope not, but I have to think something's hurting."

Later, a man close to Ellsworth advised: "That horse was sick when he got to Chicago and began to work out for the American Derby—the race he won on grass. He was off his feed for more than a week—no fever, or anything like that—just a little sick. Finally, he snapped out of it, but maybe he was sicker than anybody thought.

"They wouldn't say anything about it, but remember when the story broke before the Derby that Swaps was going to have a woman's shoe strapped around a sore foot? It could be that he's got that old injury again. That horse's foot, I know, was hurting Tuesday night."

But Ellsworth merely suggested, "It may take a little time to find out what did happen. It depends on how he'll react to this race."

(Editor's Note: Thursday noon it was revealed Swaps' right foot is injured and the horse will be rested for an indefinite period.)

Arcaro, addicted to colorful speech, did not choose this one as his greatest race, or the match victory as Nashua's greatest. He thought he preferred his performance in winning the Belmont Stakes.

"I won this race in the first three-quarters of a mile," Eddie said. "As Mr. Woodward was saying, it doesn't make any difference where you win it, just so you win it. The pace was real crazy, except for a match race. After the first half-mile, I thought Willie was riding a real good horse. At the three-quarters, I was almost sure, though, I had him. I got real sure as we turned into the stretch because I looked back and saw Willie's horse backing away from me. If he'd been a live horse, he'd have been running at me, not away.

"If there'd been other horses in the field, laying back, some clown would have whipped both of us. My horse was drunk at the finish, but I was still driving him."

In outings in earlier races, both jockeys had discovered there were two good paths on the drying-out track. "Willie," said Arcaro, apologizing for his 24-year-old opponent whom he admires greatly, "had to take the outside path, and then I guess he had the bad luck to have Swaps bear out some more into bad going."

Will they meet again? From what both stable had to say, they might—perhaps in the Sysonby in New York, Sept. 24—but neither side was particularly anxious to "go looking" for the other.

Definitely out is another match race.

Meanwhile, weep for Nashua, the winner, victorious, but welted, until Mr. Fitz smooths out Arcaro's whip marks on his hide.

Tennis

TENNIS TURNABOUT

By Allison Danzig

From The New York Times, August 28, 1955

Copyright, 1955, The New York Times

ONLY EIGHT MONTHS after it lost the Davis Cup to the United States at Sydney, Australia regained the world team tennis championship yesterday at Forest Hills.

In a truly great doubles match of two and a half hours, Lewis Hoad and Rex Hartwig defeated Tony Trabert and Victor Seixas for the clinching victory before 12,000 fans. The score was 12-14, 6-4, 6-3, 3-6, 7-5.

With the 2 points scored in the singles on Friday by Hoad and Kenneth Rosewall, Australia had the necessary 3 to give it possession of the cup. Thus it had emulated the success of the American team in 1954 in gaining the decision by the end of the second day of play.

The final two singles will be played today. Of course, they can have no bearing on the disposition of the cup, which will travel back across the far reaches of the Pacific again.

In the first match, at 2 o'clock, Hoad is scheduled to play Seixas. Then Hamilton Richardson will go on against Rosewall in the closing contest. Captain William Talbert named Richardson to replace Trabert.

The first set yesterday was the longest in doubles played in a cup challenge round since William Tilden and R. Norris Williams 2d defeated James O. Anderson and John B. Hawkes of Australia in 1923 in an opening set that went to 17-15.

Three times Hoad and Hartwig, champions of Wimbledon, stood within a stroke of winning the set. They had their first chance in the twentieth game and two more in the twenty-second.

That they rallied, after missing these opportunities, to go on to victory, was a testimonial to their spirit. Most often the team that

256

loses so prolonged an opening set becomes discouraged and yields forthwith.

Too much credit can not be given the young players from Down Under for their tenacity. At the same time, Trabert and the 32-year-old Seixas showed a fortitude of their own in the great fight they made when they seemed to be clearly on the defensive at the intermission.

So close and exciting was the battle, which had the crowd roaring throughout the five sets, that the outcome was never evident until the last stroke. Indeed, a few minutes before the end, it seemed that victory was at hand for the defending team.

To 5-all the teams fought without a breakthrough in service in this final set, just as they had fought to 12-all without a break in the long opener. Then, in the eleventh game, the Stadium was boiling with excitement.

Three times Trabert and Seixas stood within a stroke of breaking through Hoad. That practically meant they had three match points, from the way service had been standing up. But Hoad's volcanic service and the deadliness of the two young Australians at the net saved the day and killed the United States last chance.

Leading by 6-5, the Aussies broke through Seixas in the next game. Hoad whipped a backhand return of service at Seixas' feet and Hartwig scored with a backhand volley.

The next instant the two partners were throwing their arms around each other in joy and Umpire Herbert Lewis was announcing Australia as the winner of the Davis Cup.

This was the first time that Australia had won the challenge round doubles in three years. Last year Trabert and Seixas defeated Hoad and Rosewall. In 1953 they had beaten Hoad and Hartwig.

That was the first time Hoad and Hartwig had joined forces. They were hastily paired as a scratch combination against the wishes of Capt. Harry Hopman.

Yesterday Hoad and Hartwig were a far more effective team. Certainly Hartwig was a far better player. Indeed, the wiry 26-year-old Australian was the outstanding man on the court. It was to him in the main that the credit was due for the victory.

Hoad, who rose to such scintillating heights in defeating Trabert in the singles Friday, after Rosewall had beaten Seixas, was not nearly as consistent as his partner. His service was tremendous and he was great with the the volley and the smash, but off the ground he was not nearly so effective.

Hoad's return of service, chiefly from the backhand, was glaringly off until the last stages. Had his return of service not been so at fault, Australia might have won the opening set.

Hartwig was strong in every department. His return of service stood out all the more by comparison with Hoad's. Hoad seemed to be thrown off by the system of signals that the Americans used.

The man at the net signaled to the server whether or not he would cross over to protect against the cross-court return of service. Trabert often would fake crossing over. It may have been that this motion bothered Hoad.

Seixas gave a splendid account of himself until he began to tire a bit. He was in trouble more often than Trabert on his service, but he was so sterling a fighter and Trabert was so good in poaching that they were able to pull out of the hole most of the time.

The opening set was won on just one break through service, through Hartwig in the next to last game. There was just one break in the second set, also, through Seixas in the final game.

In the third set Trabert was broken through in the sixth game. Then, to the amazement and delight of the gallery, Hoad was broken through after he had led at 40-0, with Seixas magnificent on the return.

To break Hoad's service under any circumstances is an achievement. To rally from 0-40 against it is almost incredible, particularly in doubles.

But hardly had the crowd quieted down from its uproarious demonstration when the Americans were in trouble again. Seixas lost his service in the eighth game as Hoad and Hartwig did some mad volleying behind the return of service. Hartwig then served out the set in invincible style.

So the Australians, who were thought to be doomed to defeat at the end of the 57-minute opening set, left the Stadium arena with a lead of 2 sets to 1. At that time they were the decided favorites to win the match. So strong were they in service and at the net that the crowd was prepared to see them finish the match in the fourth set.

The Australians had their opportunity. They led at 30-0 on Seixas' service in the third game, but both failed with their return of service and Seixas pulled out of the hole. Then the Americans broke through Hoad in the next game.

Trabert rose to superb heights in this game. He brought off a two-handed push volley, in self defense, that sent the ball off at a tangent into the unprotected alley as the Australians stared unbelieving and the crowd gasped.

A smash by Trabert and his cross court volley contributed 2 more points. Trabert's return of service was dumped into the net by Hoad for the final point. That was the set, as it turned out, for the Australians missed an opportunity to get even when they led at 30-0 again on Seixas' service in the eighth game and lost it.

The fans cheered as the United States took the set to square the match. There was still hope, and strong hope, that the fate of the cup might be deferred until Sunday in the final singles matches.

This final set was a tense, gripping battle every minute, with the crowd hanging on every stroke. The suspense mounted every time the pitcher, meaning the server, got behind the batter, meaning the striker or receiver.

Hartwig was behind at 0-30 in the first game. Trabert was 30-40 on his serve in the second game and was carried to deuce in the sixth. Then service was devastating to 5-all, and then followed the tremendously stirring eleventh game.

Three times, as related, Trabert and Seixas stood within a stroke of breaking through Hoad after leading at 30-0. But Hoad's cannonball service and the brilliance of both Australians at the net pulled them out of the fearful situation.

It was a keen disappointment to the crowd when the game was lost by the Americans. Then followed the final blow.

Seixas, serving, netted two volleys. Hoad knocked Vic's service back for a winner from the backhand that had failed so often. Hartwig's backhand volley brought the match to an end.

Two development in the opening set remain to be commented on. In the fifteenth game Hoad hit a volley down the center of the court for a winner, but his racquet flew from his hand into the opponents' court.

At first it was ruled that the ball was dead before Hoad's racquet crossed the net. Seixas and Captain Talbert protested and the referee, Dr. S. Ellsworth Davenport Jr., ruled that the ball was still in play as the racquet crossed the net. So the Australians lost the point, but they went on to win the game.

In the twenty-fifth game, in which Hartwig was broken through, the final point was won by the United States as Hartwig put his volley into the net in answer to the return of service.

Hoad claimed that the service had been a let and both he and Seixas, who was of the same opinion, made no move to change courts. But the net umpire, Hollis Dann, ruled that the serve had not ticked the net, and so the point stood.

That was the only time in the match that Hartwig lost his service. It was the first time in twenty-seven service games against Japan, Italy and the United States that he had lost his service.

The blond, wiry Hartwig, the runner-up for the United States title last year, was judged to be too erratic for singles in spite of his great brilliance. But in doubles yesterday he was the most dependable man on the court and added greatly to his stature as an international player.

The stroke analysis shows that Trabert had the best average, with 44 earned points against forty-six errors. That is a rather remarkable percentage of winning shots. Hartwig scored 49 times and made sixty errors. Hoad had exactly the same number of earned points and seventy-one errors.

Dogs

MIDNIGHT FOR KIPPAX FEARNAUGHT

By John Rendel

From The New York Times, February 16, 1955

THE CLOCK lacked twenty-five minutes to midnight in Madison Square Garden last night when a California bulldog rose to the highest distinction American bench show competition has to offer.

He was Champion Kippax Fearnaught, a 28-month-old red and white dog. He became best in show of the Westminster Kennel Club's seventy-ninth event. He was the first of his breed to gain the honor since 1913 and the second altogether.

There were honors also for the owner, Dr. John A. Saylor of Long Beach, Calif., a young general practitioner. There were honors for the English breeder Harold Dooler, and for the professional handler, Harry Sangster. There were honors for Fearnought's sire and dam, Koper Kernal and Kippax Ann, but mostly the honors were for a fine new winner.

Secondary laurels went to a beautiful young boxer. Because an importation won, there was judging for best American-bred. That prize was taken by Barrage of Quality Hill, a fawn-colored new star owned for the time being by Mr. and Mrs. M. E. Greiner Jr. of Kansas City.

A decision by Albert E. Van Court of Los Angeles put Fearnaught among the elite. He had weighed the merits of six grand dogs in twenty minutes of judging. He had watched their movements on the green-matted arena floor. The gaiting process had told him much of what lay under those well-groomed coats.

He had evaluated them with his hands as well as his eyes. When he was done he had this to say:

"This is the best bulldog I have ever seen. His movement is ideal for a bulldog, a breed which must have certain gait and movement to be a true representative of the breed. It was the toughest deci-

261

sion I have ever had to make. The six group winners were wonderful specimens, but the bulldog stood out as the best of them."

The 10,000 spectators that included the Duke and Duchess of Windsor had watched, too, and had formed their own opinions.

They had seen a stylish Yorkshire terrier twinkle-toe before them, a bundle of animation in a small package. They had thrilled to the gaiety of an Afghan, long hair flouncing in a self-made breeze.

They had admired the even strides of an English springer spaniel. They had seen a compact, sparkling Sealyham terrier patter down the aisle on short legs. Mostly, though, they appeared to like the deep rolling gait of the phlegmatic bulldog and the smooth-flowing powerful strides of the clean-limbed boxer.

There was no question who was the people's choice. There were loud cheers and applause, even the clang of a cow bell, as Fearnaught sauntered along. He was a red and white picture of power when he moved and a stolid, impassive creature when still.

This was the second time the bulldog had been in a Garden final. He had made it last winter, too, but had gone no farther. He had captured the imaginations of Westminster regulars then. If anything, his popularity had grown with the year.

Dr. Saylor, more interested in breeding than in showing, said the dog had been in the ring fourteen times. This made his ninth and, of course, his biggest best.

The dog got to this country in rather an off-hand way. The physician said he had no intention of buying a bulldog, but had seen some photographs of this one sent by England's William Lawler. He bought the dog and never was sorry.

Future plans? About the only thing that could be said with certainty was that Easterners wouldn't see the grand house pet in a ring for a while. The doctor said the dog hasn't been entered in any Eastern shows.

There had been 2,537 dogs when the latest of Westminsters started Monday morning. Now there was only this one. Only one of so many that had started in quest of the golden crown of dogdom.

There was, however, a great deal of satisfaction for the boxer, too. He did not reach the top as so many had predicted after his victory over his sire, Ch. Bang Away of Sirrah Cress, in the breed judging Monday night. But he has time. He is only 20 months old, immature, but with vast promise.

The appearance of the boxer was the last under the ownership of the Greiners. Mr. and Mrs. Jouett Shouse of Washington had seen the quality in Barrage's sturdy frame and had bought him for $7,000 early this month for delivery after Westminster.

Fearnaught was not the only dog who had been in last year's Garden final and made it again. Another Californian, Kay Finch's Champion Taejoin of Crown Crest from Corona Del Mar, made it two in a row in the hound group and three for the breed. The other repeater was the Yorkshire terrier, Champion Star Twilight of Clu-Mor, owned by twin sisters. They are Mrs. L. S. Gordon Jr. and Janet E. Bennett of Glenview, Ill.

The other two finalists were the English springer, Champion King Peter of Salilyn and the Sealyham terrier, Champion Robin Hill Brigade.

The springer was owned by Mrs. F. H. Gasow of Birmingham, Mich., the Sealyham by Mrs. Robert B. Choate of Danvers, Mass.

There was praise enough for all. George H. Hartman, who judged the sporting group, said the home-bred Sealyham had the best topline of any of the breed he had seen. He liked the way the dog moved, his size, condition and coat. Joe Thompson was the handler.

The springer was described by Mrs. Katharine St. George in equal superlatives. She said King Peter was the best of the breed she had seen, a dog that had everything.

Taejon had a special distinction. The dog, Johnny to his friends, was said by Miss Finch to be the only dog ever to win the large Harbor Cities event in Long Beach, Calif., two years running. The 60-pound 4½-year-old Afghan turned the trick in 1952 and 1953.

The owner was the handler. The silver blond dog with the fine black mask achieved a third straight Garden breed victory in the morning. Then he came back to beat a grand bloodhound again.

Tom and Pearl Sheahan's Champion Fancy Bombardier was second to Taejon the second time. Two years ago the bloodhound had been the hound group victor. Sheahan described Taejon as a great dog.

The 4½-pound Yorkshire terrier was a pert little thing with blue and tan hair immaculately groomed and trailing to the ground. "Tuffy" sported a lavendar ribbon as a topknot and looked every inch an aristocrat in miniature.

Here, too, was an importation. Star Twilight was brought from Dublin four year ago and had fared well since leaving the Emerald Isle. His ten bests were supported by thirty-eight group victories in campaigning all around the country. Mrs. Gordon was the handler.

Hunting and Fishing

NO VICTORY AT SEA

By Grant Matthews

From The San Francisco Chronicle, August 9, 1955

Copyright, 1955, The San Francisco Chronicle

SOME DAYS a guy can't lay up a nickel.

For instance, I have a friend name of Honest John Scott who deals in stuff to catch fish with at a modest establishment in the outer Mission. He is an avid salmon fisherman and he pursues same with the tenacity of a suede shoe boy. No hour is too early; no difficulty too difficult—if he can go fishing outside the Gate. He is so enthusiastic on the subject that he sometimes becomes difficult.

Like the other afternoon. He phones me.

"The salmon are running like deer at the Farallons," he says. "They are big, fat and hungry. The are jumping into the boat. We can't miss this one."

The way he puts it, it DOES sound inviting.

"When are we leaving?" I ask.

"Tomorrow morning. Meet you in front of the Exposition Fish Grotto, Fisherman's Wharf."

"What time?"

"I'll make it easy on you," he says. "Five."

"FIVE!"

So at 5:45 I am there with bells on to meet The Honest One, Bill Blackburn, Banana Joe Novello, and Skipper Marion Beaver of the "Georgianna," a sturdy looking vessel if I ever saw one.

As we head out towards the Gate the bay is flat as a Kansan's voice and the sky is clear and everybody sits around nudging everybody else, saying "What a day" and "We'll rack 'em up today, huh boy?" It looks real good.

And real good it is, too. Until we reach that point west of the bridge where the swells come up like thunder out of China across the way. You have to admit that those big seas have had quite a running start by the time they reach this coast and when they get here and there's no more give, they start piling up on one another like cord wood.

On this memorable day, the farther out we go, the bigger the pile-up. The fair "Georgianna" begins looking less and less like a vessel and less and less sturdy. As we head west toward the ever-popular Farallons, I picture the "Georgianna" as a sand flea in the Sahara Desert.

The first man we lose is old Bill Blackburn, a seagoing Marine during the war. He makes a fight of it but it's obvious by his complexion that he ain't going to win. And he doesn't. For the first time in his life, he gets seasick.

I am very gentle with him. I tell him to go into the cabin and sack out for awhile.

"You'll feel better after a little sleep," I say, patting him on the back and leading him to a kind of seat that he can sprawl out on. I feel like a friend to man. I feel I have done a good deed. I feel it's too bad more people don't know such a lovable guy as me.

Meanwhile, the seas continued to get higher and higher and a strong wind comes up.

I observe The Honest One and The Skipper for signs of concern or fright, but Scott is having a cup of coffee and Beaver is eating a sandwich. Banana Joe is smoking a cigar. I suddenly have a strong desire to be on land.

It is right here, one-half hour from the Farallons, that I am seasick for the first time in MY life.

I sit in the stern of the boat and swallow. I swallow quite a lot. I look up at those big seas, running like wild horses and I swallow and wonder will we ever get back to Fisherman's Wharf and then I remember that on the way back these seas will be following seas and I swallow some more. Finally I make my way forward and into the cabin where The Honest One and The Skipper are still having coffee and sandwiches. Banana Joe is still smoking a cigar.

"Matter?" asks Scott. "Don't feel good?"

I try to smile, instead I swallow. I make a mental note that the life-jackets are just inside the cabin, to the right.

"Think it's a little rough for tolling?" I suggest.

"Not bad," Scott replies. "She'll flatten out when we get to the islands."

Oh, you miserable . . . , I think.

"But if you want to," he adds, "we'll give her a little try right

here and if it ain't good we can head over towards Duxbury
where it's a little more sheltered."

"Yeah, let's do her that way," I swallow.

So we troll, and we troll, and we troll. And after what must be
three days and four nights Scott finally tells The Skipper to head
over Duxbury way. Now we got the swell hitting us on our port
quarter and—this is better? Man, fetch me with a helicopter. Let
me out of this bouncing ball. Free me from this bucket.

We finally settle down off Duxbury where it really is more sheltered and Scott decides we will troll here. How eager can a guy
get?

But by that time, as far as I'm concerned, rigor mortis has set
in and salmon, schalamon—you can have my share of the biggest
salmon of them all.

Two months later, Scott decides the trolling off Duxbury isn't
too good.

"Let's move down the coast," he tells The Skipper. "Might be
some action off Slide Ranch."

One thing good about moving down the coast is it gets us nearer
to the Gate, and Fisherman's Wharf. And it is shortly after we
start moving down the coast that I lurch to the stern, grope for
the rail, and lose it all. I am transparent. "No need for an X-ray,
doctor, you can see right through me."

This is where The Honest One finally gets its through his thick
skull that I am dying.

"Don't feel good, huh?" he asks.

I will kill him but I can't raise my arms.

"Hey, skip," he yells forward, "I think we better head for home."

I love him like a brother.

. . . So we enter beautiful, placid San Francisco Bay and as
we do, we are met by the Fish and Game Department's patrol boat.
One of the wardens boards the "Georgianna," and asks for fishing
licenses. All hands come up with same except The Honest One.
He's forgotten his. He only sells about 2000 of them a year, but
he's forgotten his. I feel better.

And The Skipper? The Skipper has forgotten his Party Boat
license. Things are picking up. I look at Blackburn and he looks at
me. We smile at each other. Not brightly, but we smile.

So can you blame me when yesterday Scott phones me.

"The salmon are running like deer at the Farallons," he says.
"They are big, fat and hun. . . ."

You blame me, I hung up on him?

I'VE BEEN SKUNKED

By Ray Beck

From Outdoor Life, June, 1955

THE ONE-ROOM country schoolhouse reeked of manure on the boots of the bigger boys, rose-petal sachet on the underwear of the bigger girls, and lamp oil and turpentine on the bosoms of the little kids. But when I came in, they all took notice.

The teacher gasped, "Get out. Take those clothes home and bury them."

In those days, during the depression, skunk catching was the regular winter occupation of most of the men and boys where we lived, about 60 miles northeast of Pittsburgh. You could pretty well judge a man's success in life by your nose. When business smelled, it was good, and the biggest stinkers always had the most money.

There were trappers, dig-'em-outs, smoke-'em-outs, night hunters with dogs, night hunters without dogs, and a few professional sneak-'ems, who led an exciting dangerous life stealing from the rest of us.

Every farm publication carried the advertisements of commission houses in New York, St. Louis, San Francisco, and points between, begging us to drop a post card for their big, free catalogue of trappers' supplies and promising the highest prices for our furs.

Skunk pelts were divided into four classifications according to color, the blackest being most valuable. If the white stripes did not extend back of the shoulders, the pelt was graded black. If not beyond the middle of the skin, it was a short-stripe pelt. Narrow-stripe pelts could have white streaks of any length if they were no wider than the buyer's finger. Otherwise they were broad-stripe.

Some companies added a fifth grade, star-black, which had no stripes at all. The white star on the animal's head was its only markings.

Once a month the mailman brought a deluge of price lists quoting the prices paid by various companies (subject to change without notice), and containing valuable market forecasts. ("Strongly advise you to ship all furs without delay. Decline in prices expected.")

This expected slump invariably occurred while our furs were in transit.

The price list were masterpieces of confusion. Prices ranged from $12 to 5¢—$12 for an extra-extra-large star-black, fine-furred, well-handled, prime No. 1, and 5¢ for a little, low-grade broad-stripe. One firm listed 240 different grades, rated according to size, primeness, silkiness, how they had been handled, and the amount of white.

In those days kids didn't dream of becoming millionaires, or baseball stars. They wanted to catch that extra-extra-large, star-black, prime, fine-furred, No. 1 skunk which was listed so prominently on every price list. Statistics prove a boy is more likely to become President.

Every crossroad had its fur buyer. Traveling dealers roamed the back roads in Model T's until the mud got axle deep, and then hired a hack. Skunk hides were as good as cash at most country stores, and they could be converted into hard money.

Speculators hung barns full of skunk skins, hoping the price would go up, while others accepted orders for furs they didn't have.

The buyers cheated the trappers by undergrading the skins one grade, and the trappers cheated the buyers by blackening the white stripes in order to gain two grades.

The mail-order houses offered an imposing array of devices to make the skunk trapper's life an easier one. You didn't need money for their merchandise. They would deduct the cost of what you ordered from the value of your fur shipment. They offered lures made from "genuine animal glands and costly ingredients from all over the world" for 35¢ a bottle. There were paste baits in tubes like shaving cream, smelling faintly of anise oil, to be used during rainy weather, and there were sticks of scented tallow to rub on the soles of your boots, so an animal crossing your trail would follow it to your next trap.

There were smokers with eight feet of rubber hose to take the smoke back into the skunk den, and a picture showing two happy trappers smoking out skunks by the sackful.

There were guns and pistols enough to arm a fair-size Central American revolution. The prize of the lot was a gun for $3 to be mounted on a tree or stump and baited with a piece of meat. It was supposed to be the last word in equipment for the progressive skunk trapper. When the skunk pulled on the bait, the gun automatically aimed itself and fired. Because of its high price, few were sold, but a neighbor boy bought one and, in three successive mornings, shot the dog, the cat, and two of his own fingers.

Of course, the backbone of any trapper-supply business is traps. There were traps with long springs, short springs, coil springs, single springs, double springs, plain jaws, double jaws, notched jaws, webbed jaws, toothed jaws, offset jaws, rubber jaws, three jaws, tripple clutch, detachable clutch, high grips, and square grips.

There were folding traps which didn't take up much more space when folded than the ordinary variety and easy-set traps which were impossible to open unless you had both hands free, as I learned the hard way by spending a whole day with my thumbs in one of my own traps. That was one day I spent on the trap line when I would have preferred to have been in school.

There were also killer traps, tree traps, choker traps, and king-size rat traps.

With all this commercial skunk-taking equipment, it would hardly seem necessary to manufacture any of our own, but we did—figure-four deadfalls, pole and spindle deadfalls, two kinds of spring-pole snares, and box traps, to mention a few.

There were many experiments with ways to kill trapped skunks without creating a stink, but most of those I tried smelled things up more or less—usually more.

When I got older, I carried a .22 rifle. Theoretically, a well-placed bullet will break a skunk's neck and kill it without causing any scent. But my skunks usually moved at the wrong time, and since a hole in the neck decreased the value of the pelt, I usually shot them through the head. This results in the skunk throwing a little scent, but after all, "you can't be a trapper, and smell like a rose," as one of the boys told the schoolmarm.

The last year I was in the eighth grade at Slam Bang, as we called our school, we got a new teacher. He wouldn't allow the pupils to brings rifles and shotguns to school any more, so I bought a long-barreled .22 revolver with a shoulder holster, and carried it inside my shirt. He hadn't mentioned revolvers.

About the age when I started slowing down when the girls chased me, I noticed that the young ladies didn't try very hard to catch me during skunk season. Then an old, broken-down trapper who knew all about skunks and women (he was a bachelor) taught me how to kill skunks and still be a lady-killer. He gave me a skunk lance, a tiny two-inch knife, needle-pointed and about a quarter of an inch wide, with both edges honed to a razor edge. It was fitted to a ferrule which could be attached to a 10-foot pole. I would carefully approach the trapped skunk, not making any sudden moves to frighten him. If he raised his tail, or aimed his rear end in my direction, I stopped. When his tail dropped, I advanced. When I got close enough, I placed the point of the lance against the hollow of the skunk's throat and either thrust the knife into his jugular vein or stabbed him through the heart. Evidently the skunk never feels the keen blade, for he dies without throwing scent.

Naturally, with so many people getting sprayed by skunks, a lot of home remedies have been developed. The two most common, burying the clothes, or smoking them, are the most useless. They only postpone the day of reckoning. Buried clothing will still smell skunky if dug up six weeks later. The smell will outlast the clothes. Smoke masks the scent to a degree, but I would about as soon smell like a skunk.

Perfume and disinfectants may change the smell, but they don't improve it.

A slight taint of skunk will usually dissipate in a few days if you hang the clothing outdoors. In a warm place the smell will be stronger but will go sooner.

If your clothes are heavily sprayed, you need something like turpentine or gasoline to dissolve the oily musk. Fur buyers and others who handle skunk skins grease their hands to prevent the musk from getting into the pores. This can then be washed off with gasoline or turpentine. If the victim is your dog, wash him with vinegar. It won't remove skunk scent as efficient as turpentine, but your dog will be lots easier to catch for a second bath. Some say tomato juice is the best skunk-odor cleanser of all, but it's a fairly new formula, to me, at least, and I'm happy to say I haven't had occasion to test it.

A lot of people have the misconception that the vile scent of a skunk comes from his urine. Actually, it's produced by a pair of musk glands beside the anus, and has no connection with the bladder. Each of these glands contains about a teaspoonful of greenish-yellow fluid, which is discharged through a pair of tine jets by muscular contractions. A skunk fires both barrels at once, with about as much accuracy and range as a water pistol. He's good for half a dozen shots, but one is usually plenty.

There's no truth in the superstition that a skunk can't fire if you pick him up by the tail, but it is true that if you don't excite him by any sudden motions, you can usually handle him without danger.

A couple years ago, a photographer with a movie camera accompanied me along my trapline to get pictures of some trapped foxes. One of my sets held a skunk, and since the fur wasn't prime, I released it. A number of people who saw the pictures accused me of faking it with a descented skunk. The fact of the matter was that I simply handled the skunk carefully. The skunk is pretty much a gentleman when he has a chance to be.

Most animals relish skunk flesh, but few care to tackle the skunk. Dogs used to hunt skunks soon learn to circle around them, barking to attract the hunter, so he can kill the animal with a rifle. A dog with a shot of skunk in his eyes and mouth is a mighty sick dog, chewing ground and rubbing his face on the grass. Repeated doses can cause permanent blindness.

I remember the first time I got skunked. I had a trap set at the bottom of a 12-foot clay bank where it was protected from the weather. By standing at the edge, I could inspect it from the top. One morning, the trap was moved, and as I craned my neck to see what I had caught, I got too close to the edge, and the bank gave way. Part way down, my foot caught in a root, and I did a half-flip, landing on my neck about four feet from a big, broad-striped skunk. I snapped the .22 out of its holster with a draw that would have been the envy of Wild Bill Hickok, but the skunk was already in firing position—and he fired.

If you've ever taken a good deep breath from a jar of freshly ground horse-radish, you have some idea how I felt. My eyes burned as though they'd been scalded. I staggered around in agony for about 15 minutes before I could see anything, and my eyes hurt for a couple of days.

Under certain circumstances, the fumes are lethal. A friend of mine ran a gray fox into a hole with his dogs, and plugged it in. That evening when we returned with a shovel and mattock, we were greeted with an overwhelming odor of skunk. We dug out the hole and found a dead fox and a live skunk completely out of ammunition. Since there wasn't a mark on the fox's body when we skinned him, he had evidently been asphyxiated.

Foxes, coyotes, and wolves kill a few skunks, but horned owls, are the only creatures that habitually prey on them. The skunk's artillery can't be elevated for use as an anti-aircraft gun.

One cold January I was hunting mink in a marsh along Lake Erie. Many trees had fallen in the shallow water, making a tangle of brush that was a real mink paradise. When the dogs barked at a hole in a hollow, fallen tree I was sure they'd found one.

I shoved a couple of No. 2 traps far back in the hole and wadded my coat in the opening, so that if a mink passed the traps, he couldn't get out. Making sure there were no other openings, I started thumping the tree with my ax. In a little while I heard one trap snap, and pretty soon the second one. Then I smelled skunk. I jerked my coat away, but it was too late.

The skunk was a short-stripe, and after killing it, I pounded the tree some more. When I was about ready to quit, a black skunk came out. Figuring there might be more, I chopped a hole in the trunk, and punched out two more, both broad-stripes.

After I skinned my catch, I looked around to see how the skunks had got to the tree. There was ice in all directions. The nearest land was 20 yards away so they must have swum. I don't think they moved in after the ice formed, because they had made a good nest.

Another time, while I was trapping marten in the Rocky Mountains, I caught a spotted skunk, or civet, as they're known in the fur trade, in a marten trap I'd set on a spruce limb about eight feet above the ground. This high-climber, typical of his kind, was dark —nearly black—with irregular white markings on his back. These spotted skunks are smaller than the other varieties I've mentioned, but they smell as big as any of them.

Skunks will eat almost anything—fruit, vegetables, soft-shell nuts, small animals, including other skunks, birds, reptiles, and carrion—but they prefer insects.

A skunk will scratch at the front of a beehive and eat the bees that crawl out to investigate. He'll dig out nests of yellow jackets and devour grubs and adults alike. You often see little pockets dug in lawns and golf courses where they have been hunting grubs, and a young skunk that wandered into our bunkhouse at a logging camp and became a pet developed a fondness for roaches. It practically rid us of these pests in a couple of weeks.

In the Southwest, skunks are said to subsist largely on scorpions and rattlesnakes. I don't know about the scorpions, but I once saw a skunk kill a rattler. I first saw the animal galloping in a circle and thought it might be fast in some other trapper's set. When I got closer, I saw that it was running around a rattlesnake about 18 inches long.

The snake had its head up, ready to strike, but it had to keep turning all the time to follow the skunk. When it lowered its head, the skunk would move closer; when the snake's head was poised again, the skunk would retreat.

Finally the rattler dropped its guard and tried to escape to the safety of a near-by clump of cactus. The instant it turned, the skunk pounced on it, biting it behind the head. While the snake rolled and twisted, the skunk braced its legs wide apart and held on. It was all over in less than a minute.

It's hard to think of the skunk as a lightning-quick killer, but he belongs to the same deadly family as the weasel and marten, and he would whip the average tomcat without using his scent.

When two skunks, they apparently rule out gas attacks by mutual agreement, and settle the matter by tooth and claw. I've never seen one of these fights, but I have twice found where they took place. Both battles ended with the victor dining on the loser.

I have known a number of Indians and a few white men who ate skunks. I never tried them myself, but one Indian friend says they're delicious—"just like fat puppy dogs."

Skunk oil has been recommended for everything from waterproofing boots to taking internally for asthma. I used to sell quite a few gallons of it to a herb doctor who used it in his medicine.

An old hermit who lived in a shanty along the Allegheny River claimed that a mixture of skunk oil and skunk musk applied to the chest hot every evening would prevent colds, but nobody ever got close enough to find out if he had a cold or not.

Now I understand scientists have learned a way to remove the smell from skunk musk and use the odorless remainder as a substitute for ambergris in perfumes, to make the delicate fragrance more lasting. It looks as though skunks will be scenting up more people than ever.

General

THE IMPORTANT PART

By Art Rosenbaum

From The San Francisco Chronicle, May 23, 1955

PEOPLE WHO KNOW the Olympic Games best cannot help but be amused by the deep and constant cries of horror about the possibility of the United States losing to Russia. Fact is Russia has developed some great athletes and stands a fine chance of dominating in certain classifications—but even if Russia does "win" the Olympics it doesn't mean the end of the democratic world as we know it.

Permit me to clear the books. I love to sing "The Star-Spangled Banner" when the band plays it in honor of an American conqueror on the victory stand. One of my heart-thumpiest Olympic thrills in the 1952 Games came in the 3000-meter steeplechase—an event I can normally do nicely without—when Horace Ashenfelter, an F.B.I. agent from New Jersey and Pennsylvania, overtook the great Soviet star, V. Kazantsev, to win the first distance title by an American in 44 years of Olympics. It was the least expected of all United States victories, and we all roared until our throats were lost when the time of 8:45.4 was announced as the fastest steeplechase ever run, anywhere.

Ashenfelter's surprising triumph emphasizes the Olympic ideal as well as any, and it proves again why we needn't fear a Russian team victory—or a victory by any other nation. To understand why, we must understand the Olympic ideal. A Frenchman named Baron de Coubertin revived the modern Olympics, and he stated its purpose: "The important thing in the Olympic Games is not winning but taking part. The essential thing in life is not conquering but fighting well."

Cynics will call it corn. Most Americans think they believe themselves when they say, "Forget the glory—just put my name on the check every payday."

It's not entirely true, and you know it.

But the Baron's insistence on individual glory, overriding national pride, makes sense in international athletics.

The way it's set up, everybody and nobody wins the Olympic Games. The glory and garlands are there for all.

In the first place, there is no official team score. How can there be? Newspaper services have concocted a scoring plan but it is merely a device by which they can interlock the Games, on paper. Most scoring gives 10 points for the win, 8 for second, and so on down the line. Yet a basketball team that plays through half a dozen eliminations and finally wins receives only 10 points, no more than a man who takes the 100-yard dash or a bantamweight boxing title. In the '52 Olympics, the Russians scored heavily in gymnastics because 10 points were given to each winner in horizontal bar, parallel bar, rings, pommelled horse, long horse, etc., etc. The Russians won hundreds of mythical points in combined events that did not equal (theoretically) Bob Mathias' 10-event decathlon for which he received 10 newspaper points.

But the Baron spoke of taking part, and of individual glory. In the 1948 Games at London, Argentine correctly considered it had "won" the Olympics because Cabrera won the marathon. After all, the marathon run of 26 miles 385 yards is based on the original Grecian run and is the key to the Olympic Games. Ergo, Argentine and South American captured the most important event of all.

Turkey won the 1948 Olympics. As far as the Turks were concerned, Greco-Roman wrestling is the only manly event of any consequence on the program, and they dominated that sport. Or perhaps you didn't know Greece-Roman wrestling was part of the Olympics?

Italy had its glory. A. Consolini won the discus, and in ancient days the No. 1 hero was the man who threw the classic discus wore the garland wreath.

Headlines in The Netherlands danced for Fanny Blankers-Koen, for in this race of individual glory Fanny had won four gold medals—more than any other person. While we were screaming for Bob Mathias and Sammy Lee and the American basketballers, Czechoslovakia went wild about Emil Zatopek, Belgium declared a holiday for Gaston Reiff and Sweden unfurled its flags for H. Eriksson.

In the Olympics, there is boxing, swimming, bicycle riding,

horsemanship, etc., etc. Hitler in 1936 tried to include knitting, tatting and sewmanship in order to increase the national score. It didn't work. Jesse Owens was still Our Hero.

Victories—individual or national—will not come easily, but three world records in Saturday night's Modesto Relays indicate United States athletes are as robust as ever. The United States will dominate where the United States has interest, such as in men's track and field. I have yet to hear anyone moan because the Russians will beat us badly in women's track and field, because we simply dismiss women's track and field from important consideration in discussing the Olympic Games.

So I say, let the Russians win a few. Let Luxembourg and Gold Coast and Pakistan take some medals, too. But don't sell the U. S. short—and don't count the points.

THE SAGA OF PLAINFIELD TEACHERS

By Bob Cooke

From The New York Herald Tribune, August 28, 1955

Copyright, 1955, The New York Herald Tribune

THE ENTIRE football world was saddened the other day when Morris Newburger announced his retirement from football. Oh, you've heard of Knute Rockne, Walter Camp, Alonzo Stagg and the like, but I'll make a bet you never thought of putting Newburger up there on the list. Fact is, I'll wager you never heard of Newburger.

Football was blessed with Newburger many years after Rockne, Stagg, Camp and their kind had become famous in song and story. It remained for Newburger, a citizen of quiet renown, to provide an everlasting memorial to the game as we know it today.

Newburger was always a fellow who shied away from praise. He never played football. He is not a spotlight seeker. Yet, the advent of a football season, with no mention of Newburger, is more than a fan can stand.

Newburger once coached a team that was never beaten, never tied. He needed no assistant coaches, no stadium, no customers, and no players.

It was in the fall of 1941 when Newburger was seized by an uncontrollable desire to build an undefeated eleven.

So he created one which he called Plainfield State Teachers. Sounds like a college, doesn't it? Newburger thought so, and so did a number of metropolitan sports writers.

Having founded Plainfield State, Newburger needed only a schedule to get his season started. Swiftly he improvised some "tough opposition" not to mention "traditional rivals." When he had completed his work, Plainfield State had an eight-game itinerary against such teams as Scott, Chesterton, Fox, Randolph Tech, Ingersoll, Benson, Appalachian and Harmony U. (homecoming).

The above institutions were as mythical as Plainfield State but they appeared to be football teams. Newburger, working fiendishly, had given them names which carried a trace of the familiar thus leading to the illusion of the authentic.

In the opener against Scott, Plainfield State got off to a "terrific" start by whipping its "bigger opponents," 20 to 0. At this stage of the game, Newburger displayed a talent amounting to genius.

After he'd phoned the result of the Plainfield State-Scott game to the New York Herald Tribune, the New York Times, the Associated Press, and other news media, he created the celebrated fullback, John Chung.

"Can't have a miracle team without a miracle player," Newburger whispered to himself as he began to make an accounting of Chung's assets.

Chung was a 205-pound, full-blooded Chinese fullback. He was the star of the Plainfield State team, the crowbar which pried victory from defeat, the shining white horse on which the team rode forth to battle. According to Plainfield State's statistics, Chung gained an average of 9.3 yards every time he carried the ball, due largely, so Newburger said, to Chung's habit of eating rice between the halves.

Herb Allan, former sportswriter on the New York Post, received a publicity release on Chung and wrote a glowing feature about the star of the Orient. This was one week prior to the revelation that neither Chung nor Plainfield State existed.

Six victories had been recorded before Caswell Adams, then of the Herald Tribune, scooped the town with his story of the Plainfield State hoax.

Plainfield had trampled on Scott, Chesterton, Fox, Randolph Tech, Ingersoll and Benson. Appalachian was to have been beaten, 20 to 2. Then, in the final, Harmony was to put up a great game but was succumb to Chung's wizardry, 40 to 27, before an enthusiastic homecoming crowd.

The cancellation of the games against Appalachian and Harmony saddened Mr. Newburger. He was also downhearted over the sudden end to the career of John Chung, the indestructible Chinese. So retirement has claimed Mr. Newburger.

Always and forever, Newburger will recall the time he telephoned a local paper with the score of the Plainfield State-Randolph Tech game. The score was Plainfield State Teachers, 35; Tech, 0.

"Where's Plainfield State?" asked the rewrite man. "In Plainfield, N. J.?"

"No, just outside," said Newburger and hung up.

BACK TO CAP AND GOWN

By Walker Stewart

From The Memphis Commercial-Appeal, November 6, 1955

FOR THE FIRST TIME in a lot of years (none of them quite collectors' items) we have returned to the fountain-head of our Bachelor of Science degree and things have changed pretty shockingly. It was in 1930 that we returned the cap and gown to the rental agency and were unleashed upon a world which began to regret it almost immediately.

But we didn't recognize the campus until we looked twice. To begin with, the school buildings have been moved and are much farther apart than they used to be. Back in our undergraduate time, we could walk from the Architecture Building to the Old Gym in a shade under eight minutes. This morning, the safari used up almost half an hour. Of course, we stopped to admire the landscape, but that wasn't because we were tired.

The fraternity house looks just the same from the outside, but we discovered that two more stories had been added when we climbed to the top floor. They've redesigned the stairs, too, and the things are like ladders with steps at least 10 inches higher than they were in 1930.

Modern youth now writes in almost microscopic fashion and entirely without firmness—allows the pencil to waver all over the place. We learned this when we entered the fraternity telephone cubicle. Could hardly read the numbers on the wall—had to back out into the hall before they came into focus.

Then we saw the label of the Theta sorority house dimly enclosed in what we had meant to be a heart. There it lingered like the painting of a prehistoric bison clinging to the wall of a cave which had been redecorated and lit with neon. Lovely girl she was, too, with tiny laughter wrinkles at the corners of the eyes. Bet those wrinkles look like plow furrows now. Women age faster than men, you know. We've discovered that she lives in Buffalo now and has five kids. This news cheered us immensely, for, with a wife and brood, we wouldn't be able to dedicate two December weeks to the wild waterfowl population.

And the brothers in the fraternity house. They call us "sir" and we wouldn't be too amazed if one of them offered to help us across the street. But, after all, they're the merest children. Rather astonished us, however, when shrewd cross-questioning revealed that their ages are similar to ours when we went to Illinois.

Well, men matured earlier in our day. The coeds are younger, too. Can't think what their mothers are thinking about—letting them run about without nurses.

But what saddens us is the condition of the classmates who have come back to help celebrate the Illinois-Michigan football match. Hope they take it slow up the ramps, or some of them won't make it.

The years have dealt pretty harshly with all the rest of them and here they are bouncing about in sports jackets and acting the fool. Of course, our own plaid is a bit on the pronounced but— well, it becomes us and rather seems to blend in with our personality.

Some of these characters from the class of '30 look as though they'd fallen into the hands of hostile Indians. Our own hair may be a trifle thin in a few spots, but you'd never guess it unless the light happens to be strong and unfriendly.

We caught one quarter of a "B" game yesterday afternoon and were amazed at the small fry taking part. The program indicated that they were as large or larger than we were when we sat on the bench here. But you know how coaches lie about weights.

The dyes they use in pennants and flags isn't nearly as bright as they were back in the jolly old days and the bands don't play with the same shrill spirit.

And the weather is a good deal more penetrating than it used to be. Why, we used to stroll from the stadium to the fraternity house wearing a T-shirt through this sort of temperature and now this heavy-duty tweed overcoat isn't quite sufficient. Probably more humidity than there once was.

The quality of hot dogs has fallen off, too. Time was when we gulped half a dozen at a time and they tasted like porterhouse steak with caviar sauce. Just insulted the inner man with a singleton and feel as though we'd swallowed a porcupine without pausing to remove the bark. Had all the noble succulence of old sunflower stalks. The dogs looked just like they once did, however. Must be the fault of communism.

Acoustics of the fraternity house aren't what they once were, either. During the homecoming night of our freshman year, we slumbered peacefully in a nook under the window-seat while a 30-man crap game raged on the billiard table, a quarter fought it out with a jug band near the door and someone with feet like steam shovels danced a passionate buck-and-wing within inches of our nose. At 1 a.m. Saturday, some cad knocked over an ash tray in the living room three stories below our bedroom and we couldn't sleep a wink the rest of the night.

The game hasn't even begun and there's an idiot boiled to the ears and waving a pennant and wearing a blue and orange hat and begging any member of the Class of '38 to have a snort. We just can't understand why people refuse to admit that they're getting old.

FUN WEEK

By Franklin (Whitey) Lewis

From The Cleveland Press, May 11, 1955

AT THE RISK of offending the intellectual giants who conceived
the ideas for Doughnut Week, National Pickle Week, Plant-a-
Rose-a-Day Week, Mother-in-Law Week, Dog Week and other
forms of celebration based on food and affection, this unworthy
peasant would like to suggest some weeks in sports.

National Shotgun Week: For seven days we would have open
season for shooting the big mouths with raucous voices who always
sit just behind you at baseball and football games.

Out-of-Bounds Week: This is not quite what you might think.
I would enjoy playing golf for one week without having to take a
two-stroke penalty whenever I hooked or sliced a ball beyond the
white stakes. I would suggest a half a stroke penalty instead of two
strokes. Being sure to hit two out, I thus would lose one full stroke.
If I hit three out, I can always walk in.

Anti-Tout Week: Without penalty to myself, I would be able to
belt on his kisser the first bum who told me at the race track that a
certain horse couldn't lose.

Journalism Week: Expulsion to the Silver Gulch (Ariz.) Weekly
Vindicator would be automatic to all baseball writers who quote a
winning pitcher, "I really had it out there today." The same ban
would be placed upon boxing writers who quote a victorious tramp,
nose bleeding, eyes bulging, mouth red-smeared, "He never hurt
me once in de whole fight."

Bleacher Week: This would be in honor of those hardy souls
who pick up splinters while they watch and never complain, even
when they can't understand the gibberish that comes through the
public-address system horns out their way.

Anti-Burp Week: A 30-day sentence on either bread and water
or Scotch and water for anyone who still believes pro rassling is
on the level.

Snicker Week: Let's all join in feeling sorry for the U. S. tennis
bums who are touring foreign lands, especially those who get out
of line and have their expense money cut off. In South Pacific,

there was nothing like a dame. In the United States, there is nothing like an amateur.

Special Award Week: All persons who discover within a seven-day period what makes trotting horses "break," especially as they are leaving the barrier, and thus stick the gullible folks who bet on them with a sure-fire loss, will receive citations from Felix Suspicion, president of Suckers Anonymous.

Anti-Boo Week: The ears of sports headliners burn brightly with the inverted cheers of their constituents, so they deserve a break. Instead of booing baseball players, fighters, et al., save the boos for bankers who refuse you a loan, gas station attendants who slop up your car while overfilling the tank, bus drivers who pass you up, sports writers who don't have to pay to get in, and dames over 30 who wear their hair down their back.

Hold-Your-Temper Week: When a golf pro shows you how to hit a ball a certain way, and you can't, and he says, "Look it's so simple, just swing like I do," you are not to kick him on the Argyles. Instead, you are to lead him to a portable typewriter and tell him to write a 1000-word column just like you do.

Love-and-Kisses Week: Not once in this given period will criticism be leveled at the general manager, the manager, a coach or a ticket seller at the ball park. There will be special cages for columnists who simply won't be able to last out the week.

Laugh Week: Let's all just bust our buttons, especially if we win.

THEY DRAG OUT THE DEAD

By Jack Clowser

From The Cleveland Press, March 30, 1955

Copyright, 1955, The Cleveland Press

BULLFIGHTS are not for the squeamish. Nor are they for lovers of fine animals. The bullfight is said to be Mexico's national sport, but the natives compare it to a ballet, or a ritual dance.

I saw my first corrida while in Mexico City recently, attending the Pan-American Games. I was prepared to be shocked, and I was. You do not sleep well, if you have a sensitive nature, after your first mingling with blood and sand.

Yet I came away fascinated.

The bulls, bred through generations to develop fighting instincts, spend their first four years living regally. They get the finest food and care. On the day when the last 15 minutes of their lives are devoted to mortal combat, they carry about 1600 pounds on their splendidly-muscled frames.

Matadors are leaders of the fighting teams. They are assisted by peones, who do the first cape work; picadors, the armored mounted men who wield long pikes, and banderilleros, who thrust their darts into the heavy muscles of the bull's neck.

I felt particularly sorry for the first bull. Even I, a novice aficionado, could tell he had no great relish for the fray. The senior matador, who fights first, dispatched him speedily. I glanced away as the matador, cape low to keep the bull's eyes down, went in over the horns.

It was a powerful thrust, missing the bones. The mist of death quickly blurred the animal's eyes.

With the second bull, it was different. Snorting and pawing, el toro burst into the bright sunshine and raced fiercely toward any sign of movement. One peon drew shouts of "Ole!" from the crowd as the bull missed him narrowly with opening charges. The word is the Mexican equivalent for high approval.

The first picador maneuvered badly as the bull hit his horse. The smashing impact lifted and turned the horse, exposing its left, or relatively unprotected flank. Recovering fast, the bull got to the unpadded side and, with both horns, delivered fatal wounds. The death agonies of the blindfolded horse were sickening.

It is considered no disgrace if the matador fails to kill with his first sword thrust. At the moment, the bull must be standing with forefeet together, thus opening the shoulder blades and leaving passage to the heart.

So it was with the third bull. It was the junior matador's turn. He was opposed to a fast and courageous animal. It wheeled so sharply the banderilleros had to pivot for their lives as they placed their darts. The youthful matador played him long and dangerously. It seemed the strength and savagery of el toro would never abate sufficiently to permit the execution.

Three times the man went in over the horns. Three times the bull dislodged the sword with violent shrugging. He had a dread habit, hooking with one horn. Only a week before, in the same ring, a difficult bull had pierced a matador's abdomen. The aficionados were tense, remembering.

Even after the fourth plunge over the horns, this very brave bull gave trouble. He sank to his knees once. His fighting heart brought him up again for one last feeble move. But this time the matador was sure, and disdainfully reached out to touch the lowering horn.

Thus it went. The dead were dragged out. The unsuspecting living, avid for the next combat, whirled in and breathed defiance. Only once in a very great while does a bull so capture the crowd with its great spirit that they importune the judge for the animal's life. Then he is taken away, his wounds dressed, and his bravery and strength poured into succeeding generations.

But the odds are stacked very high against him. He has been born to meet death in the afternoon, amid gay colors and shrill trumpet calls. It is not a pretty sight.

For the Record

CHAMPIONS OF 1955

ARCHERY

World Champions

Men's Individual—Nils Andersson, Sweden.
Women's Individual—Katarzyna Wisniowska, Poland.

United States Champions

Target

Men—Joe Fries, Los Angeles.
Women—Mrs. Ann Clark, Cincinnati.
Men's Team—Cleveland Archery Club.
Women's Team—Cleveland Archery Club.

AUTO RACING

Indianapolis Winner—Bob Sweikert, Indianapolis.

BADMINTON

Thomas Cup (men)—Malaya.

National Champions

Men's Singles—Joseph Alston, South Pasadena, Calif.
Women's Singles—Margaret Varner, El Paso, Tex.
Men's Doubles—Wynn Rogers, Arcadia, Calif., and Joseph Alston.
Women's Doubles—Judy Devlin and Susan Devlin, Baltimore.
Mixed Doubles—Dorothy Hann, Los Angeles, and Wynn Rogers

BASEBALL

World—Brooklyn Dodgers.
National League—Brooklyn Dodgers.
American League—New York Yankees.
All-Star Game—National League.
Leading Batsman, N. L.—Richie Ashburn, Philadelphia.
Leading Batsman, A. L.—Al Kaline, Detroit.
Little World Series—Minneapolis Millers.
International League—Montreal (regular season); Rochester (play-offs).
American Association—Minneapolis (regular season and play-offs).
Pacific Coast League—Seattle.
Dixie Series—Mobile (S. A.).

Colleges

N. C. A. A.—Wake Forest.
Eastern League—Yale.

BASKETBALL

National Collegiate—San Francisco.
National Invitation—Duquesne.
Eastern Intercollegiate League—Princeton.
Yankee Conference—Connecticut.
Atlantic Coast Conference—N. C. State.
Southeastern Conference—Kentucky.
Southern Conference—West Virginia.
Western Conference—Iowa.

Big Seven Conference—Colorado.
Missouri Valley Conference—Tulsa.
Southwest Conference—Southern Methodist.
Skyline Conference—Utah.
Rocky Mountain Conference—Idaho State.
National Assn. (N. A. I. A.)—East Texas State.
A. A. U.—Phillips Oilers, Bartlesville, Okla.
Women's A. A. U.—Wayland Queens, Plainview, Tex.

Professional

National Association—Syracuse.

BILLIARDS

World Champions

Three-Cushion—Ray Kilgore, San Francisco.
Pocket—Willie Mosconi, Philadelphia.

BOBSLEDDING

World Champions

Two-Man—Switzerland (Fritz Feierabend and Harry Warbourton).
Four-Man—Switzerland.
Skeleton—Douglas Connor, Canada.
National A. A. U. Champions
Two-Man—Bud Washbond, Keene Valley, N. Y., and Pat Martin, Massena, N. Y.
Four-Man—Saranac Lake (N. Y.) Bobsled Club.

BOWLING

American Bowling Congress

Champions

All-Events—Fred Bujack, Detroit.
Singles—Eddie Gerzine, Milwaukee.

Doubles—George Pacropis and Harry Zoeller, Wilkes-Barre, Pa.
Five-Man Team—Pfeiffer Beer, Detroit.
Women's International Congress
All-Events—Mrs. Marion Ladewig, Grand Rapids, Mich.
Singles—Nellie Vella, Rockford, Ill.
Doubles—Mrs. Marion Ladewig and Wyllis Ryskamp, Grand Rapids.
Team—Fallstaff, Chicago.

BOXING

World Champions

Flyweight—Pascuel Perez, Argentina.
Bantamweight—Robert Cohen, France.
Weatherweight—Sandy Saddler, New York.
Lightweight—Wallace Smith, Cincinnati.
Welterweight—Carmen Basilio, Canastota, N. Y.
Middleweight—Ray Robinson, New York.
Light Heavyweight—Archie Moore, San Diego.
Heavyweight—Rocky Marciano, Brockton, Mass.

National A. A. U. Champions

112-Pound—Heji Shimabukuro, Honolulu.
119-Pound—John Cereghin, U. S. Air Force.
125-Pound—Joe Charles, U. S. Air Force.
132-Pound—Jack Puscas, Portland, Ore.
139-Pound—Robert Cofer, Philadelphia.
147-Pound—Walter Sabbath, Detroit.
156-Pound—Frank Davis, U. S. Air Force.

165-Pound—Paul Wright, U. S. Air Force.

178-Pound—John Horne, Washington.

Heavyweight—George Moore, Detroit.

National Collegiate Champions

119-Pound—Robert McCullom, Idaho State.

125-Pound—Seiji Naya, Hawaii.

132-Pound—Vincent Polumbo, Maryland.

139-Pound—John Granger, Syracuse.

147-Pound—Herbert Odom, Michigan State.

156-Pound—Tony DiBiase, Virginia.

165-Pound—Max Voshall, San José State.

178-Pound—Gordon Gladson, Wash. State.

Heavyweight—Robert Hinds, Wisconsin.

Team—Michigan State.

CANOEING

U. S. Paddling Champions

One-Man Single Blade—George Byers, Samoset C. C.

One-Man Double Blade—John Pagkes, Yonkers (N. Y.) C. C.

Tandem Single Blade—John Pagkes and Tom Budrock, Yonkers C. C.

Tandem Double Blade—John Pagkes and Russell Dormond, Yonkers C. C.

Four-Man Single Blade—Philadelphia C. C.

Four-Man Double Blade—Yonkers C. C.

Team—Yonkers C. C.

U. S. Sailing Champions

Decked—Adolph Morse, Phoenix C. C., Lindenhurst, L. I.

Cruising—Stephen Lysak, Yonkers C. C.

International Challenge Cup—United States.

CASTING

National Association Champions

All-Around—Marion Garber, Toledo.

All-Distance—Jon Tarantino, San Francisco.

All-Accuracy—Jim Kangas, Toledo, and Robert Budd, Jeffersonville, Ind.

Distance Baits—William J. Lovely, St. Louis.

Distance Flies—Jon Tarantino.

Accuracy Baits—Roland Williams, Baytown, Tex.

Accuracy Flies—Jim Kangas.

COURT TENNIS

World Open—James Dear, England.

American Open—Albert Johnson, New York.

National Singles—Alastair B. Martin, Glen Head, L. I.

National Doubles—William L. Van Alen and F. Hastings Griffin, Philadelphia.

Tuxedo Gold Racquet—Alastair B. Martin.

Intercollegiate Team (Van Alen Trophy)—Harvard.

CROSS-COUNTRY

National A. A. U.—Horace Ashenfelter, New York A. C.

National A. A. U. Team—New York A. C.

National Collegiate—Charles Jones, Iowa.

National Collegiate Team—Michigan State.

I. C. 4-A—Henry Kennedy, Michigan State.

I. C. 4-A Team—Pittsburgh.

Heptagonal—Dave Eckel, Cornell.
Heptagonal Team—Cornell.

CURLING

Gordon International Medal—Canada.
Women's U. S. Champion—Wauwa-
tosa (Wis.) Granites

CYCLING

Tour de France—Louison Bobet,
France.

U. S. Amateur Champions

Senior Open—Jack Disney, Pasadena,
Calif.
Junior Open—Pat DeCollibus, De-
troit.
Girls' Open—Jeanne Robinson, De-
troit.

DOG SHOWS

Best-in-Show Winners

Westminster—Dr. John A. Saylor's
bulldog, Ch. Kippax Fearnaught,
Long Beach, Calif.
Morris and Essex—Mr. and Mrs. John
P. Wagner's boxer, Ch. Baroque of
Quality Hill, Chicago.

FENCING

United States Champions

Foil—Albert Axelrod, Salle Santelli.
Epee—Abram Cohen, Fencers Club.
Saber—Richard Dyer, Phila. F. C.
Women's Foil—Mrs. Maxine Mitchell,
Hollywood, Calif.

Team

Foil—Fencers Club, New York.
Epee—Salle Santelli, New York.
Saber—Salle Santelli.

Women's Foil—Salle Santelli.
Three-Weapon Team—Fencers Club.

National Collegiate Champions

Foil—Herman Valesco, Illinois.
Epee—Donald Tadrawski, Notre
Dame.
Saber—Barry Pariser, Columbia.
Three-Weapon Team—Columbia.

Intercollegiate Association

Foil—Aubrey Seaman, C. C. N. Y.
Epee—Richard Pew, Cornell.
Saber—John Parker, Navy.
Three-Weapon Team—Cornell.
Foil Team—Navy.
Epee Team—Columbia.
Saber Team—Columbia.

FOOTBALL

National—Oklahoma (Associated
Press and United Press polls).
Eastern (Lambert Trophy)—Pitts-
burgh.
Ivy League—Princeton.
Western Conference—Ohio State.
Pacific Coast Conference—U. C. L. A.
Southeastern Conference—Mississippi.
Atlantic Coast Conference—Maryland
and Duke (tie).
Southern Conference—West Virginia.
Southwest Conference—Texas Chris-
tian.
Big Seven Conference—Oklahoma.
Skyline Conference—Colorado A. & M.
Missouri Valley Conference—Detroit
and Wichita (tie).
Rocky Mountain Conference—Idaho
State.
Border Conference—Texas Tech.
Mid-American Conference—Miami
(Ohio).
Canadian Intercollegiate—Queens.
Canadian Professional (Grey Cup)—
Edmonton Eskimos.

National Football League

Eastern Conference—Cleveland Browns.

Western Conference—Los Angeles Rams.

League Champion—Cleveland Browns.

GOLF

Ryder Cup—United States.

Walker Cup—United States.

Canada Cup—United States.

Hopkins Trophy—United States.

National Open—Jack Fleck, Davenport, Iowa.

National Amateur—Harvie Ward, San Francisco.

National P. G. A.—Doug Ford, Yonkers.

British Open—Peter Thomson, Australia.

British Amateur—Joe Conrad, San Antonio.

Augusta Masters—Cary Middlecoff, Memphis.

World Pro (Tam O'Shanter)—Julius Boros, Southern Pines, N. C.

World Amateur (Tam O'Shanter)— Doug Sanders, Cedartown, Ga.

All-American Open—Doug Ford.

All-American Amateur—Doug Sanders.

Canadian Open—Arnold Palmer, Latrobe, Pa.

Canadian Amateur—Moe Norman, Kitchener, Ont.

Eastern Open—Frank Stranahan, Toledo, Ohio.

Western Open—Cary Middlecoff.

North and South Amateur—Don Bisplinghoff, Orlando, Fla.

Trans-Mississippi—Jimmy Jackson, St. Louis.

N. C. A. A.—Joe Campbell, Purdue.

N. C. A. A. Team—Louisiana State.

National Junior—William Dunn, Duncan, Okla.

National Public Links—Sam Kocsis, Detroit.

Women

National Amateur—Pat Lesser, Seattle.

National Open—Fay Crocker, Montevideo, Uruguay.

British Open—Mrs. George Valentine, Scotland.

World Pro (Tam O'Shanter)—Patty Berg, Chicago.

World Amateur (Tam O'Shanter)— Wiffi Smith, St. Clair, Mich.

All-American Amateur—Wiffi Smith.

All-American Pro—Patty Berg.

Western Open—Patty Berg.

Western Amateur—Pat Lesser.

Canadian Amateur—Marlene Stewart, Fonthill, Ont.

North and South—Wiffi Smith.

Southern Amateur—Mrs. Scott Probasco, Chattanooga, Tenn.

Trans-Mississippi—Polly Riley, Fort Worth.

United States Seniors—Mrs. Harrison Flippin, Ardmore, Pa.

Titleholders—Patty Berg.

Eastern Amateur—Mary A. Downey, Baltimore.

U. S. Junior—Carol Jo Kabler, Roseburg, Ore.

U. S. Intercollegiate—Jackie Yates, Hawaii.

GYMNASTICS

National A. A. U. Champions

All-Around—Karl K. Schwenzfeier, Penn State.

Free Exercise—John Beckner, U. S. Army.

Horizontal Bar—Abie Grossfeld, West Side Y. M. C. A., New York.

Tumbling—James H. Sebbo, Jersey City Dept. of Rec.

Long Horse—John Miles, Florida State Gymkana, Tallahassee.

Trampoline—Robert Elliot, Maverick Boys' Club, Amarillo, Tex.

Side Horse—James Brown, Los Angeles State College.

Parallel Bars—Edward Scrobe, St. Mary's Recreation Center, N. Y.

Still Rings—John Miles.

Rope Climb—Robert Hammond, U. C. L. A.

Swinging Rings—Samuel Bailie, Iowa University.

Team—Florida State Gymkana.

National Collegiate

All-Around—Karl Schwenzfeier, Penn State.

Flying Rings—George Wikler, So. California.

Free Exercise—Don Faber, U. C. L. A.

Horizontal Bar—Carlton Rintz, Michigan State.

Parallel Bar—Carlton Rintz.

Rope Climb—Robert Harmmond, U. C. L. A.

Side Horse—Carlton Rintz.

Trampoline—Richard Albershardt, Indiana.

Tumbling—Lloyd Cochran, So. California.

Team—Illinois.

HANDBALL

National A. A. U. Champions

Four-Wall

Singles—Sam Costa, New York.

Doubles—John Abate and Joe Ingrassia, New York.

One-Wall

Singles—Harold Hanft, New York.

Doubles—Rubrecht Obert and Oscar Obert, New York.

U. S. Association Champions

Four-Wall

Singles—Jimmy Jacobs, Los Angeles.

Doubles—Sam Haber and Ken Schneider, Chicago.

HARNESS RACING

Mile Tracks

2-Year-Old Pacer—Greentree Adios.

2-Year-Old Trotter—Egyptian Princess.

3-Year-Old Pacer—Meadow Ace and Frisco Creed (tie).

3-Year-Old Trotter—Scott Frost.

Aged Pacer—Adios Harry.

Aged Trotter—Prince Victor.

Half-Mile Tracks

2-Year-Old Pacer—Belle Acton.

2-Year-Old Trotter—Gratis Hanover.

3-Year-Old Pacer—Dottie's Pick.

3-Year-Old Trotter—Galophone.

Aged Pacer—Adios Harry.

Aged Trotter—Lady's First.

Other Champions

Leading Money-Winner—Scott Frost.

Leading Driver—Billy Haughton.

HOCKEY

Stanley Cup—Detroit.

National League—Detroit.

World Amateur—Penticton V's, Canada.

Allan Cup—Kitchener-Waterloo Dutchmen.

Memorial Cup—Toronto Marlboros.

Intercollegiate

National Collegiate—Michigan.

Pentagonal League—Harvard.
Canadian—Toronto.

HORSE RACING

T. R. A. Champions

American Champion—Nashua.
Handicap Champion—High Gun.
Handicap Filly or Mare—Parlo.
3-Year-Old Colt—Nashua.
3-Year-Old Filly—Misty Morn.
2-Year-Old Colt—Nail.
2-Year-Old Filly—Nasrina.
Steeplechaser—Neji.

Other Champions

Money-Winning Owner—Belair Stud.
Money-Winning Horse—Nashua.
Trainer (winners saddled)—Frank
Merrill, Jr.
Jockey (winners ridden)—Willie Hartack.

HORSE SHOWS

National Horse Show Champions

International Individual Championship
Trophy—Brig. Gen. Humberto Mariles, Mexico, with ch. g. Chihuahua II.
International Perpetual Trophy
(Team—Mexico.
Open Jumper—Mr. and Mrs. Bernie
Mann's gr. g., Riviera Wonder, Port
Washington, L. I.
Conformation Hunter—Mrs. Morton
S. Smith's b. g., Jazz Session, Cobham, Va.
Working Hunter—Eleonora Sears'
ch. m., Reno, Pride's Crossing, Mass.
Green Conformation Hunter—John S.
Pettibone's br. g., The Duke of Paeonian, Middleburg, Va.
National Horse Show Equitation

(Good Hands)—Mikee McCormack, Mountain Lakes, N. J.
A. S. P. C. A. Equitation (Maclay
Trophy)—Wilson Dennehy, Lake
Forest, Ill.
A. H. S. A. Medal (Hunter Seat)—
Wilson Dennehy.
A. H. S. A. Medal (Saddle Seat)—
Sandra Harris, Indianapolis.

P. H. A. Season Jumping Trophy

Irl A. Daffin's bl. g., Bedford, Lititz,
Pa.

HORSESHOE PITCHING

World Champions

Men—Ted Allen, Boulder, Colo.
Women—Mrs. Hazel Harris, Denver.

ICE SKATING

Figure

World Champions

Men—Hayes Alan Jenkins, United
States.
Women—Tenley Albright, United
States.
Pairs—Frances Dafoe and Norris Bowden, Canada.
Dance—Jean Westwood and Lawrence
Demmy, England.

United States Champions

Men—Hayes Alan Jenkins, Colorado
Springs, Colo.
Women—Tenley Albright, Newton
Center, Mass.
Pairs—Carole Ann Ormaca and Robin
Greiner, Berkeley, Calif.
Gold Dance—Mr. and Mrs. Edward L.
Bodel, Berkeley, Calif.

North American Champions

Men—Hayes Alan Jenkins.
Women—Tenley Albright.

Pairs—Frances Dafoe and Norris Bowden, Toronto.

Dance—Mr. and Mrs. Edward L. Bodel.

Speed

World Champions

Men—Sigge Ericsson, Sweden.
Women—Rimma Zhukova, Russia.

United States Champions

Men's Outdoor—Ken Bartholomew, Minneapolis.

Women's Outdoor—Pat Gibson, West Allis, Wis.

Men's Indoor—Bill Disney, Pasadena, Calif., and Jay Hasbrouck, Newburgh, N. Y.

Women's Indoor—Mrs. Barbara M. DeSchepper, Detroit.

North American Champions

Men's Outdoor—Jay Hasbrouck.
Women's Outdoor—Pat Gibson.
Men's Indoor—Bill Disney.
Women's Indoor—Mrs. Barbara M. DeSchepper.

LACROSSE

U. S. Open—Mt. Washington Club, Baltimore.
U. S. Intercollegiate—Maryland.
North-South Game—South.

LAWN BOWLING

National Champions

Singles—Harry P. Hope, St. Petersburg, Fla.

Doubles—Jeff Smith and Frank C. Wilson, London, Ont.

Triples—John Chisholm, Isaac Balmain and Alexander L. Ripley, New York.

MODERN PENTATHLON

World Champions

Individual—Konstantin Sainykov, Russia.
Team—Hungary.

MOTOR BOATING

Gold Cup—Gale V, owned by Joseph L. Schoenith; driven by J. Lee Schoenith.

President's Cup—Tempo VII, owned by Guy Lombardo; driven by Danny Foster.

Silver Cup—Tempo VII.

Detroit Memorial Cup—Gale IV, owned by Joseph L. Schoenith; driven by W. J. Cantrell.

Maple Leaf Cup—Miss Cadillac, owned and driven by Frank Saile Jr.

International Cup—Tempo VII.

Governor's Trophy (Indiana)—Tempo VII.

Imperial Gold Cup (7 litres)—Miss De Soto, owned and driven by George Byers Jr.

Unlimited Class (championship regatta)—Tempo VII.

Unlimited Class (high points for season)—Gale V.

POLO

National Outdoor Champions

Open—Triple C, Detroit.
20-Goal—Triple C, San Antonio, Tex.
12-Goal—Farmington, Conn.
Handicap—Meadow Brook, L. I.
Inter-Circuit—Woodside, Calif.

Indoor Champions

National Senior—Squadron A, New York.

National 12-Goal—New York Athletic Club.

National Intercollegiate—Cornell.

Sherman Memorial—Huntington, L. I.

Eastern 12-Goal—New York A. C.

RACQUETS

World Open—Geoffrey W. T. Atkins, Chicago.

National Singles—Geoffrey W. T. Atkins.

National Doubles—Geoffrey W. T. Atkins and William Wood-Prince, Chicago.

Tuxedo Gold Racquet—Geoffrey W. T. Atkins.

ROWING

United States Champions

Single Sculls—Jack Kelly Jr., Vesper, B. C., Philadelphia.

Assn. Single Sculls—Tom McDonough, Fairmont R. A., Philadelphia.

Assn. Single Sculls Team—Undine B. C., Philadelphia.

Double Sculls—Walter Hoover Jr. and James McIntosh, Detroit B. C.

Quadruple Sculls—Vesper B. C.

Pair-Oared Shell With Coxswain—Fairmont R. A.

Pair-Oared Shell Without Coxswain —New York A. C.

Eight-Oared Shell—Vesper B. C.

Intermediate Eight-Oared Shell—Vesper B. C.

150-Pound Single Sculls—Tom Smith, Hamilton, Ont.

Four-Oared Shell With Coxswain—West Side R. C., Buffalo.

Four-Oared Shell Without Coxswain —West Side R. C.

Team—Vesper B. C.

Intercollegiate

I. R. A. Varsity—Cornell.

Eastern Association—Pennsylvania.

Harvard-Yale—Yale.

Adams Cup—Pennsylvania.

Blackwell Cup—Pennsylvania.

Carnegie Cup—Cornell.

Childs Cup—Pennsylvania.

Compton Cup—Harvard.

Dad Vail Trophy—Dartmouth.

Goldthwait Cup—Princeton.

Oxford-Cambridge—Cambridge.

Eastern Association Lightweight— Penn.

SHOOTING

United States Champions

Rifle

Small-Bore—Mrs. Viola Pollum, Brookville, Pa.

High Power (Match)—Sgt. Lloyd G. Crow, Jr., U. S. Army.

High-Power (Service)—Capt. John W. Kolb, U. S. Army.

Women's Small-Bore—Mrs. Viola Pollum.

Women's High-Power (Match)— Marlene Bellinger, Seattle.

Women's High-Power (Service)— Ruth I. Sawyer, Dayton, Ohio.

Pistol

Service—Master Sgt. Huelet Benner, U. S. Army.

Women—Mrs. Gertrude Backstrom, Hoquiam, Wash.

Civilian—Robert K. Fisher, Los Alamos, N. M.

Police—Joseph C. White Jr., U. S. Border Patrol.

Trap

Grand American Handicap—Logan Bennett, Hodgenville, Ky.

Women's Grand American Handicap
—Mrs. Dolly Isetts, Kenosha, Wis.
North American Clay Targets—Ned
Lilly, Stanton, Mich.
Women's North American Clay Targets—Helen Thomas, Los Angeles.

Skeet

All-Around—Robert E. Rath, Winetka, Ill.
Women's All-Around—Mrs. Alphonso
Ragland Jr., Dallas.
All-Gauge—Alex H. Kerr, Beverly
Hills, Calif.
Women's All-Gauge—Mrs. Leon Mandel, Chicago.
Industry All-Around—Fred Missildine,
Sea Island, Ga.
Industry All-Gauge—Fred Missildine.
Champion of Champions—Louis Gordon, Texarkana, Ark.

SKIING

United States Champions

Jumping—Rudy Maki, Ishpeming,
Mich.
Downhill—Chiharu Igaya, Hanover,
N. H. and William Beck, Mount
Mansfield, Vt. (tie).
Slalom—Ralph Miller, U. S. Army.
18-Kilometer Cross-Country—Tauno
Pulkkinen, New York.
30-Kilometer Cross-Country—Tauno
Pulkkinen.
Alpine Combined—Chiharu Igaya.
Giant Slalom—Ralph Miller.
Women's Downhill—Mrs. Andrea
Mead Lawrence, Parshall, Colo.
Women's Slalom—Mrs. Andrea Mead
Lawrence.
Women's Alpine Combined—Mrs. Andrea Mead Lawrence.

North American Champions

Downhill—Ralph Miller and William
Beck (tie).
Slalom—Ralph Miller.
Alpine Combined—Ralph Miller.
Women's Downhill—Cathy Carey,
Denver.
Women's Slalom—Skeeter Werner,
Steamboat Springs, Colo.
Women's Alpine Combined—Skeeter
Werner.

National Collegiate Champions

Jumping—William Olson, Denver.
Downhill—Chiharu Igaya, Dartmouth.
Slalom—Chiharu Igaya.
Cross-Country—Larry Damon, Vermont.
Combined—John Cress, Denver
Team—Denver.

SOCCER

National Challenge Cup—Eintracht,
New York.
National Amateur Cup—Heidelberg
(Pa.) Tornadoes.
National Junior Cup—Gottschee, New
York, and Schwaben, Chicago (tie).
Lewis Cup—Philadelphia Uhriks.
American League—Philadelphia Uhriks.
National League—Ukrainians, New
York.

SOFTBALL

Amateur Association

Men—Raybestos Cardinals, Stratford,
Conn.
Women—Orange (Calif.) Lionettes.

SQUASH RACQUETS

Lapham Trophy (men)—Canada.
Wolf-Noel Cup (women)—England.

National Champions

Open—G. Diehl Mateer Jr., Philadelphia.

Amateur—Henri Salaun, Boston.

Doubles—Ed and Joe Hahn, Detroit.

Professional—Hashim Khan, Pakistan.

Veterans'—Germain G. Glidden, Norwalk, Conn.

Women's Singles—Janet Morgan, England.

Women's Doubles—Janet Morgan and Sheila Speight, England.

Women's Senior—Mrs. Ellwood I. Beatty Jr., Cynwyd, Pa.

Intercollegiate—Roger Campbell, Princeton.

Intercollegiate Team—Princeton.

Other Champions

Cowles Invitation—Henri Salaun.

Canadian Singles—G. Diehl Mateer Jr.

Howe Cup (women)—New York.

SQUASH TENNIS

National Singles—H. Robert Reeve, New York.

SWIMMING

Men's National Senior Outdoor Champions

100-Meter Free Style—Hendrik Gideonse, New Haven S. C.

200-Meter Free-Style—Bill Woolsey, Hawaii.

400-Meter Free-Style—Ford Konno, Hawaii S. C.

1,500-Meter Free-Style—George Onekea Jr., Hawaii S. C.

100-Meter Back-Stroke—Yoshi Oyakawa, Hawaii S. C.

200-Meter Back-Stroke—Yoshi Oyakawa.

200-Meter Butterfly—Bill Yorzyk, New Haven S. C.

200-Meter Breast-Stroke—Bob Mattson, North Carolina State.

400-Meter Medley—George Harrison, Berkeley (Calif.) City Club.

400-Meter Medley Relay—New Haven S. C.

400-Meter Relay—New Haven S. C.

Three-Meter Dive—Don Harper, Palo Alto, Calif.

Ten-Meter Dive—Gary Tobian, Los Angeles A. C.

Team—New Haven S. C.

Long Distance—Frank Brunell, Philadelphia.

Long-Distance Team—Huntington (Ind.) Y. M. C. A.

Men's National Senior Indoor Champions

100-Yard Free-Style—John Glover, New York A. C.

220-Yard Free-Style—Ford Konno.

440-Yard Free-Style—Ford Konno.

1,500-Meter Free-Style—George Breen, Cortland State T.

100-Yard Back-Stroke—Yoshi Oyakawa.

220-Yard Back-Stroke—Yoshi Oyakawa.

220-Yard Butterfly—Eulalio Rios, Mexican Swimming Federation.

220-Yard Breast-Stroke—Robert Gawboy, Minneapolis.

400-Yard Individual Medley—Jack Wardrop, Ann Arbor, Mich.

400-Yard Free-Style Relay—New Haven S. C.

400-Yard Medley Relay—N. C. State A. A.

One-Meter Dive—Gerry Harrison, Columbus, Ohio.

Three-Meter Dive—Gerry Harrison.

Team—New Haven S. C.

Women's National Outdoor Champions

100-Meter Free-Style—Wanda Werner, Walter Reed S. C., Washington.

400-Meter Free-Style—Dougie Gray, Walter Reed S. C.

800-Meter Free-Style—Carolyn Green, Fort Lauderdale (Fla.) S. A.

1,500-Meter Free-Style—Carolyn Green.

100-Meter Back-Stroke—Carin Cone, Ridgewood, N. J.

200-Meter Back-Stroke—Carin Cone.

100-Meter Butterfly—Betty Mullen, Walter Reed S. C.

200-Meter Breast-Stroke—Mary Jane Sears, Walter Reed S. C.

400-Meter Medley—Marie Gillett, Walter Reed S. C.

400-Meter Medley Relay—Walter Reed S. C.

800-Meter Relay—Walter Reed S. C.

One-Meter Dive—Mrs. Pat McCormick, Los Angeles A. C.

Three-Meter Dive—Mrs. Pat McCormick.

Ten-Meter Dive—Mrs. Juno Stover Irwin, Pasadena (Calif.) S. C.

Team—Walter Reed S. C.

Long Distance—Kitty Kannary, Women's City Club, Detroit.

Long-Distance Team—Riviera Club, Indianapolis.

National Collegiate Champions

50-Yard Free-Style—Kerry Donovan, Yale.

100-Yard Free-Style—Rex Aubrey, Yale.

220-Yard Free Style—Jack Wardrop, Michigan.

440-Yard Free-Style—Ford Konno, Ohio State.

1,500-Meter Free-Style—Ford Konno.

100-Yard Back-Stroke—Yoshi Oyakawa, Ohio State.

200-Yard Back-Stroke—Yoshi Oyakawa.

200-Yard Butterfly—Phil Drake, North Carolina.

200-Yard Breast-Stroke—Bob Mattson, North Carolina State.

150-Yard Medley—Al Wiggins, Ohio State.

300-Yard Medley Relay—Ohio State.

400-Yard Free-Style Relay—Yale.

One-Meter Dive—Fletcher Gilders, Ohio State.

Three-Meter Dive—Gerry Harrison, Ohio State.

Team—Ohio State.

TABLE TENNIS

World Champions

Men's Singles—Tashiaki Tanaka, Japan.

Women's Singles—Angelica Rozeanu, Rumania.

United States Champions

Men's Singles—Richard Miles, New York.

Women's Singles—Mrs. Leah Neuberger, New York.

Men's Doubles—Erwin Klein, Los Angeles, and Richard Bergmann, England.

Women's Doubles—Mrs. Leah Neuberger, and Peggy Folke, New York

Mixed Doubles—Mildred Shahian, Chicago, and Richard Miles.

TENNIS

Davis Cup—Australia.

Wightman Cup (women)—United States.

Wimbledon Champions

Men's Singles—Tony Trabert, United States.

Women's Singles—Louise Brough, U. S.

Men's Doubles—Lewis Hoad and Rex Hartwig, Australia.

Women's Doubles—Angela Mortimer and Ann Shilcock, England.

Mixed Doubles—Victor Seixas and Doris Hart, United States.

United States Outdoor Champions

Men's Singles—Tony Trabert, Cincinnati.

Women's Singles—Doris Hart, Coral Gables, Fla.

Men's Doubles—Kosei Kamo and Atsushi Miyagi, Japan.

Women's Doubles—Louise Brough, Beverley Hills, Calif., and Mrs. Margaret Osborne du Pont, Wilmington, Del.

Mixed Doubles—Victor Seixas, Philadelphia, and Doris Hart.

CLAY COURTS

Men's Singles—Tony Trabert.

Women's Singles—Mrs. Dorothy Head Knode, Alameda, Calif.

Men's Doubles—Hamilton Richardson, Baton Rouge, La., and Tony Trabert.

Women's Doubles—Janet Hopps, Seattle, and Mrs. Dorothy Head Knode.

Mixed Doubles—Yola Ramirez, Mexico City, and Sam Giammalva, Houston.

TENNIS

Collegiate

Singles—Jose Aguero, Tulane.

Doubles—Pancho Contreras and Joaquin Reyes, So. California.

Team—Southern California.

United States Indoor Champions

Men's Singles—Tony Trabert.

Women's Singles—Kay Hubbell, Conway, N. H.

Men's Doubles—Tony Trabert and Victor Seixas.

Women's Doubles—Ruth Jeffrey, Melrose, Mass., and Kay Hubbell.

Mixed Doubles—Wallace McIntyre, Chestnut Hill, Mass., and Ruth Jeffrey.

TRACK AND FIELD

Men's National Senior Outdoor Champions

100-Yard Dash—Bobby Morrow, Abilene Christian.

220-Yard Dash—Rod Richard, U. S. Army.

440-Yard Dash—Charles Jenkins, Villanova.

880-Yard Run—Arnold Sowell, Pittsburgh.

Mile Run—Wes Santee, U. S. Marine Corps.

Three-Mile Run—Horace Ashenfelter, New York A. C.

Six-Mile Run—Dick Hart, Collegiate Track and Field Club, Philadelphia.

120-Yard Hurdles—Milt Campbell, Indiana.

220-Yard Low Hurdles—Charles Pratt, Pioneer Club.

440-Yard Hurdles—Josh Culbreath, Morgan State.

Two-Mile Steeplechase—Ken Reiser, Town Club, Eugene, Ore.

Two-Mile Walk—Henry Laskau, 92d Street Y. M. H. A., New York.

Broad Jump—Gregory Bell, Terre Haute, Ind.

High Jump—Ernie Shelton, Los Angeles A. C., and Charles Dumas, Compton, Calif. (tie).

Hop, Step and Jump—Victor Paredes, Cuba.

Pole Vault—Bob Richards, Los Angeles A. C.

Hammer Throw—Harold Connolly, Boston A. A.

Shot-Put—Parry O'Brien, U. S. Air Force.

56-Pound Weight Throw—Bob Backus, New York A. C.

Discus Throw—Parry O'Brien.

Javelin Throw—Franklin Held, San Francisco Olympic Club.

Team—New York A. C.

Decathlon—Bob Richards.

Pentathlon—Des Koch, Southern California.

All-Around—Lyman Frazier, Baltimore O. C.

Marathon—Nick Costes, Farrell, Pa.

440-Yard Relay—N. Y. Pioneer Club.

One-Mile Relay—Pioneer Club.

One-and-⅞-Mile Relay—University of Chicago Track Club.

10-Kilometer Walk—Henry Laskau.

15-Kilometer Walk—Henry Laskau.

20-Kilometer Walk—Henry Laskau.

25-Kilometer Walk—James Hewson, Buffalo.

30-Kilometer Walk—Alex Oakley, Ontario.

35-Kilometer Walk—Leo Sjogren, Finnish-American A. C., New York.

40-Kilometer Walk—Guillermo Weller, Argentina.

50-Kilometer Walk—Leo Sjogren.

15-Kilometer Run—Browning Ross, Penn A. C., Philadelphia.

20-Kilometer Run—Dr. Charles Robbins, Pioneer Club.

25-Kilometer Run—Browning Ross.

30-Kilometer Run—Browning Ross.

Men's National Senior Indoor Champions

60-Yard Dash—John Haines, Pennsylvania.

60-Yard High **Hurdles**—Harrison Dillard, Cleveland.

600-Yard Run—Charles Jenkins.

One-Mile Run—Wes Santee.

Three-Mile Run—Horace Ashenfelter.

One-Mile Walk—**Henry Laskau**.

Sprint Medley Relay—Pioneer Club.

One-Mile Relay—Morgan State.

Two-Mile Relay—Syracuse.

Broad Jump—Roselyn Range, U. S. Army.

High Jump—**John Hall, U. S.** Army, and Ernie Shelton (tie).

Pole Vault—Bob Richards.

Shot-Put—Parry O'Brien.

35-Pound Weight—Robert Backus.

Team—Pioneer Club.

National Collegiate Champions

100-Yard Dash—Jim Golliday, Northwestern.

220-Yard Dash—Jim Golliday.

440-Yard Run—J. W. Mashburn, Okla. A. & M.

880-Yard Run—Tom Courtney, Fordham.

One-Mile Run—James Bailey, Oregon.

Two-Mile Run—Keneth Reiser, Oregon.

120-Yard Hurdles—Milt Campbell, Indiana.

220-Yard Hurdles—Charles Pratt, Manhattan.

Broad Jump—Joel Shankle, Duke.

High Jump—Ernie Shelton, So. California.

Pole Vault—Don Bragg, Villanova.

Discus—Des Koch, Southern California.

Shot-Put—Bill Nieder, Kansas.

Javelin—Les Bitner, Kansas.
Team—Southern California.

Intercollegiate A. A. A. A. Outdoor Champions

100-Yard Dash—John Haines.
220-Yard Dash—Art Pollard, Penn State.
440-Yard Run—Charles Jenkins, Villanova.
880-Yard Run—Arnold Sowell.
One-Mile Run—Burr Grim, Maryland.
Two-Mile Run—George King, N. Y. U.
120-Yard Hurdles—Joel Shankle, Duke.
220-Yard Hurdles—Charles Pratt, Manhattan.
One-Mile Relay—Villanova.
Broad Jump—Joel Shankle.
High Jump—Wilfred Lee, Pennsylvania.
Pole Vault—Don Bragg.
Shot-Put—Roosevelt Grier, Penn State.
Hammer Throw—Donald Seifert, Brown.
Discus Throw—Roosevelt Grier.
Javelin Throw—Al Cantello, La Salle.
Team—Manhattan.

VOLLEYBALL

Open—Stockton (Calif.) Y. M. C. A.
Y. M. C. A.—Stockton, Calif.
A. A. U.—Wilson Avenue Y. M. C. A., Chicago.

WATER POLO

A. A. U. Champions

Outdoor—Illinois A. C., Chicago.
Indoor—Illinois A. C.

WEIGHT LIFTING

World Champions

Bantamweight—Vladimir Stogov, Russia.
Featherweight—Rafael Tchimichkian, Russia.
Lightweight—Nikolau Kostylev, Russia.
Middleweight—Pete George, United States.
Light Heavyweight—Tommy Kono, U. S.
Middle Heavyweight—Arkadii Vorobiev, Russia.
Heavyweight—Paul Anderson, United States.
Team—Russia.

National A. A. U. Champions

123-Pound—Charles Vinci, Cleveland.
132-Pound—Isaac Berger, New York.
148-Pound—Joseph Pitman, Vero Beach, Fla.
165-Pound—Richard Giller, Akron, Ohio.
181-Pound—Tommy Kono, Sacramento, Calif.
198-Pound—Dave Sheppard, Astoria, Queens.
Heavyweight—Paul Anderson, Toccoa, Ga.

WRESTLING

National A. A. U. Champions

Free Style

114.5-Pound—Katsutoshi Yokoyama, Japan.
125.5-Pound—Etsuma Iwano, Japan.
136.5-Pound—Motoichi Motohashi, Japan.
147.5-Pound—Joe Scandura, New York A. C.

160.5-Pound—Dr. Melvin Northrup, Olympic Club, San Francisco.
174-Pound—Wenzel Haber, U. S. Army.
191-Pound—Tim Woodin (Ithaca (N. Y.) Grapplers.
Heavyweight—Bill Kerslake, Cleveland.
Team—New York A. C.
National Collegiate Champions
115-Pound—Terrance McCann, Iowa.
123-Pound—Ed Peery, Pittsburgh.
130-Pound—Myron Roderick, Oklahoma A. & M.
137-Pound—Lawrence Fornicola, Penn State.
147-Pound—Edward Eichelberger, Penn State.
157-Pound—Bill Weick, Iowa State.
167-Pound—Fred Davis, Oklahoma A. & M.
177-Pound—Dan Hodge, Oklahoma.
191-Pound—Peter Blair, Navy.
Heavyweight—William Oberly, Penn State.
Team—Oklahoma A. & M.

YACHTING

Distance Races

Newport to Marstrand, Sweden—Richard S. Nye's yawl, Carina, Greenwich, Conn.
Havana to San Sebastian, Spain—Enrique Urrutia's yawl, Mare Nostrum, Spain.
Los Angeles to Honolulu—Ira P. Ful-

mor's ketch, Staghound, Newport, Calif.
Fastnet (England)—Carina.
Gotland (Sweden)—W. S. Gubelmann's yawl, Windigo, Oyster Bay, L. I.
New London to Annapolis—Henry Sears' sloop, Actaea, Greenwich, Conn.

North American

Adams Trophy (women)—Toni Monetti, Manhasset Bay Y. C., Port Washington, L. I.
Mallory Cup (men)—William Buchan Jr., Seattle.
Sears Cup (juniors)—Skippy Leonard, Toronto.

One-Design

World Star—Charles de Cardenas, Havana.
North American Star—Jorge de Cardenas, Havana.
World Snipe—Mario Capio, Italy.
National Snipe—Harry Allen, Westport, Conn.

International

One-Ton Cup (six-meter)—Andre Firmenich's Ylliam IX, Switzerland.
British-American Cup (six-meter)—United States.
New York Canoe Club Cup—North Shore Y. C., United States.
Amorita Cup (International Class)—Spring: Bermuda. Fall: United States.
Norway-United States Team (International Class)—Norway.

(In Alphabetical Order)

JESSE ABRAMSON (The Checkered Flag) who shares in the news coverage award this year, has appeared in every one of the twelve volumes in the Best Sports Stories series—and with stories on all sorts of sports, too. In 1949 and 1953 he won the prizes for news coverage. As a sports writer for the New York Herald Tribune for more than thirty years, he is regarded as one of the top reporters of the nation.

RAY BECK (I've Been Skunked) is 41 years of age and spent his youth in western Pennsylvania. After high school graduation he became a professional trapper for eight years, a guide and prospector. Following his military discharge he took advantage of the G.I. Bill to enroll in a correspondence writing course and eventually he started selling to the better magazines. At present he is free lancing and lives in Knox, Pennsylvania.

ROGER BIRTWELL (Two Men Gambled) was educated at Exeter and Harvard. He worked, in order, for the Boston Transcript, Boston Post, New York Telegram, New York Times, New York News, Ned York American, New York Herald Tribune, New York Daily News again and now the Boston Globe. Magazine stories have appeared in Collier's, Liberty, Esquire and Vanity Fair. He was the only sports writer mentioned in the Bookman Magazine's selections of best newspaper stories in America, 1928. Third time in Best Sports Stories.

SI BURICK (Weep for the Winner) is sports editor of the Dayton News. He attended the University of Dayton as a pre-med, turned to the newspaper business and since 1930 has covered practically every major sports event, including the Kentucky Derby and Big Ten and Notre Dame football games.

ROBERT L. BURNES (All-Star Accolade) has been away from "Best Sports Stories" much too long—in fact we haven't had him around since the first edition in 1944 . . . that would make him 42 years of age. He was 30 when we first heard from him. He was

303

graduated from the University of St. Louis and worked for the St. Louis Post Dispatch and Globe-Democrat in the same city. He was appointed sports editor in 1943. He is a proud devotee of the Cardinals and has done extensive reportage of their fortunes and misfortunes.

AL CARTWRIGHT (The Merciful Executioner) is thirty-eight years old and has been the sports editor of the Journal-Every Evening in Wilmington, Delaware since 1947. His newspaper career started with the Reading (Pa.) Times in '33 and he also put in some writing time with the Dayton (Ohio) Herald and the Philadelphia Record. In 1949 he received the Headliner's Award, succeeding Dan Parker as the most consistently outstanding sports columnist. In '55 he won the annual award of the Thoroughbred Racing Association. Loves his wife and three children and dislikes the Phillies, Marciano, and the University of Delaware in football.

JACK CLOWSER (They Drag Out the Dead) has been a sports writer for 27 years, both on the Cleveland News and the Cleveland Press, with which he is now associated. He covers golf, football and track mainly. He has also covered the Olympic and Pan-American Games for the Press and was a member of the five-man commission that represented Cleveland (where the Pan-Am Games will next be held) to study facilities and organization in Mexico City. There's where he saw his first bullfight.

TIM COHANE (College Football's Greatest Folly) is a familiar name to all sports lovers. He has written in many of our outstanding newspapers and magazines and at present is the sports editor of Look Magazine. He graduated from Fordham University in New York and began his newspaper career with the New York World Telegram. Cohane is also the author of two books on sports "Gridiron Grenadiers; The Story of West Point Football" and "The Yale Football Story."

DAVID CONDON (Thunder in Los Angeles) is making his first appearance in Best Sports Stories. Educated at Notre Dame, he joined the staff of the Chicago Tribune in 1944 and since July of 1955 has conducted the column, In the Wake of the News, as well as covering important assignments. He also worked on the Las Vegas, N. M. (where he was born) Daily-Optic and the South Bend Tribune. Has four daughters and a son.

BOB COOKE (The Saga of Plainfield Teachers) joined the staff of the Herald Tribune shortly after his graduation from Yale and became its sports editor in 1948. He covered the Dodgers until '48 with the exception of a three-year hitch as a combat pilot of a B-26. He was an all around athlete in college, played baseball and hockey, but he has no preference as to the sport he covers when writing. He likes them all.

ALLISON DANZIG (Tennis Turnabout) has appeared in all of the anthologies of "Best Sports Stories". He won the newspaper coverage award in 1950 with his exciting tennis report on the Gonzales-Parker semi-final match in the national tennis championships. Born in Texas, graduated from Cornell, has authored and edited some fine sports books in addition to being a working newspaper man on the sports department of the New York Times for almost thirty years.

LEO FISCHER (All Is Confusion) is one of the oldest writers, from point of service, in the Middle West. In 1923 he joined the old Chicago Herald-American and became its sports editor after it changed its name to the Chicago American. He has won many sports readers with his excellent writing.

STANLEY FRANK (Coaching the Pros Is a Cinch, He says) got his baptism in newspaper work with the New York Post. However since leaving that paper shortly after the second World War, he has been free lancing. He has appeared in every major magazine in the country. He is a most versatile and prolific writer who can ghost a best seller for Elsa Maxwell or do a brilliant personality study of any of our great sports figures.

JACK GALLAGHER (He Wouldn't Harm a Fly), at 32 makes his first appearance in "Best Sports Stories." He is a graduate of the University of Texas and wrote for his school paper while an undergraduate. He later did short stints for the Austin American-Statesman and the Citizen, suburban newspapers. He has been with the Houston Post since 1949, writing a column and covering the Southwest Conference.

JOHN B. GILLOOLY (Sox Apollo) has been with the Record-American-Sunday Advertiser since 1925 when he began working his way through Boston College at 25 cents an inch as the B.C.

correspondent. His dad, who died in '24, was sports editor of the American. He has covered a variety of sports and travelled eight years with the Braves before they took their safari to Milwaukee. Age 47, five feet ten inches and a calorie watcher. Won the Best Sports Stories award for coverage last year.

Bob Goethals (Locker Room), who shares the feature award, is a newcomer to this series of annual sports stories. He is 30 years of age and a native of San Francisco. He joined the Chronicle in 1948 after attending the University of San Francisco. His stories have appeared in many national magazines. Served in the Navy during World War II and is the father of two children, a girl and a boy.

Curley Grieve (Yankees Never Die) is 53 years of age and has been sports editor of the San Francisco Examiner for the past twenty-five years. He has covered every major sport, including the Olympics, and edits a sports column entitled "Sports Parade". In '24 he was graduated from the University of Utah and went to work with Salt Lake Tribune, thence to the sports editorship of the Rocky Mountain News. He moved to the Examiner in '41. Married and the father of one child, Vernon David Jr.

W. C. Heinz (Young Fighter) started his newspaper career with the now defunct New York Sun. He earned himself four prizes from the volumes of "Best Sports Stories". He won outright in 1948, 1950 and 1954 and shared the award in '52. He is a free lance writer at present. He is a graduate of Middlebury College and served as a war correspondent. Lives in Connecticut.

Al Hirshberg (Roommate: Bob Cousy) won a "Best Sports Stories" award in 1953. At present he is free lancing. His last newspaper writing was with the Boston Post. He has been printed by almost every major magazine in this country and a book that he wrote, "Fear Strikes Out," is being made into a movie. He has done a number of juvenile books for Atlantic-Little Brown and his latest, "Varsity Double Play," appeared in the Spring.

Bob Hunter (A Life for the Dodgers) attended the University of Southern California and Southwestern Law School, which he left when offered a job as a sports writer with the Los Angeles Examiner in 1933. He covers baseball, college football and basketball and conducts a column for the Examiner called "Bobbin' Around." He also wrote the script for the Laraine Day and Leo Durocher TV series.

JOHN LARDNER (Perilous Plight of the Pitcher) is one of America's great sports writers and perhaps inherited more than a modicum of his talent from his dad, the great Ring Lardner. His column in Newsweek always contains a fresh slant on the current sports situation and his fine book, "It Beats Working," won him a host of new readers.

HAL LEBOVITZ (Why Do Bunts Roll Foul in Cleveland), who was last printed in "Best Sports Stories" in '52, holds a masters degree in chemistry and looks like a football player. He was graduated from Western Reserve University, coached athletics and taught high school for a while. He left the academic life when the Cleveland News offered him a chance as a sports reporter. Married and the father of two children.

BILL LEISER (Forget the "Was") was born in Kansas, attended schools in Wisconsin and Idaho and graduated from Stanford. In San Francisco he wrote for the Examiner in 1925 and joined the Chronicle in '34, where he has remained since. He is the past president of the San Francisco Press Club and also headed the Football Writers Association of America. "Best Sports Stories" has included Mr. Leiser six times in the series.

FRANKLIN (WHITEY) LEWIS (Fun Week) has made a handsome reputation for himself as one of Cleveland's finest sports columnists. He lives in Shaker Heights just outside of Cleveland. Purdue University is his Alma Mater and Bob Hope was once his cue partner in the local pool-rooms. He has worked as an actor, life-guard, sports reporter and (sotto voce) a poet.

WHITNEY MARTIN (The Biggest Victory) is represented for the fifth time in "Best Sports Stories" and was a winner in the news-feature competition in 1952 with his study of Eddie Stanky. He was born in Chicago in 1896 and is a graduate of Coe College. For the past seventeen years he has been writing a sports column out of the New York office of the Associated Press.

GRANT MATTHEWS (No Victory at Sea) made his debut in "Best Sports Stories" in '55 and is with the San Francisco Chronicle writing fish and game news. He was born and bred in the Far West. Seattle is his original state and he attended Washington State College. He is 44 years of age, married and the father of a sixteen year old boy.

TEX MAULE (They Never Hurt Me) is with the Dallas Morning News, having come that distance by way of press agent of the now defunct Dallas Football Club. He is forty-one years of age and married. He has had a rather checkered career, holding down such variegated jobs as trapeze artist, hand balancer, flight purser, war department investigator, press agent and newspaperman.

ANDY McCUTCHEON (The Kid They Call 'The Hot Rod') was born twenty-eight years ago in a very small mining town in West Virginia and at present is attached to the sports desk of the News-Leader in Richmond (Va.) The Rose Bowl was the scene of some of his football activity when he played with the University of Tennessee during the war. In '48, after war service, he graduated (cum laude) from Washington and Lee to which he had transferred.

JERRY MITCHELL (The Saga of 'Davy' Berra) has been with the New York Post for over twenty years and his readers are kept constantly amused and informed by his clever reporting. All of his earlier newspaper writing was done with New York papers including the now defunct Graphic. He comes from upstate New York, Plattsburgh, is married and the father of a foine broth of a boy, Michael Patrick. Past president of New York Baseball Writers Association.

JERRY NASON (12 Minutes Short of 70 Days) won the news coverage award for his story of the Army-Notre Dame football game in '45. His fine writings have merited him inclusion in practically every one of the "Best Sports Stories" editions. He originally was a sports cartoonist and has been associated with the Boston Globe, of which he is sports editor, since 1941. He is forty-six years of age.

HENRY T. PAXTON (Football's Biggest Show) is sports editor of the Saturday Evening Post and has been a member of its editorial staff since 1942. He became the sports editor in '49 and writes a major part of the thirty odd sports articles that the periodical runs each year. He broke in with newspapers in the Philadelphia suburbs and wrote for Tide Magazine before coming to New York. He is a graduate of Haverford College.

DICK PEEBLES (The Will to Win) was born in Oil City, Pa. on July 4, 1918. He started writing sports for the Erie Dispatch-Herald in 1929. In 1941 he worked for the Sharon (Pa.) Herald as sports editor and following his discharge from service in 1946 he was named sports editor of the San Antonio Express, where he is at present. He married a Texas gal in 1950 and is the father of two boys. First appearance in "Best Sports Stories".

JANE PERRY (Brooklyn's Mad Golf Course) is one of the few members of the distaff side to grace this series. Her first novel, "The Savage City," was published in 1955 under her real name, Jean Paradise. She was born in Brooklyn and has dabbled in all forms of sports, including ju jitsu. She has been a gag writer, published fiction and articles in the Atlantic and several of the literary quarterlies.

SHIRLEY POVICH (Up from the Floor) was born in Bar Harbor, Maine, studied law at Georgetown, turned his back on jurisprudence and became a very young sports editor for the Washington Post. For the last 25 years he has covered every major sports event except for a stint as war correspondent. After returning to civilian duty he relinquished his sports editorship to devote full time to a daily column. He has received the National Headliners Sports Writing award and in '55 was elected National President of the Baseball Writers Association of America.

ED PRELL (No Hitter) has been writing sports for the Chicago Tribune since 1939. Before that he was a newsman with a host of papers throughout the Middle West and the South. He was born in Pittsburg, Kansas, married a resident of Skokie, Illinois and is the father of two sons, one an electronic engineer and the other a student at Northwestern University.

HOWARD PRESTON (Who's Excited?) has been regaling Cleveland News readers for nineteen years with his splendid sports writing. During the last decade his column has been one of the fine features of that paper. As a matter of fact he does two columns . . . one a general essay type which won him a Newspaper Guild Award in '55. This is his second appearance in "Best Sports Stories" and as a verse writer he has been included in an anthology of American poets.

JOHN RENDEL (Midnight for Kippax Fearnought) has been a member of the New York Times sports staff for 30 years. He became a dog specialist about ten years ago and since then has written a book about canines and another on horses. In 1955 he was awarded the Kilbon Award. Another of his specialties is yacht racing.

ART ROSENBAUM (The Important Part), winner of the 1952 E. P. Dutton Award for news coverage, has been with the San Francisco Chronicle for more than twenty years. He was absent three years ('42 to '45) on U. S. Maritime Service duty. In addition to his coverage he writes a daily column, "Overheard," which has appeared since 1936. He covered Olympic Games in London, 1948 and Helsinki, 1952. He is married and has a teen-age (13) daughter.

HAROLD ROSENTHAL (Farm Boss with a Green Thumb) who has been represented in a half-dozen editions of "Best Sports Stories," used the distillation of countless story-telling sessions while covering the Brooklyn Dodgers for the New York Herald Tribune as a basis for his article on the slightly-fabulous Fresco Thompson. A member of the Herald Tribune's sports staff for two decades, with time out for a three-year Army hitch, he is currently assigned to the Yankees.

EARL RUBY (The Comet from California) has been sports editor of the Louisville Courier-Journal for seventeen years and a member of the staff twenty-seven. He was born within five miles of Churchill Downs. He has seen every Derby since he was 12. He is now 52. He won the National Headliners Award in 1945 for having the "most consistently good" sports column in America. He holds two commissions from Governors of Kentucky—as a Colonel and Ambassador of Good Will at Large. He attended the University of Louisville and has a son in that school now.

DICK SEAMON (Big Man from Nicetown) is a native New Yorker born in 1919 and a graduate of Yale University, Class of '40. He saw a great deal of flying service in the Pacific and holds the rank of Lt. Colonel in Marine Reserve. After the war he indulged in a variety of reading and editorial chores and in 1951, came to Time magazine, where he wrote for almost every section of the periodical. He was named sports editor of the Time in 1954.

BLACKIE SHERROD (The Raving) is a native Texan, thirty-five, who has been the sports editor and daily columnist of the Fort Worth Press for the past six years. This is his third straight appearance in "Best Sports Stories". He is president of the Texas Sportswriters Association; president of the Texas League Baseball Writers Association; did a four year Navy hitch as aerial gunner. He worked as a police reporter, rewrite man, radio script writer before returning to his first love—sports writing.

MARSHALL SMITH (Cowboy Race Kings) has been sports editor of Life since 1950 after serving with the Providence Star-Tribune, Providence Journal and Time. A Baltimorean by birth, he is the son of a stockbroker who later became a horse trainer. He himself worked as a groom for a short time. He began his journalistic career by "carrying a typewriter" for the Baltimore Sun's racing writer.

WALTER W. (RED) SMITH (The Cook Was from Richmond, Ky.) came to the New York Herald Tribune as a sports columnist from the Philadelphia Record. Previously he had worked in St. Louis and Milwaukee, after graduating from Notre Dame. He has appeared in all of the editions of the "Best Sports Stories" and has been a three-time winner in the series. He is the author of two books of his columns, is a prolific magazine writer and lecturer, is married and the father of a son and daughter.

WALTER STEWART (Back to Cap and Gown) is a familiar name to those who know good sports writing, particularly in the South, where he toils for the Commercial Appeal in Memphis as sports editor. He was graduated from the University of Illinois class of '30, saw newspaper service in New York City with the World-Telegram and came out of the Pacific war theatre a full colonel. He covers all areas of sports, particularly boxing. Upon his graduation at Illinois he received a commission in the Horse Cavalry.

JOE TRIMBLE (Paradise at Last) makes his third appearance and wins his first award in Best Sports Stories—1956. He began

work for the New York Daily News in '37 and has regularly
covered the Yankees and Giants. He is an alumnus of St. John's
University, class of '36. His vocational background is enhanced by
experience as a stevadore, actor and finance operator. He hangs
his hat in Flushing, is forty-one years of age and has no use for
the Dodgers.

GENE WARD (The Gay Gob) was born in Oneonta, New York
in 1913, went West almost immediately and appeared in "Our
Gang" comedy series. Attended Colgate and Columbia where he
was active in athletics and in '35 he joined the New York Daily
News. He is also known as a TV and radio commentator on the
"Big Fight" series and his writing stints include a column, "Inside Sports". He lives in Jackson Heights . . . an important suburb
of Brooklyn.

MAURY WHITE (Odd Fellows These Coaches) is 36 years of
age, played football and baseball at Drake before graduation in
1942, spent four years in the Navy and then went to work at the
Des Moines Register and Tribune in 1946. He is still there. His
great-grandfather started a paper in 1869 and the family never got
out of the habit. This is his third story in "Best Sports Stories".

HERBERT WARREN WIND (Jack the Giant Killer) started as a
sports reporter with the Brockton (Mass.) Enterprise and was on
the staff of the New Yorker from 1948, writing Profiles. At present
he is associate editor of Sports Illustrated. He is the author of two
books on golf, "The Story of American Golf," and, with Gene
Sarazen, "Thirty Years of Championship Golf," a biography of
Gene. He is thirty-seven years old and is single.

STANLEY WOODWARD (Flippin the Executioner) has labored
as sports writer and editor for many of the finest papers in the
country. He himself has won a host of readers for his fine reportage
and columns. His excellent book, "Sports Page," is a must for
anyone interested in the "behind the scenes" of a sports department.
On two occasions, 1948 and 1950, he won two of the prizes this
series offers, one for a newspaper article and the other for a magazine piece. The Newark Star and Ledger is the scene of his present
sports reporting.

FRANKLIN YEUTTER (They Even Cheered Generals) has been
with the Philadelphia Evening Bulletin for more than thirty years.

He has covered all types of news stories and has reported on twenty World Series. Harvard is his college and he served in both World Wars. He emerged from the second as a Lieutenant Colonel. He has travelled with both the Phillies and Athletics.

DICK YOUNG (The Outlawed Spitball), winner of the magazine prize, has amused the readers of the New York Daily News since 1941 with his pointed barbs concerning the foibles of the Brooklyn Dodgers. He is married, in his thirties and a graduate of New York University. He has appeared in Best Sports Stories before, but this is the first year he has won an award.

Thirty of the Year's Best Pictures

PHOTOGRAPHERS

HAL BURGERT, *Detroit News*
BOB DOTY, *Dayton Journal Herald*
ED STISO, *Newark News*
CHARLIE HOFF, *New York Daily News*
BARNEY STEIN, *New York Post*
JACK FRANK, *New York Herald Tribune*
FRANK HURLEY, *New York Daily News*
SAM MYERS, *The Associated Press*
JOHN LINDSAY, *The Associated Press*
ED JERRY, *United Press Associations*
ANTHONY SANDE, *United Press Associations*
MARK KAUFFMAN, *Sports Illustrated*
ANDREW LIPEZ, *United Press Associations*
MATHEW ZIMMERMAN, *The Associated Press*
DAVID DAVIS, *United Press Associations*
JACK O'CONNELL, *Boston Globe*
CLINT GRANT, *Dallas Morning News*
BILL SAURO, *United Press Associations*
HOWARD SWIFT, *Des Moines Register and Tribune*
ERNEST SISTO, *The New York Times*
BOB EAST, *Miami Herald*
BILL SEAMAN, *Minneapolis Star and Tribune*
WAYNE BELL, *Minneapolis Star and Tribune*
JOHN AHLHAUSER, *Milwaukee Journal*
EARL SEUBERT, *Minneapolis Star and Tribune*
P. H. REICHARD, *Columbus Citizen*
BOB LONG, *Des Moines Register and Tribune*
HY PESKIN, *Sports Illustrated*
ROLF GILLHAUSEN, *The Associated Press*
PAUL VATHIS, *The Associated Press*

PHOTOGRAPH WINNERS

HAROLD C. BURGERT, staff photographer of the Detroit News, began taking press pictures with the Tampa (Fla.) News in 1924. He learned his profession from his father and grandfather and, in fact, comes from a long line of photographers, including his mother, who, with five uncles were in the photo studio business. He has been on the staff of the Detroit News since 1929. A brother, Thel, joined that staff in 1931.

BOB DOTY is chief photographer of the Dayton (Ohio) Journal, with which he has been associated for seventeen years except for the time he was an instructor in the Marine Corps, photo division. His work has appeared in Life and other national magazines and he has received numerous photography awards. This is the third straight year he has been in Best Sports Stories but it is the first time he has won or shared an award.

WHEEL OF (MIS)FORTUNE
By Hal Burgert,
Detroit News

The tremendous violence depicted in this crash made it a stand-out photo of the year and a co-winner of the "Best Sports Stories" picture contest. The crackup occurred at the Michigan State Fair when a wheel flew fifty feet into the air. The driver Dick Jeannette suffered a fractured vertebra.

© 1955, *The Detroit News*

WALTER E. ALSTON

WALTER E.
ALSTON.
4340
CHERRY ST.

GOOD NEWS! By Bob Doty, *Dayton Journal Herald*

The viewer of this photo does not have to be a Dodger rooter to appreciate this irresistible shot. On this most wonderful of days Walter Alston did have some important news for his grandson and Mr. Doty earned himself a share in co-winner this year's "Best Sports Stories" photo award. © 1955, *Dayton Journal Herald*

SANDY SAVES THE SERIES By Ed Stiso, *Newark News*

This photo is certainly one of the year's finest and is excellent testimony to one of
the key plays of the 1955 world series. © 1955, *Newark News*

FINISHING TOUCHES By Charlie Hoff, *New York Daily News*

This scene was caught on a Sunday as Leo Durocher headed for the Giant clubhouse
for the last time to bow out as the manager at the Polo Grounds.
© 1955, *New York Daily News*

RACE TO FIRST

By Barney Stein

New York Post

Pictured here is Pee Wee Reese and pitcher Bob Grim racing madly towards first base during the 1955 World Series at Ebbets Field.

© 1955, *Barney Stein, New York Post*

SCREEN PLAY

By Jack Frank

New York Herald Tribune

Dodger catcher Roy Campanella about to snare ball batted foul by Don Mueller of the Giants. Umpire Barlick disallowed the catch after some fancy juggling and thereafter Don singled, scoring Hank Thompson with the first run of the game.

© 1955, *New York Herald Tribune*

THE LAST SAY
By Frank Hurley
New York Daily News

This is the scene just before Umpire Flaherty dismissed Casey Stengel from the game. The altercation was started by a slight difference of opinion about balls and strikes.

© 1955, *New York Daily News*

OOMPH!
By Sam Myers
The Associated Press

Cubs pitcher Dave Hillman (top) crashes into Stan Lopata in an attempt to score from first base in a game between Chicago and Philadelphia.

© 1955, *The Associated Press*

THE HAT TRICK

By John Lindsay

The Associated Press

This enthusiastic baseball fan thinks more of Senator's Clint Courtney's foul ball than of his hat. The scene includes the rival Yanks Bill Skowron and Gil McDougald.

© 1955, *The Associated Press*

TIGER TANGLE

By Ed Jerry

United Press Associations

Detroit's catcher, Bob Wilson, and first baseman J. W. Porter get tangled up while reaching for Hank Bauer's pop-up during the first inning of a game with the Yankees.

© 1955, *United Press Associations*

FANCY FOOTWORK
By Anthony Sande
United Press Associations

Yank catcher Charlie Silvera makes like a danseuse after tagging Ferris Fain in a rundown at the Yankee Stadium.

© 1955, *United Press Associations*

SYMPATHIZER
By Mark Kauffman
Sports Illustrated

When Archie Moore was counted out in the ninth round, his victorious opponent, Rocky Marciano, rushed over to the stricken fighter and poured out his solicitation.

© 1955, *Sports Illustrated*

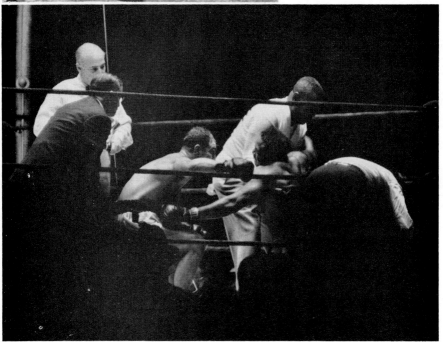

THE BITTER END
By Andrew Lopez
United Press Associations

The light-heavyweight champ, Archie Moore, lies against the ropes, a helpless, beaten fighter. Rocky Marciano, the heavyweight titleholder, floored Moore four times during the bout in which he retained his championship.

© 1955, *United Press Associations*

THE BLOOD FLOWS
By Mathew Zimmerman,

The Associated Press

Rudy Garcia's face has just stopped a left thrown by Lulu Perez in the final round of their ten round bout at Eastern Parkway Arena. Perez won a unanimous decision.

© 1955, *The Associated Press*

THE CLINCHER
By David Davis
United Press Associations

This tender scene was enacted between Artie Towne, the recipient of the sweet nothings in his ear, and Milo Savage. Towne won the fight at St. Nick's.

© 1955, *United Press Associations*

TAKING THE COUNT
By Jack O'Connell
Boston Globe

The referee, Del Manning, is deliberately giving a finger count to stricken Tony DeMarco, who has just been floored by Carmen Basilio.

© 1955, *The Boston Globe*

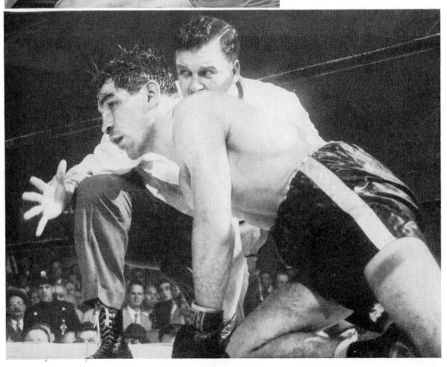

"'TILL I WALTZ AGAIN WITH YOU"

By Clint Grant

Dallas Morning News

These two obscure club fighters are caught in a stag version of a popular song hit.

© 1955, *Dallas Morning News*

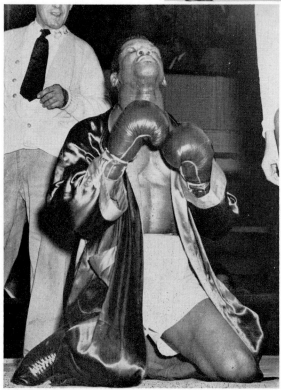

WINNER'S THANKS

By Bill Sauro

United Press Associations

Sammy Walker kneels on the canvas of St. Nick's arena and says a prayer after gaining a decision over Milo Savage. Walker hit the deck twice, not reverently but involuntarily and came on strong in the late rounds to win.

© 1955, *United Press Associations*

NO STRINGS ATTACHED By Howard Swift, *Des Moines Register*

Rex Fischer, Nebraska's halfback, takes a "flier" against Iowa State. He landed in the arms of waiting Cyclone guard Jim Lyons. © 1955, *Des Moines Register*

FIVE-YARD PLUNGE By Ernest Sisto, *The New York Times*

Buddy Epps, of the New York Giant football team, without the aid of fins or mask makes a five-yard gain under water against the Cardinals. © 1955, *New York Times*

S-T-R-E-T-C-H By Bob East, *Miami Herald*

This humorous shot has one sad aspect. There aren't too many spectators around—
but the photographer certainly latched on. © 1955, *Miami Herald*

SITTEN ON AIR By Bill Seaman, *Minneapolis Star and Tribune*

When the high school all stars played their annual game in Minneapolis, one of the
backs emulated Peter Pan long enough for the photographer to come away with this
beauty. © 1955, *Minneapolis Star and Tribune*

BLOCKED PUNT
By Wayne Bell
Minneapolis Star and Tribune

In the Minnesota-Michigan State game at East Lansing, Michigan, this blocked punt was converted into a touchdown in the first quarter.

© 1955, *Minneapolis Star and Tribune*

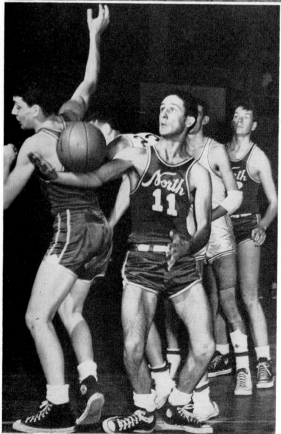

BALANCED BALL
By John Ahlhauser
Milwaukee Journal

In a game between North and South Division High in Milwaukee, a ball bounced off the backboard, struck Jim Grayson's arm and came to rest there.

© 1955, *The Milwaukee Journal*

GET OFF MY BACK!

By Earl Seubert

Minneapolis Star and Tribune

The Minnesota State High School basketball tournament came up with this strange action.

© 1955, *Minneapolis Star and Tribune*

NO TIME FOR REFLECTION

By P. H. Reichard

Columbus Citizen

In a moment there is going to be a big splash as these Big Ten hurdlers pause momentarily for this excellent shot.

© 1955, *Columbus Citizen*

SIX INCHES SHORT

By Bob Long

*Des Moines Register
and Tribune*

Art Henze of Grundy Center takes a spill only six inches from the tape in the two mile relay at Ames, Iowa. Bud Toms of Lake City came on to win in the record-breaking time of 8 minutes 19.6 seconds.

© 1955, *The Des Moines Register and Tribune*

BOOM BOOM
GOES BOOM!

By Hy Peskin

Sports Illustrated

Bernie (Boom Boom) Geoffrion plays with zest. So does Leaping Lou Fontinato of the Rangers. This scene occurred when the two met at Madison Square Garden. Geoffrion was out of action for one week.

© 1955, *Sports Illustrated*

SWISS MISS By Rolf Gillhausen, *The Associated Press*

Swiss goalie Charles Burger dives in vain attempt to block ball during world championship handball tournament final between Switzerland and Germany. The handball game is similar to soccer, except that the ball is propelled by hands instead of feet.

© 1955, *The Associated Press*

PARTING COMPANY By Paul Vathis, *The Associated Press*

Larry J. McGuinness of the Canadian Horse Show team and his mount, Dark Horse, part company on a jump during the Harrisburg Horse Show.

© 1955, *The Associated Press*

Date Due

DEC 3			
NOV1 7			
FEB1 9			
MAR1 8			
APR5			
OCT 3 0			
OC27 '65			
NO22 '65			
Demco 293-5			